1–2–3 GO!

1-2-3™ GO!

JULIE E. BINGHAM

Addison-Wesley Publishing Company

Reading, Massachusetts ★ Menlo Park, California
Don Mills, Ontario ★ Wokingham, England ★ Amsterdam
Sydney ★ Singapore ★ Tokyo ★ Madrid ★ Bogotá
Santiago ★ San Juan

This book is in the **Addison-Wesley Microcomputer Books** Popular Series

Marshall Henrichs, *Cover Design*
Bookwrights, Inc., *Production Coordination*

1–2–3 is a trademark of Lotus Development Corporation, Cambridge, Massachusetts.

IBM is a trademark of International Business Machines, Inc.

WordStar is a trademark of MicroPro International, San Rafael, CA.

The screen images of 1–2–3, and other Lotus created materials shown in this book are copyright ©, 1984 by Lotus Development Corporation and used here with permission.

All of the 1–2–3 tables in this book are copyright ©, 1984 by Forum/Nevison Executive Computing and Julie E. Bingham, used here with permission.

Eleventh Printing, July 1986

Library of Congress Cataloging in Publication Data

Bingham, Julie E.
  1–2–3 Go!

  (Addison-Wesley microcomputer books popular series)
  Includes index.
  1. LOTUS 1–2–3 (Computer program) 2. IBM Personal
Computer—Programming. I. Title. II. Title: One–two–
three go! III. Series.
HF5548.4.L67B56   1984   001.64'25   83-19735
ISBN 0–201–13047–5

ISBN 0-201-13047-5
KLMNOP-HA-89876

To my family and Joe

Foreword

The fledgling computer user is usually surprised, if not overwhelmed, at how much there is to learn and how little help is available in learning it.

Because there is so much to learn, what beginners desperately need is an understanding friend who'll explain patiently each part of the program, provide a step-by-step demonstration, and suggest additional exercises for learners to try on their own. This is especially true for 1–2–3, a large business tool with a number of different parts. Julie Bingham's *1–2–3 Go!* fills this need.

This book introduces you to each new idea—be it spreadsheet, database, or graphics—by explaining where you are going and leading you on a step-by-step journey through the new territory. In each case the new territory will be a combination of 1–2–3 features and a basic business application. Next you will review what you have covered and learn why it is important. Finally, before you leave each idea, you will be shown several side trips that you can make on your own to test your new skills.

1–2–3 Go! is more than a simple tutorial; it is also a source of ideas. Several of the exercises offered at the end of each chapter can be the beginning of useful models for your business. A good example is the PROJDATA exercise in Chapter 6, which allows you to track work by individual and by project. You can apply this model to your own department and track your staff's progress on several projects.

Because you must do quite a bit of hands-on computing as you go, you will not merely *read* this book; you will *experience* it. As you practice on your computer, you'll enhance your ability to work productively—perhaps even to a dramatic degree. In fact, *1–2–3 Go!* may do more for your personal business productivity than any book you have read in the last five years.

Concord, Massachusetts
August 1983

John M. Nevison
Chairman, Forum/Nevison
Executive Computing

Acknowledgements

My heartfelt thanks go to my employers at Forum/Nevison Executive Computing, Jack Nevison and Tim Stein, who gave me both the opportunity and the technical ability to write this book. Tim and Jack and my other colleagues at Forum/Nevison Executive Computing were always there to inspire and encourage me. They gave me invaluable assistance as programmers, educators, editors, and friends. Sally Elkind suffered as first reader and editor, and John Kenower created the book's title.

Special thanks to Joe Finnegan for his support, faith, and understanding, and to my parents and family for their encouragement.

1–2–3 Go! was written on an IBM™ Personal Computer with the WordStar™ word processing program.

J. E. B.

Contents

PART I

Introduction

Introduction

1. Why 1–2–3?

A program created by Lotus Development Corporation, 1–2–3 is a tool for making better decisions. Like any tool, 1–2–3 aids its user in getting work done. It can not replace the work you do, but it can make your work easier, faster, and more reliable.

Unlike many programs (ones that print mailing lists, for example), 1–2–3 performs a number of seemingly unrelated functions. In fact, the capabilities of 1–2–3 are so varied that it resembles a small computer language.

- It can perform a wide variety of functions.
- It can be personalized to fit your needs.
- It makes very efficient use of the computer's power.

Though it is less comprehensive than a full-fledged computer language, 1–2–3 has some advantages over languages.

- It is easier to learn.
- It enables you to do useful work with greater speed and less effort.
- It tailors the computer to the way *you* do work.

Choosing a good piece of software is always difficult. There is little standardization in the computer industry, and this is perhaps most true in the area of software. 1–2–3 is a particularly good piece of software because it meets these criteria:

Simplicity   1–2–3's commands are easy to learn and understand.

Independence   You can tailor your 1–2–3 worksheet to your specific needs, even to the point of creating applications that can be used by a novice.

Economy   1–2–3 is reasonably priced.

Reliability   1–2–3 has extensive, dependable controls against errors.

For many businesses 1–2–3 meets these criteria, as well:

Ability   1–2–3 can handle the work you do now.

Continuity   1–2–3 allows you to work in much the same way you do now. (You should not have to change your procedures to suit software; software should be chosen because it suits your methods.)

Flexibility   The many varied functions of 1–2–3 make it adaptable to new tasks.

2. 1–2–3: The Decision-Maker's Tool

What does it mean when we say that 1–2–3 is a "decision-making tool"? In other words, what does 1–2–3 really do?

Let's answer these questions by taking a look at the way you make decisions. Suppose you want to buy a new car. What steps will you take before you come to a decision about which car is best for you?

First, you'll gather information about what cars are available. Second, once you get some idea of what you're looking for, you'll start analyzing your information; this means you'll compare various options, prices, finance deals, and so on. Third, you'll clarify your analysis. (If you must present your decision to someone else, this final step will take the form of a chart or list.) Then, equipped with a clear, comparative analysis of your options, you'll be ready to make your decision and buy a car.

Thus we see that the decision-making process has three steps:

1. Gather information about your options.
2. Analyze and summarize the information in such a way that options can be compared.
3. Clarify the information by putting it in some presentable form.

Actually, these are the three steps we would *like* to take when we make a decision. Tedium and lack of time frequently cause us to skip a step or to act hurriedly. For most of the decisions we're asked to make, we must commit some time to making a sound decision—or take a well-intentioned guess and hope for the best.

With its ability to perform three major kinds of work, 1–2–3 can help at each stage of your decision making:

1. **Data management** helps you gather and order information.
2. **Spreadsheet** commands help you analyze the information.
3. **Graphics** help you present the information in a meaningful way.

1–2–3 helps you work the way you normally do; the computer and 1–2–3 simply extend the capabilities of pencil, paper, and calculator. And *1–2–3 Go!* is your introduction to this versatile business tool.

3. About this Book

1–2–3 Go! is an introduction to the features, commands, and functions of 1–2–3; its aim is to teach you how to use 1–2–3. The book is a tutorial; so if you have 1–2–3, you should follow along, typing the commands and other information covered in the lessons. The book will tell you what to type and how 1–2–3 will respond, and its numerous illustrations will show you what your computer screen should look like. If you don't have 1–2–3, the pictures and diagrams will give you a good idea of how 1–2–3 works.

1–2–3 Go! is for the novice user who doesn't want to read the full *User's Manual* in order to work with 1–2–3. The *1–2–3 User's Manual* is a reference to everything you need to know about 1–2–3, whereas *1–2–3 Go!* is a tutorial on the most common and useful 1–2–3 commands. But since the *User's Manual* is more complete than this book, do keep it handy for reference as you read.

If you use your computer and follow along with the book, you'll get a solid workout on the major 1–2–3 commands. You'll also build two small but sophisticated business models for a fictitious company. One model summarizes the company's quarterly financial data, and the other compares this year's profits with last year's profits. As you develop these models, you'll learn how 1–2–3 can help you

- build and manipulate a spreadsheet,
- ask what-if questions about your spreadsheet,
- build graphs that provide a pictorial representation of your spreadsheet,
- query and summarize collections of data,
- write a memo to accompany your summary tables, and
- customize menu options to your worksheet.

4. Exercises

At the end of Chapters 3 through 9 you'll find exercises relevant to the procedures you've learned there. Some of these exercises will suggest changes to your current model. Others will show different models you can build with 1–2–3. After each model, you'll find several comments and suggestions about how to build, use, and alter it.

Try to build each exercise model on your own, using the model picture and comments as a guide. If you have trouble completing a model, check your version against the cell-by-cell formula listings in Appendix C. You'll find that many of the exercise models are added to and altered in exercises following subsequent chapters. All exercises can be built with the commands you learned in the particular chapter.

5. Saving Models

As you learn about 1–2–3, you'll build and manipulate the two fictitious models that we mentioned earlier. Each section of this book builds on the previous section; so if you are a novice, you should work through the book front to back. If you're an experienced 1–2–3 user, you'll find it possible to jump to a particular section to learn about a specific command—but you'll need a copy of the model used in that section. Use the listings in Appendix C to build the model used in the particular section on which you focus.

Before you begin working with 1–2–3, format at least one disk to save your models on. The procedure for saving a model is described only once (in Chapter 3, section 7), but you should save the model often as you progress.

- Always save the model before taking a break. Try to time your breaks at the end of a section or a chapter.
- Always save the model before trying modifications not described in the book. If something goes wrong with what you're trying, you'll be able to recall the saved model and try again.
- Save the model at the end of each chapter, whether or not you're taking a break. That way you'll always have a copy of the model from the end of the previous chapter.

Saving a model on a disk is like saving a document in a filing cabinet. In fact, models saved on a disk are *called* **files.** When you save a 1–2–3 model, you tell 1–2–3 what to name the file. Depending on what you name the file, one of two things can happen:

a) If the name you give the new file is the same as that of a previously saved file, the earlier file is overwritten.

b) If there is no other file on the disk with the same name, 1–2–3 saves the new file under the name you specified.

You'll notice that when you tell 1–2–3 to save a file, it first checks the disk for files with the same name. If 1–2–3 finds a matching file name, it asks you whether to Cancel the command or Replace the old file. If you select Cancel, the Save command is canceled and the model is not saved. If you select Replace, the old file is overwritten with the current worksheet.

You may wish to save updated versions of your file over your original, or you may save updates as new files. To overwrite the old file with your updated worksheet, simply call it by the same name and tell 1–2–3 to Replace the old file. To save the updates in separate files, assign each update a new name. It doesn't have to differ radically; for example, you might have one file with the name FINANCE and then save subsequent updates as FINANCE2, FINANCE3, and so on. In any case, save at least one file as it is shown in the book; you'll need a version that follows along with the modifications made in each section.

P A R T **II**

Basics of 1–2–3

From Information to Knowledge

In Chapter 1, we'd like to take you quickly through a hypothetical problem so you can observe how it is solved with the help of 1–2–3. This chapter will not teach you how to use 1–2–3, but it should give you a feeling for how 1–2–3 works and what the program can do. We'll describe parts of this problem–solution in more detail in subsequent chapters. The two models presented here are very similar to the models you will build and modify as you progress through the book. If you're eager to get right to work with 1–2–3, you can skip this chapter; but if you'd like a better idea of how 1–2–3 works and how it can work for you, you'll find it worthwhile to read on.

1. Year-End Reporting

At the end of each year Jim Bickford must produce a profit analysis of Music Corporation. He is given twelve months of revenue and cost figures for his company's four divisions. From this information, he is asked to produce several tables and graphs that analyze company profits.

- The *Profit Breakdown* shows profits by division and by quarter.
- The *Profit Performance Summary* compares profit margins of the four divisions.

- The *Change Summary* compares each division's current-year profits with its profit of the preceding year.

Fig. 1.1   The Year-End Reports

```
PROFIT BREAKDOWN                        1983

Division                      Quarter              Division
********                1      2      3      4      Totals
CLASSICAL              140    168    196    271      775
COUNTRY                80     80     78     62       300
JAZZ                   30     36     45     89       200
ROCK                   90     105    108    127      430

Corporate
Totals                340    389    427    549      1705


PROFIT PERFORMANCE SUMMARY       1983

Division   Revenue   Profit       Profit
*****************************Performance
CLASSICAL   1070      775          72%
COUNTRY     1570      300          19%
JAZZ        540       200          37%
ROCK        1390      430          31%

Corporate
Totals      4570      1705         37%


            1983 CHANGE SUMMARY
                 ($000)

Division  Last Year This Year    Change  % Change
-------------------------------------------------
CLASSICAL      620      775         155      25%
COUNTRY        280      300         20        7%
JAZZ           120      200         80       67%
ROCK           470      430        (40)      -9%

CORPORATE     1,490    1,705        215      14%
```

In the past, Jim prepared rough drafts of these tables and graphs and asked his secretary and the graphics department to produce final copies. The task of boiling down data to arrive at the summary figures and then creating presentation-quality tables and graphs usually took a day or two to complete. Last-minute changes to fourth-quarter data often added several hours of correcting figures and reproducing the reports. This year Jim has a computer and 1–2–3, and he's hoping to use the program to speed up production, make more dependable calculations, and make late changes easier to handle. By printing the tables and graphs directly from 1–2–3 he hopes to eliminate retyping entirely.

2. The Corporate Financial Report

Music Corporation's data-processing department passes the monthly revenue and cost data to Jim's microcomputer, where it is entered into a 1–2–3 worksheet. Jim's first cut at the worksheet looks like this:

Fig. 1.2   FINANCE with Database Only

DATA	DIVISION	QTR	REVENUE	COST	PROFIT
	JAZZ	1	30	20	10
	ROCK	1	100	50	50
	JAZZ	1	35	25	10
	ROCK	1	100	85	15
	JAZZ	1	35	25	10
	ROCK	1	100	75	25
	CLASSICAL	1	60	20	40
	CLASSICAL	1	65	17	48
	COUNTRY	1	135	110	25
	COUNTRY	1	150	110	40
	COUNTRY	1	115	100	15
	CLASSICAL	1	70	18	52
	ROCK	2	125	80	45
	COUNTRY	2	140	110	30
	ROCK	2	100	80	20
	JAZZ	2	40	30	10
	CLASSICAL	2	70	20	50
	JAZZ	2	40	29	11
	CLASSICAL	2	85	27	58
	JAZZ	2	40	25	15
	COUNTRY	2	130	105	25
	COUNTRY	2	130	105	25
	CLASSICAL	2	85	25	60
	ROCK	2	125	85	40
	JAZZ	3	45	35	10
	ROCK	3	110	84	26
	ROCK	3	130	83	47
	JAZZ	3	55	35	20
	ROCK	3	120	85	35
	COUNTRY	3	130	107	23
	CLASSICAL	3	95	31	64
	CLASSICAL	3	90	25	65
	JA77	3	50	35	15
	COUNTRY	3	130	105	25
	COUNTRY	3	130	100	30
	CLASSICAL	3	95	28	67
	CLASSICAL	4	125	29	96
	JAZZ	4	55	30	25
	ROCK	4	140	82	58
	ROCK	4	110	84	26
	CLASSICAL	4	100	25	75
	JAZZ	4	55	26	29
	COUNTRY	4	130	103	27
	CLASSICAL	4	125	25	100
	ROCK	4	130	87	43
	JAZZ	4	60	25	35
	COUNTRY	4	125	105	20
	COUNTRY	4	125	110	15

The worksheet includes five columns of financial information, including the division name, quarter number, revenue amount, and cost amount. Jim gets revenue and cost data reported on a monthly basis, but his year-end reporting is concerned only with quarterly figures. (Therefore his database includes a quarter column but not a month column.) Because each quarter is made up of three months' data, there are three quarter-1 entries, three quarter-2 entries, and so on.

The fifth column contains formulas that subtract cost from revenue to get profit. Jim enters only the first profit formula, then instructs 1–2–3 to copy the formula down the column. Each copied formula is adjusted by 1–2–3 to refer to the revenue and cost figures in its particular row.

Jim's financial data is listed in order of quarter, but he is also interested in the breakdown by division. With this in mind, he reorders the data alphabetically by division and by quarter within each division. Reordering the data is a simple task with 1–2–3 and takes less than two seconds of sorting to complete.

Jim builds a table summarizing profits by division and quarter.

Fig. 1.3 FINANCE Sorted with Data Table

DATA DIVISION	QTR	REVENUE	COST	PROFIT
CLASSICAL	1	60	20	40
CLASSICAL	1	65	17	48
CLASSICAL	1	70	18	52
CLASSICAL	2	85	25	60
CLASSICAL	2	70	20	50
CLASSICAL	2	85	27	58
CLASSICAL	3	90	25	65
CLASSICAL	3	95	28	67
CLASSICAL	3	95	31	64
CLASSICAL	4	125	29	96
CLASSICAL	4	125	25	100
CLASSICAL	4	100	25	75
COUNTRY	1	115	100	15
COUNTRY	1	135	110	25
COUNTRY	1	150	110	40
COUNTRY	2	130	105	25
COUNTRY	2	140	110	30
COUNTRY	2	130	105	25
COUNTRY	3	130	100	30
COUNTRY	3	130	105	25
COUNTRY	3	130	107	23
COUNTRY	4	130	103	27
COUNTRY	4	125	110	15
COUNTRY	4	125	105	20
JAZZ	1	35	25	10
JAZZ	1	30	20	10
JAZZ	1	35	25	10
JAZZ	2	40	25	15

PROFIT BREAKDOWN

		QUARTE		
*********	1	2	3	4
CLASSICAL	140	168	196	271
COUNTRY	80	80	78	62
JAZZ	30	36	45	89
ROCK	90	105	108	127

```
JAZZ      2     40     30     10
JAZZ      2     40     29     11
JAZZ      3     55     35     20
JAZZ      3     45     35     10
JAZZ      3     50     35     15
JAZZ      4     55     26     29
JAZZ      4     55     30     25
JAZZ      4     60     25     35
ROCK      1    100     75     25
ROCK      1    100     85     15
ROCK      1    100     50     50
ROCK      2    125     85     40
ROCK      2    125     80     45
ROCK      2    100     80     20
ROCK      3    130     83     47
ROCK      3    110     84     26
ROCK      3    120     85     35
ROCK      4    130     87     43
ROCK      4    140     82     58
ROCK      4    110     84     26
```

He uses 1–2–3 commands to extract the division names and list them to the left of the table. Then he enters a formula that 1–2–3 uses to sum profit entries for each division in each quarter. The individual sums in the table are calculated and displayed by 1–2–3. Jim adds formulas that sum each row and column of the table; if the table entries change, the totals will be recalculated automatically.

Fig. 1.4   Profit Breakdown with Totals

```
PROFIT BREAKDOWN                    1983

Division                  Quarter              Division
********      1        2        3        4      Totals
CLASSICAL    140      168      196      271      775
COUNTRY       80       80       78       62      300
JAZZ          30       36       45       89      200
ROCK          90      105      108      127      430

Corporate
Totals       340      389      427      549     1705
```

This table shows that CLASSICAL, Music Corporation's oldest and most solid division, is the big seller. ROCK division is running a poor second, and the newer JAZZ and COUNTRY divisions follow.

Jim also wants to evaluate each division's profit performance. He builds a second table summing revenues and profits and adds a column that calculates profit as a percent of revenue. After adding titles and formatting some of the numbers, he prints the completed report.

15

Fig. 1.5   Profit Performance Summary

```
PROFIT PERFORMANCE SUMMARY      1983

Division  Revenue  Profit    Profit
*******************************Performance
CLASSICAL   1070    775       72%
COUNTRY     1570    300       19%
JAZZ         540    200       37%
ROCK        1390    430       31%

Corporate
Totals      4570   1705       37%
```

This second table adds some color to the picture. Not only is CLASSI-CAL a big money-maker, it is also a highly *efficient* money-maker, with a 72-percent margin. Jim wonders what to do to boost the other divisions' profitability.

From the corporate summaries Jim builds and prints several graphs, as shown in Fig. 1.6:

a) A pie chart, showing how profits are distributed among the four divisions. (CLASSICAL division is the comany's bread and butter.)

Fig. 1.6   Profit Analysis Graphs

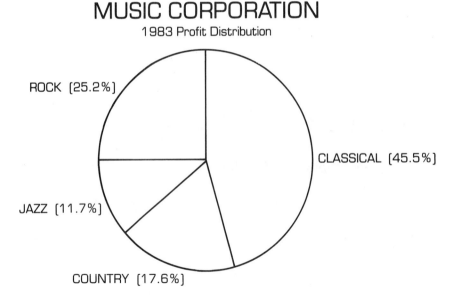

MUSIC CORPORATION
1983 Profit Distribution

ROCK [25.2%]

CLASSICAL [45.5%]

JAZZ [11.7%]

COUNTRY [17.6%]

b) A bar chart, comparing profit as a percent of revenue for the four divisions. (CLASSICAL is the ideal, and COUNTRY needs the most help.)

Fig. 1.6 (Cont.)

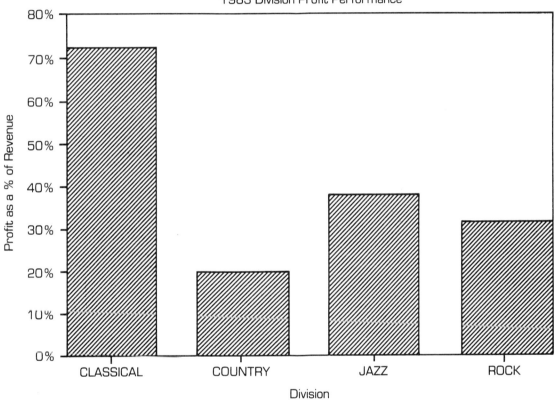

MUSIC CORPORATION
1983 Division Profit Performance

c) A stacked-bar chart, comparing the divisions' profits in each quarter. (COUNTRY and ROCK didn't have the expected fourth-quarter Christmas surges.)

Fig. 1.6 (Cont.)

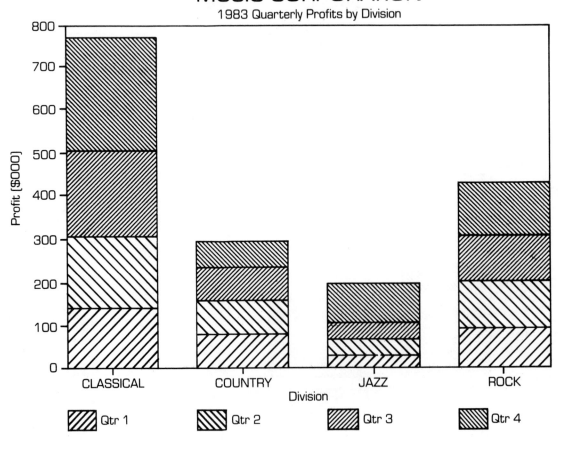

d) A line graph, showing quarterly profit growth. (COUNTRY division actually lost money in the fourth quarter.)

Fig. 1.6 (Cont.)

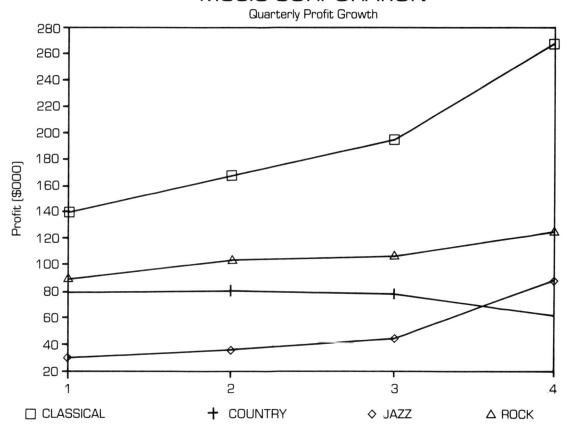

MUSIC CORPORATION
Quarterly Profit Growth

□ CLASSICAL   + COUNTRY   ◇ JAZZ   △ ROCK

Jim uses 1–2–3 to print a copy of the summary tables and the graphs and sends them to Bill, his boss. The calculations and production for the corporate financial summaries are done. What once took Jim and his staff most of a day is accomplished in only an hour.

3. The Change Summary

In preparation for the next table, Jim does two things:

1. He saves the final version of his current worksheet on two disks (a master copy and a backup copy) to be sure he doesn't lose his work.

2. He copies the total-profits-by-division column into a separate worksheet.

Jim erases the 1–2–3 worksheet and enters two new columns, listing the division names and their profits for last year; 1–2–3 copies the total profits for this year into his new worksheet. He adds two more columns to compute the change and percent change in profit. Then, on the same worksheet, he writes a short memo decribing what the figures mean (Fig. 1.7a) and highlights his discussion with a bar graph (Fig. 1.7b).

Fig. 1.7(a) THISYR Memo

```
Dear Bill,

There's good news and bad news when you compare our 1983
performance with last year's figures. CLASSICAL division,
always our biggest seller, shows a healthy 25% growth in
this year's profits. The flashy good news is that we are
bouncing back with the new interest in Jazz and our JAZZ
Division is up an impressive 67%. (Though its margins
aren't what they could be.)

                    1983 CHANGE SUMMARY
                         ($000)

Division  Last Year This Year    Change   % Change
--------------------------------------------------------
CLASSICAL      620       775        155        25%
COUNTRY        330       300       (30)        -9%
JAZZ           120       200         80        67%
ROCK           400       430         30         8%

CORPORATE    1,470     1,705        235        16%


The bad news is that ROCK is only up 8% (I would blame that
on the economy) and COUNTRY is down 9% (I would blame that
on us). The attached graph makes it hard to avoid the
conclusion that we should do a serious review of our
COUNTRY Division with an eye to selling it.

                              Sincerely,

                              Jim Bickford
```

Fig. 1.7(b)   THISYR Graph

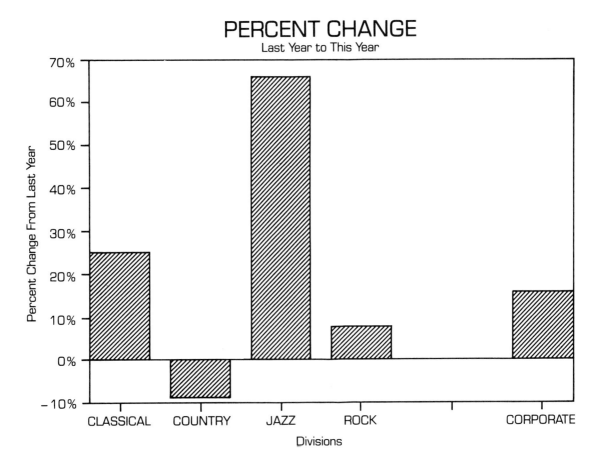

Jim prints the memo and graph and sends them to Bill. He prints the table and the graph a second time for inclusion in his annual report. Again, Jim saves copies of the worksheet on two disks.

Jim completes all this work in record time. In the process, he has developed a set of tools that will be useful when it's time to produce next year's profit analysis. As a further advantage, he can adapt them to quarterly reporting, as well. And because there was no need to transcribe or retype anything, Jim feels more confident that his figures are correct.

Last-minute changes are much easier to handle now because all the worksheets have been saved. Data changes are easy to enter, and 1–2–3 can produce new tables and graphs in very little time. In fact, Jim can generate new reports and graphs in less than an hour.

Throughout the pages of *1–2–3 Go!* you'll learn how to use 1–2–3 by doing the kind of work Jim did. You will use all the commands Jim used in his work, and you'll become familiar with many others. Like Jim, you'll build your worksheets to summarize and manipulate financial data in many ways. As the basis for your work, you'll use Music Corporation's four divisions.

CHAPTER 2

Getting Started with 1–2–3

1. The Pieces of 1–2–3

The basis for all 1–2–3 work is called the **worksheet.** A 1–2–3 worksheet looks much like a paper spreadsheet: it has rows and columns that you fill in with labels, numbers, and formulas. Most 1–2–3 **commands** give you control over the worksheet. They perform three major kinds of business work—spreadsheet, data management, and graphics—as well as such tasks as text processing.

There are also commands for handling the computer's work. These commands control 1–2–3's communication with the disk drives and the printer. They can be used to save a worksheet on disk for later use, to reload a worksheet that you saved earlier, or to print a worksheet.

The list of commands available to you is called a **menu.** There are nine commands in 1–2–3's main menu. You tell 1–2–3 what to do by selecting a command from the menu. Some of these commands perform special kinds of work (though there is often some crossover), while some perform general-purpose work on the entire worksheet. We can classify the nine main-menu commands in the following way:

1. General Purpose:

    WORKSHEET   RANGE   MOVE   COPY   QUIT

2. Specialized:

Data Management	Graphics	Communication
DATA	GRAPH	FILE PRINT

Because it requires no one specific command, spreadsheet work isn't easily classified. To build a simple graph, you must use the GRAPH command; but to build a simple spreadsheet, you might not use *any* commands (although they would probably make your task easier). To better understand what 1–2–3 can do, let's define three kinds of work.

1. *Spreadsheet.* The 1–2–3 worksheet is particularly well-suited to tabular work such as accounting. You can enter numbers, labels, and even formulas into the worksheet. For example, you can define one number in the worksheet as the sum of the ten numbers entered above it. When one of the initial ten numbers is changed, the sum adjusts automatically (and *very* quickly). Figure 2.1 is a 1–2–3 spreadsheet that compares two years of profits.

Fig. 2.1 Spreadsheet

A1:   READY

	DIVISION	LAST YEAR	THIS YEAR	CHANGE	% CHANGE
	JAZZ	123.00	200.00	77.00	63%
	ROCK	456.00	500.00	44.00	10%
	CLASSICAL	789.00	800.00	11.00	1%
	COUNTRY	444.00	400.00	(44.00)	−10%
	CORPORATE	1,812.00	1,900.00	88.00	5%

CAPS

2. *Data Management.* Data-management (DATA) commands allow you to sort, summarize, and extract portions of a collection of information (or data). The collection of data is known as a **database** and is stored on the 1–2–3 worksheet. Figure 2.2 is a 1–2–3 database containing Music Corporation's financial information.

Fig. 2.2 Financial Database

A1: "DATA   READY

	A	B	C	D	E	F	G	H	I
1	DATA	DIVISION	QTR	REVENUE	COST				
2		ROCK	1	300	210				
3		ROCK	2	350	245				
4		ROCK	3	360	252				
5		CLASSICAL	1	200	60				
6		CLASSICAL	2	240	72				
7		CLASSICAL	3	280	84				
8		JAZZ	1	100	70				
9		JAZZ	2	120	84				
10		JAZZ	3	150	105				
11		COUNTRY	1	400	320				
12		COUNTRY	2	400	320				
13		COUNTRY	3	390	312				
14									
15									
16									
17									
18									
19									
20									

CMFS

3. *Graphics.* Through the use of GRAPH commands, you can plot and draw graphs on your computer screen or your printer. You specify the pertinent numbers from your 1–2–3 worksheet, and 1–2–3 will graph them. Figure 2.3 is a bar graph comparing revenues for the company's four divisions.

Fig. 2.3 Bar Graph

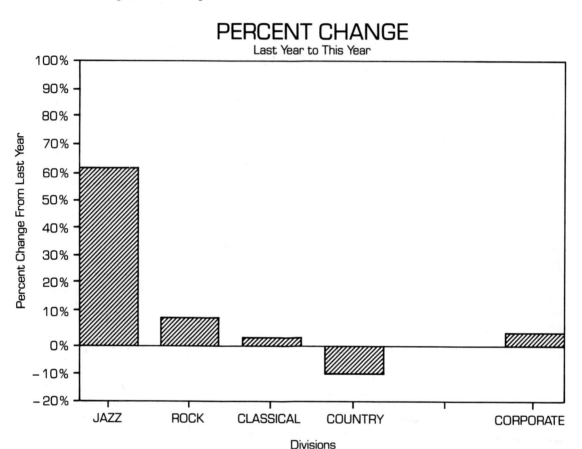

PERCENT CHANGE
Last Year to This Year

In addition to performing these three functions, you can do other things with 1–2–3. Some of its commands handle simple text processing. Figure 2.4 is a memo written on the 1–2–3 worksheet.

You can even use 1–2–3 as a simple calculator; it performs arithmetic very quickly.

Fig. 2.4   Memo

M3: 'Dear Bill,   READY

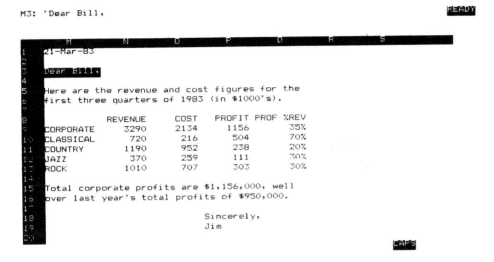

2. The Keyboard Layout

The 1–2–3 program assigns special meaning to several keys on your computer keyboard. Appendix B defines the special keys for the IBM Personal Computer. If you are using a computer other than the IBM PC, read Appendix B and your *1–2–3 User's Manual* to find the special keys defined there.

3. The 1–2–3 Worksheet

Let's take another look at the 1–2–3 worksheet we saw in Fig. 2.1. If you own 1–2–3, you should get it out and load it into your computer now. If this is your first time using 1–2–3, read the section in your *User's Manual* on how to customize 1–2–3 to your equipment ("Getting Started"). Once you have carried out the instructions in "Getting Started," you can follow the summary procedure below:

1. Put your 1–2–3 disk in drive A and turn the computer on.
2. The computer will display the Lotus Access System menu.
3. Select 1–2–3 from the Lotus menu. You can select 1–2–3 by typing [Enter] or by typing a 1.
4. You should now be looking at the Lotus 1–2–3 logo. Type any key to clear the logo and display the 1–2–3 worksheet.

The 1–2–3 screen display has three parts:

1. The **control panel** takes up three lines at the top of the screen. It displays information about where you are, what you are doing, and what you can do next.

Fig. 2.5   The Control Panel

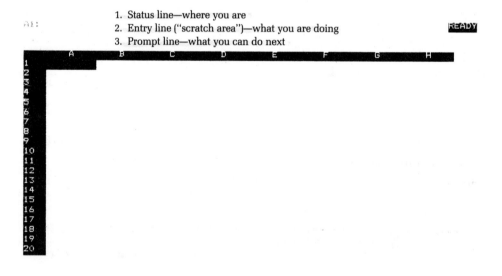

2. The **border** labels the rows and columns of your worksheet. Columns are labeled with letters (A, B, C, etc.), and rows are labeled with numbers (1, 2, 3, etc.).

3. The rest of the screen is called the **worksheet** because it is the area in which you do your work.

Fig. 2.6   The Screen Display

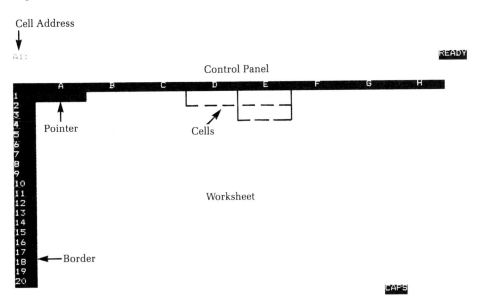

The worksheet is divided into rows and columns. The intersection of a row and a column is called a **cell,** and it is referred to by its **cell address.** A cell address is like a home address: it tells you where the cell is. A1 is the address of the first cell in the worksheet—the cell that is the intersection of column A and row 1.

On cell A1 is a reverse-video bar called the **pointer.** The pointer highlights the cell or cells you are working on. To enter a value in the worksheet, you usually follow this procedure:

1. Move the pointer to the cell in which you want the entry to appear.

2. Type the entry.

3. Type [Enter].

29

You can always tell where the pointer is in the worksheet by looking in the upper left-hand corner of the screen. Right now the pointer is on cell A1, and the upper left-hand corner of the screen reads "A1:."

Move the pointer one cell to the right by typing the Right Arrow key. Remember, the Right Arrow key is on the pointer movement keypad at the right of the keyboard. So you type [→].

Fig. 2.7 Pointer Movement

Look at your screen. Two things should have changed. First, the pointer is now on cell B1. Second, the message in the upper left-hand corner of the screen now reads "B1:."

Move the pointer down one cell by typing a Down Arrow: [↓]. Now the pointer is on cell B2 and the message reads "B2:." Type an Up Arrow to move back to B1. Now move to the edge of the worksheet and see what happens. Move right by striking the Right Arrow key seven times. Watch the screen as you type the seventh arrow. Notice that you have just gone "over the edge" of your screen, but you're still on the 1–2–3 worksheet.

Fig. 2.8 Pointer in Column I

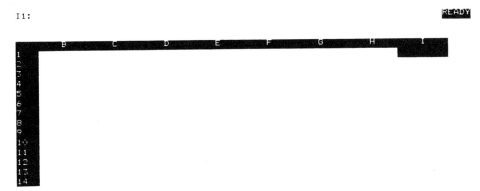

To find out how big the worksheet really is, hold down the Right Arrow key. When you hold a key down, it repeats. If you hold a key down too long, the computer will give you a high-toned beep. This means that it can't keep up with all the commands you're giving it (move right, move right, move right, etc.). If the computer beeps like this, stop typing until the screen and pointer stop moving.

When you reach one of the boundaries of the worksheet, the computer will beep at you in a lower tone. You should be able to move all the way to column IV.

Fig. 2.9 Worksheet's Last Column

The next logical question is, "How many *rows* are in the worksheet?" Move the pointer down several rows using the Down Arrow key. This soon becomes tiresome, so move down faster using the Page Down key [PgDn]. This key moves you down one page, or 20 lines, at a time.

The fastest way to get to the end of the worksheet is by typing two keys in succession: first the End key and then the Down Arrow key [End] [↓]. This moves you immediately to the last row in the worksheet: row 2048.

Fig. 2.10   Worksheet's Last Row

By now it's apparent that you are dealing with a huge worksheet— 256 columns by 2048 rows, or a total of 524,288 cells! What you see on the computer screen at any given time is just a small portion of the whole. Think of the screen as a "window" on the larger worksheet (Fig. 2.11).

Fig. 2.11   Screen as Window

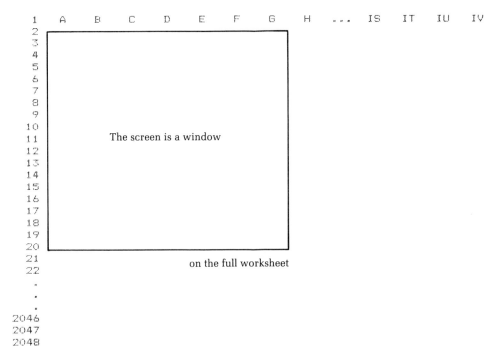

You can move back to the first cell in one of three ways:

- Hold the Up Arrow and then the Left Arrow keys down until you get to A1.
- Type the Home key on the pointer movement keypad. Home is the first cell in the worksheet—A1.
- Tell the pointer to Goto A1 by typing the Goto function key and then typing A1 [Enter].

Use either the second or third method to get the pointer back to cell A1. Take a few minutes to move around the worksheet using the other pointer movement keys until you understand what they do.

4. Correcting Errors

Errors are a fact of life. Before you begin entering real data, you should know how to correct the occasional mistakes you'll make. Let's create a few intentional errors and examine the different ways to correct them. As you learn about error correction, you'll also learn something about how data is entered in the worksheet.

With the pointer on A1, type 123. Notice that as you type them, these three numbers appear in the second line of the control panel.

Fig. 2.12   The Control Panel—Entering Data

Think of this as a "scratch area" where you can figure out what you want to put in a cell. Once the scratch area has the right data in it, you can "send" that data to the worksheet by typing [Enter]. Type [Enter] now.

In response to your command, 1–2–3 sends the number from the scratch area to the worksheet and then displays the contents of A1 in the top line of the control panel.

Fig. 2.13   Control Panel During Data Entry

The top line is a status line. Right now, the status line says:

A1:	123	READY
(the pointer is on A1)	(A1 contains the value 123)	(the program is ready to do more work)

Move the pointer to B1 and type 456. Look at the upper right-hand corner of the control panel. The word displayed is called the **mode indicator** because it tells you what you are now doing (that is, what mode you are in). The mode indicator says VALUE because you are now typing a number, or value, in the scratch area.

Fig. 2.14   Value Entry

Before you type [Enter], however, you spot an error: the number you *should* have typed is 467. Correct this by striking the Backspace Delete key twice to erase 5 and 6 in the scratch area; then type 67 [Enter].

Fig. 2.15   Correcting Errors During Data Entry

Suppose it turns out that the number 123, in cell A1, was also a mistake—the correct number is 234. How can you fix it? You can't use the Backspace Delete key, because it works only to erase things in the scratch area.

The fact is, you don't have to "correct" the first number. Instead, you can just "type over" the value in cell A1. Move the pointer back to A1 and type 234 [Enter]. The old number is replaced by the new (correct) number.

Fig. 2.16   Corrected Worksheet

3 5

Suppose you don't want any number at all in cell A1. To clear a cell entirely, you must use one of the special 1–2–3 commands. First, type a slash: /. What now appears in the control panel is the 1–2–3 main menu. We're not going into detail about the menu here, but soon we'll take a closer look at it.

Type R to select the RANGE command. (We're showing the commands in uppercase, but lowercase works just as well). Next, type E to select the ERASE command; then type [Enter] to say that you want to erase only one cell.

The number is erased from A1 and from the control panel, and the mode indicator is set back to READY.

Fig. 2.17   Worksheet After Range Erase

That sequence involved a lot of activity that you haven't learned yet. Don't worry about it; we'll look at menus before long. For now, remember that you can erase the contents of a cell by typing / R E [Enter].

But what if you start to erase a cell and then change your mind? Let's find out. Type / R. At this point suppose you decide not to erase the cell. Type the Escape key once. You have now *backed up one step* in your command sequence. Type the Escape key again, and the menu will disappear. You can always back out of a command sequence by typing Escape until the menu is gone and the mode indicator says READY.

There is also a command that erases the entire worksheet. You should use this command only when the worksheet contains *nothing* that you want to keep. If you want to erase everything on the worksheet and start with a clean slate, type / W, for WORKSHEET; E, for ERASE; and Y, for YES. The Y tells 1–2–3 that you really do want to erase everything.

Fig. 2.18   Erasing the Worksheet

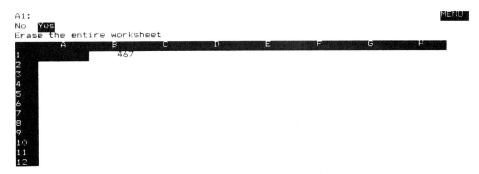

Remember, once you have erased the worksheet there's no getting it back unless you have saved it on a disk. So be careful with this command.

Here is a quick summary of the methods you've learned for correcting errors:

1. If you make an error while typing something in the scratch area of the control panel,

   use the Backspace Delete key to erase the mistake, then finish the entry correctly and type [Enter].

2. If you have entered something in the worksheet and you want to replace it with other data,

   move the pointer back to that cell, then type the new entry and [Enter]. The new entry will replace the old entry.

3. If you have entered data in a cell of the worksheet and you want to make the cell blank,

   type / R E [Enter] to erase the one-cell range.

4. If you start a command sequence and don't want to complete it,

   type the escape key until the menu is gone and the mode indicator says READY.

5. If you want to erase the entire worksheet,

   type / W E Y. (Remember—when you erase the worksheet, *everything* on it is gone. Use this command with care!)

3 7

5. Getting Help

The 1–2–3 program contains 110 built-in commands and subcommands. It's only reasonable to expect that sometimes you'll forget how a particular command works. To help you remember how to use the commands, 1–2–3 provides a very comprehensive Help option. To use the Help option, you must have the 1–2–3 program disk in the drive. Make sure it's there now, and we'll give it a try.

Type / R, as though you were going to erase a cell. Now, suppose you can't remember what to do next . . .

Ask for help by pressing the Help key. What you see now is a **Help screen.**

F1 must have a disk in a B drive

Fig. 2.19   Help Screen

```
A1: 123                                                               HELP
Format  Label-Prefix  Erase  Name  Justify  Protect  Unprotect  Input
Format a cell or range of cells
                                                            145
Range commands -- Process the entries, format, or assign a name
                  to a range of cells.

A Range command affects a particular range of cells.  In many cases, a
corresponding Worksheet command affects the entire worksheet.

The Range commands are:

Format                     Justify
Label-Prefix               Protect
Erase                      Unprotect
Name                       Input




Ranges                 Help Index
```

Think of this display as a page in a very helpful and easy-to-use manual. This "manual" always opens conveniently to the page that explains the command you are working on. In other words, the Help function is context-sensitive.

Notice that the Help screen also has a pointer. Since you want to get help with the ERASE command, move the Help-screen pointer down to ERASE by typing two Down Arrows.

When the pointer is on ERASE, type [Enter]; 1–2–3 now shows you a screen of information about the RANGE ERASE command. Notice that there are more options at the bottom of the screen in case you want help with related commands.

Fig. 2.20   RANGE ERASE Help Screen

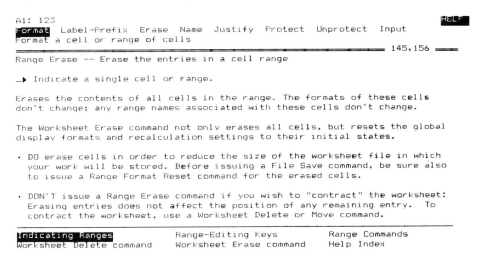

When you are finished looking at the Help screen, type the Escape key. Escape returns you to *exactly where you were before you asked for help,* which in this case is in the middle of a RANGE ERASE command. You can now go on and complete the command, or you can back out of it by typing Escape. Type Escape until the menu is gone and you are in READY mode (that is, until the mode indicator says READY).

For practice, type some numbers and try changing and erasing them. If you forget how to use the ERASE commands, ask for help by striking the Help key. When you're through making corrections, clear the entire worksheet with the WORKSHEET ERASE command.

3 9

6. Menus and Commands

You have already glimpsed the 1–2–3 menus and have actually used two commands: RANGE ERASE and WORKSHEET ERASE. These are just two examples of the many available commands. Now we're about to take a closer look at commands and menus, but first let's establish some definitions:

- A **command** is an order that you give 1–2–3 when you want some function performed. Each primary command has sublevel commands and prompts, which let you specify further what you want done.

- A **menu** is a list of the commands from which you can choose. Menus are structured in a hierarchy; a main menu connects to second-level menus, which connect to third-level menus, and so on. A menu may also branch to a **prompt,** asking for further detail about the function you want performed. Prompts let you *specify* a function, whereas menus let you *select from a list* of functions.

To select an option from a 1–2–3 menu, you can follow either of these approaches:

a) Type the first letter of the option (e.g., type R to select RANGE).

b) Move the menu pointer to the desired option and type the [Enter] key.

For reasons we'll explain shortly, we recommend method (a).

The menu pointer works like the worksheet pointer. You can move it to the left or the right with the appropriate Arrow key. If you move to the end of the menu line, the pointer will loop around to the first option again. The Home key will move the pointer to the first menu option, and the End key will move it to the last.

There are two lines in a menu. The first line lists available options. The second line describes what each option does. This line shows only one description at a time: that of whatever option the pointer is on. If you move the pointer to a new option, the description changes.

Prompts for more information usually take just one line. Different commands elicit different prompts, but they will become familiar to you as you learn.

To take another look at the sequence of commands you used to clear the worksheet, type a Slash, [/]. The Slash key invokes the main command menu. Your control panel should look like Fig. 2.21. (If your worksheet pointer isn't on A1, don't worry.)

Fig. 2.21   Control Panel with Main Menu

Notice that the mode indicator now says "MENU."

There are nine commands in the main menu. The menu pointer is on the WORKSHEET command, so the descriptive line lists the options in the WORKSHEET sub-menu.

Type a Right Arrow to move the menu pointer to the right. Now the pointer is on the RANGE command, and the descriptive line lists the commands in the RANGE sub-menu.

Fig. 2.22   RANGE Sub-Menu

By moving your pointer to the right, look at each command and command description. Notice that some commands don't have sub-menus, or the list of subcommands is not displayed. The COPY command, for example, does not have any sub-menus. The GRAPH command leads to a sub-menu, but its options are not displayed in the descriptive line.

Fig. 2.23 All Menus

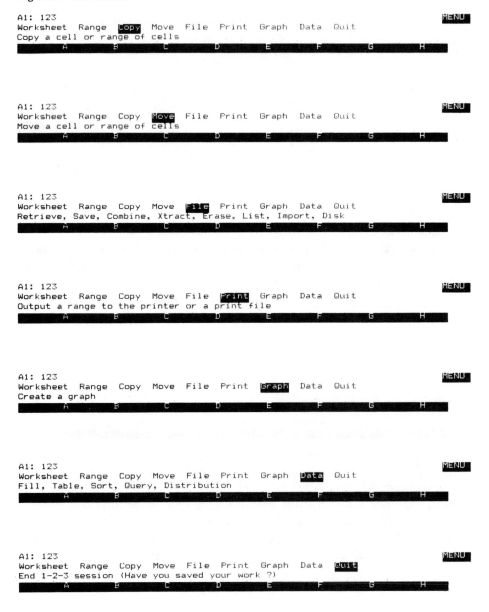

If you continue to move the pointer to the right, it will eventually come back around to WORKSHEET again.

You could select the WORKSHEET command by typing [Enter], but it's a good idea to establish the habit of selecting commands by typing the appropriate letter. This way you'll learn what the letters do, and you won't slow yourself down moving the menu pointer around.

So type W to select WORKSHEET. Now you are looking at the second-level WORKSHEET menu. It lists the subcommands from which you can choose. Notice that each subcommand also has a description in the second menu line.

Fig. 2.24   WORKSHEET Menu

Type E to select the ERASE command. Now 1–2–3 displays a prompt, asking you to confirm that you really do want to erase the whole worksheet. This is unusual; 1–2–3 rarely asks you to confirm commands. It requests confirmation here because an erased worksheet is irretrievable. The program is asking you to really think about whether or not you want to erase your worksheet.

In this case you *do* want to erase the worksheet, so type Y. Now 1–2–3 clears the screen and redisplays it with an empty worksheet. The

4 3

mode indicator is back at READY to show that you have completed the command sequence and have left the menu.

Fig. 2.25 Menus

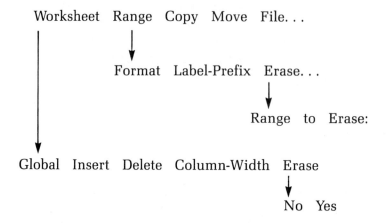

Worksheet   Range   Copy   Move   File. . .

Format   Label-Prefix   Erase. . .

Range   to   Erase:

Global   Insert   Delete   Column-Width   Erase

No   Yes

Your 1–2–3 program tries to be smart about exiting or remaining in MENU mode. For example, if you are in the second-level GRAPH menu and you complete a command, 1–2–3 will remain in the menu. Why? Because in many cases you will want to execute more graphing commands. However, if 1–2–3 remains in a menu for which you have no further commands, you can leave the menu by typing the Escape key until you're back in READY mode. Or you can select the QUIT option, if one is available.

Unlike menus in many programs, 1–2–3 menus are made up of full-word commands and include a line of description. As you work, you can get an immediate explanation of any command simply by typing the Help key. Conveniently, Help is context-sensitive, so it always turns to the screen that describes the command you're working on.

From now on we'll instruct you to invoke commands merely by telling you which one to select—for example, "select WORKSHEET ERASE." Take a minute to review the procedure you'll follow.

1. Type a slash: [/].

2. Type a W to select WORKSHEET.

3. Type an E to select ERASE.

You'll find that it doesn't take long to become adept at selecting menu options. Remember that you can always back out of a menu sequence by typing the Escape key, though often you'll have to type Escape several times to clear the menu and return to READY mode.

Look around the menus and use the Help key to find out more about the command options. But don't spend too much time figuring out how to use a command. The best way to learn is by doing, and that's what this book is all about.

PART **III**

Problem-Solving
with 1–2–3

Building a Spreadsheet

1. Comparing Yearly Profits

In this chapter, we're going to build a fairly complex (though small) spreadsheet. Building a spreadsheet is a good way to start using 1–2–3 for a number of reasons:

- You can build your spreadsheet from scratch. (Simple databases and graphics work on information already present in the worksheet.)

- The 1–2–3 worksheet looks like a paper spreadsheet, so it is easy to understand what data we need and why.

- You can use all the general purpose commands to make the spreadsheet easy to build and use.

The best way to begin working with 1–2–3 is to define what you want to end up with. Remember the old saying, "If you don't know where you're going, you won't know when you've arrived."

Figure 3.1 is a picture of the spreadsheet we're going to build.

Our initial task is to compare this year's sales performance of Music Corporation's four divisions. The spreadsheet includes sales figures for last year and this year, as well as two columns showing dollar change and percent change in sales. There is also a row of totals and a corporate percent-change figure.

Fig. 3.1 THISYR

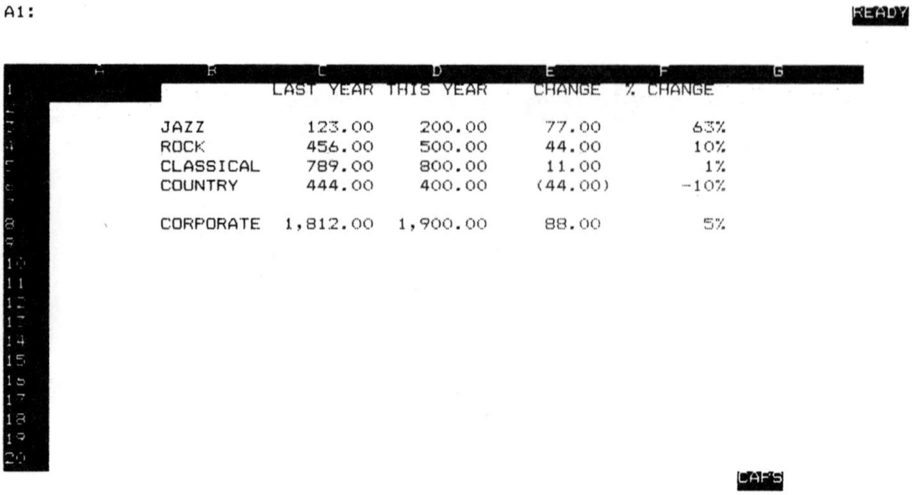

A1:   READY

```
        A          B          C          D          E         F         G
1                        LAST YEAR  THIS YEAR    CHANGE   % CHANGE
2
3            JAZZ        123.00     200.00       77.00        63%
4            ROCK        456.00     500.00       44.00        10%
5            CLASSICAL   789.00     800.00       11.00         1%
6            COUNTRY     444.00     400.00      (44.00)      -10%
7
8            CORPORATE  1,812.00   1,900.00      88.00         5%
9
10
11
12
13
14
15
16
17
18
19
20
```

                                                                          CAPS

2. Building a Sum

If there is anything on your worksheet, erase it now by selecting WORK-
SHEET ERASE YES.

Move the pointer to C3, type 123, and [Enter] it.

Now move the pointer down to C4, type 456, and, instead of typing
[Enter], simply type a Down Arrow. 1–2–3 enters the value and moves
the pointer, and you've saved yourself a keystroke. Now enter 789 in C5,
444 in C6, and move the pointer to C8.

Fig. 3.2 Entries to Sum

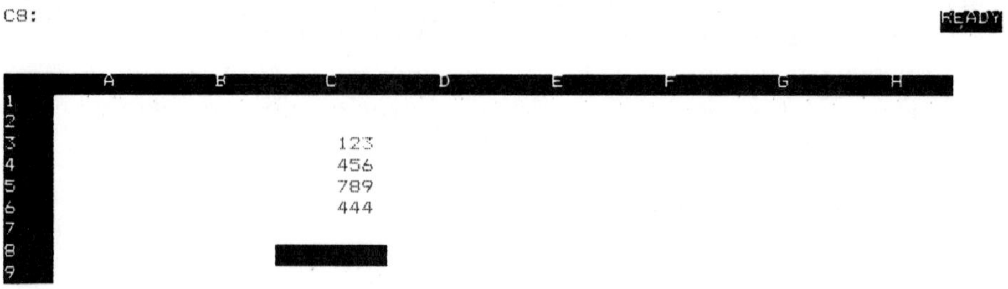

C8:   READY

```
        A          B          C          D         E         F         G         H
1
2
3                              123
4                              456
5                              789
6                              444
7
8
9
```

We want C8 to contain the total of our last year's sales figures, and we want 1–2–3 to figure out that total. What we really want in C8 is a **formula** that tells 1–2–3 to sum the numbers in cells C3 through C6 and display the sum in C8. A formula performs some arithmetic (such as addition or subtraction) on entries in the worksheet; it uses numbers you already know to calculate numbers you want to know. There are three formulas for calculating a total, and we're going to try them here. (We'll build the second formula two different ways.)

FIRST FORMULA

Type this formula in cell C8:

123 + 456 + 789 + 444

Type [Enter], and 1–2–3 performs the arithmetic and displays the answer: 1812.

Fig. 3.3   First Sum Formula

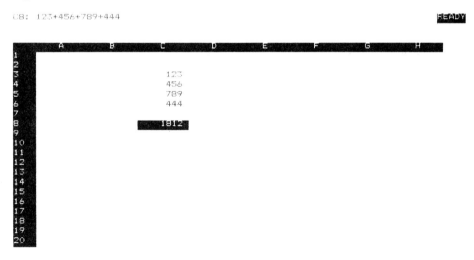

Notice that the original equation is displayed in the status line of the control panel. Whenever you want to know the formula behind a value, move the pointer to the cell and look at the status line.

SECOND FORMULA

The answer 1812 is correct, but we didn't use the special features of our "electronic spreadsheet." Let's try it another way by typing this formula in cell C8:

+C3+C4+C5+C6

Now type [Enter]. Again 1–2–3 performs the arithmetic and displays the answer.

Fig. 3.4 Second Sum Formula

C8: +C3+C4+C5+C6

Formula two has a very nice advantage over formula one. Move the pointer up to C3. Suppose you find out that the first division's last-year sales were actually 150. How will you fix the number and the sum?

With the pointer on C3, type 150; watch the sum as you type [Enter].

Fig. 3.5 New Data

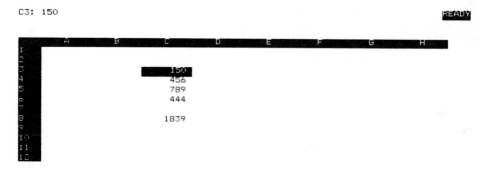

C3: 150

Notice how quickly the sum changed? Imagine using a very large spreadsheet with hundreds of numbers and formulas. By simply retyping a single number we can correct a bad entry (or try an alternative estimate) and all dependent numbers are instantly adjusted. Enter 123 in C3 again, and the sum is adjusted back to 1812. This is the real bonus behind an electronic spreadsheet: formulas that quickly adjust to new data.

Second Formula: a Variation

Because it allows you to change the data easily, formula two makes better use of the 1–2–3 electronic spreadsheet. However, it is often difficult to remember which cell addresses to put in the formula. In fact, formula one was probably easier to build, because you didn't have to think about where the numbers were entered in the worksheet.

You can build formula two in another way; it takes longer but doesn't require you to think about cell addresses. This method is called ''pointing''; it lets you use the pointer to specify which cells are included in the formula.

If you were summing a list of numbers on paper, you would probably point to each number with your finger as you added it to the sum in your head. The pointing keeps track of where you are and which numbers you have left to sum. 1–2–3 lets you use the worksheet pointer the same way you would use your finger.

With the pointer in cell C8:

a) Type a plus sign [+] to tell 1–2–3 you're going to type a formula.

b) Move the pointer up to cell C3 with the Up Arrow key [↑]. Notice that you are now in POINT mode because you are pointing to a cell you want to include in the sum formula.

Fig. 3.6   Building the Sum with Pointing

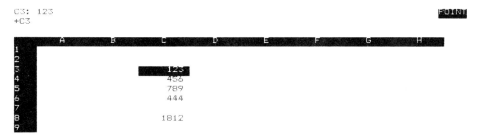

c) Since you haven't finished with the list of numbers, type [+] again. The pointer jumps back to C9 and the control panel shows both the old sum formula and the partial formula that you're building now.

Fig. 3.7 First Entry Point Complete

d) Move the pointer up to C4, the second value to sum. Notice that the control panel shows the C4 entry, 456, and the partial sum. Again the mode indicator is set to POINT.

Fig. 3.8 Pointing the Second Entry

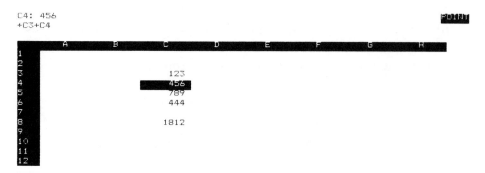

Type another [+], point to C5, type [+] again, and point to C6, the last of the values to sum.

e) When you enter the formula, the sum is calculated once again, and the completed formula is displayed in the status line of the control panel.

Fig. 3.9   Second Formula Complete

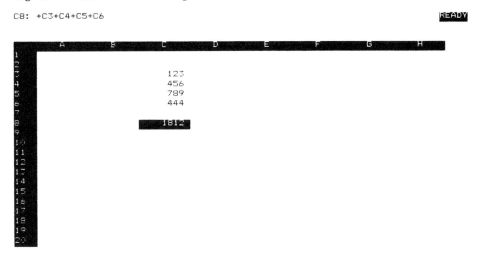

This time the readily adjustable formula was easier to build, because it followed your usual way of working.

THIRD FORMULA

Formula two and its variation may be easy to understand, but the process can become quite cumbersome. What if there were fifty values to sum! Formula three provides an easier way.

a) Move the pointer to C8 and type an "at" sign: [@] (Shift 2). The @ sign tells 1–2–3 that you are going to use a special 1–2–3 function—in this case, the @SUM function.

b) Type the word SUM immediately after the @ (no spaces) and then type an open parenthesis (Shift 9). The formula in the status line should look like this:

@SUM(

5 5

Fig. 3.10   Third Sum Formula

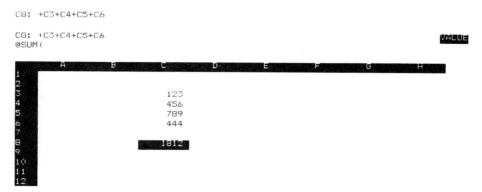

c) Move the pointer to cell C3. You want to tell 1–2–3 to sum all the values from C3 to C6. You can do this by tacking the pointer down at C3, then stretching it to cover cells C4, C5, and C6. Tack the pointer down by typing a Period. Notice that 1–2–3 displays another period and another C3 to show that you are defining a range of cells, and the range is currently one cell long.

Fig. 3.11   Pointing the Third Sum

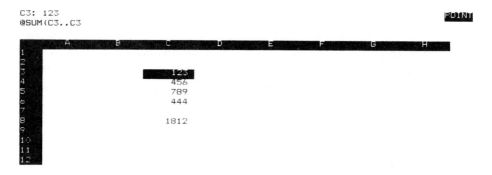

d) Now move the pointer down to C6. You should see the pointer stretching out to cover all the cells from C3 to C6. Because it highlights a block of cells, this is called a **block pointer.** The block pointer is especially convenient because it shows you

5 6

exactly what range you have specified; this means you can check and correct it if necessary. Your screen should look like this:

Fig. 3.12   Block Pointer

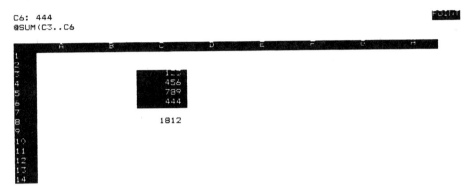

e) Close the parentheses by typing Shift 0, then [Enter] the formula. The sum appears in D8 and the new formula is displayed in the status line.

Fig. 3.13   Third Formula Complete

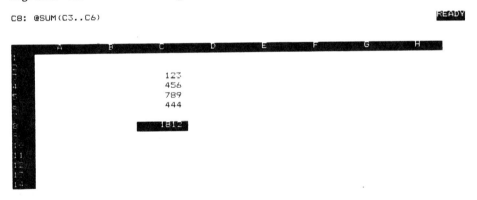

Like formula two, formula three will adjust the sum if we go back and change an initial value. Formula three is easy to create, easy to adjust, and has other advantages that we'll talk about later.

3. Labels and Column Width

Now that you have some numbers in the spreadsheet, you need labels to show what the numbers represent. Move the pointer to C1 and type LAST YEAR. Notice that as soon as you type the first letter, the mode indicator reads "LABEL."

Fig. 3.14 Label Entry

1–2–3 makes certain assumptions about what you enter in a cell:

• If the entry begins with a letter, 1–2–3 assumes it is a label.

• If the entry begins with a number or an arithmetic symbol (such as + or –), 1–2–3 assumes it is a value.

• If the entry begins with the "at" sign (@), 1–2–3 assumes it is a formula using one of the 1–2–3 functions. When you are entering a formula, the mode indicator says "VALUE," since all formulas result in values.

Remember when you entered formula 2 (+ C3 + C4 + C5 + C6) in the preceding section. The initial plus sign told 1–2–3 that we were entering a formula. If you had typed just C3, 1–2–3 would assume that the C indicated a label entry.

If you want to type a formula that begins with a letter, precede the letter with an arithmetic symbol (such as +). If you want to type a label that begins with a number, precede the number with a Single Quote mark (').

Enter the label in C1 and move to cell D1. Type THIS YEAR and [Enter] it.

Fig. 3.15   Second Label Entry

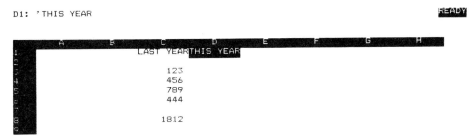

It helps to have labels here; but as you can see, the labels are too close together. You can fix this in one of two ways: either abbreviate the label or make the column wider (1–2–3 columns are nine spaces wide to start). Let's expand the column width to ten spaces throughout the worksheet. To do this, we'll have to use a new command sequence.

Type [/] to invoke the main menu. Select WORKSHEET. We want to set the column width for the whole worksheet, so we must use the GLOBAL command. When we ask 1–2–3 to do something **globally** we mean, "Do it everywhere."

Select GLOBAL COLUMN-WIDTH. Now you could just type in the new width for the columns, but you may not be sure how wide you want them. To avoid trial-and-error guessing, 1–2–3 lets you define the width using the arrow keys. Type the Right Arrow once to make the column one character wider. If you continue to type Right Arrows, the columns will continue to expand (up to a width of 72 characters). Left Arrows will make the column narrower again. Set the column width so that it is ten characters wide and [Enter] it.

Fig. 3.16   Expanding Column Width

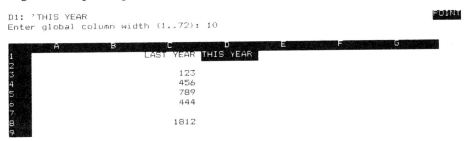

59

Finally, you can add some row labels to identify the four divisions. Move the pointer to B3 and type these labels and arrows:

JAZZ[Down]

ROCK[Down]

CLASSICAL[Down]

COUNTRY[Down]

[Down]

CORPORATE[Enter]

Fig. 3.17   Division Titles

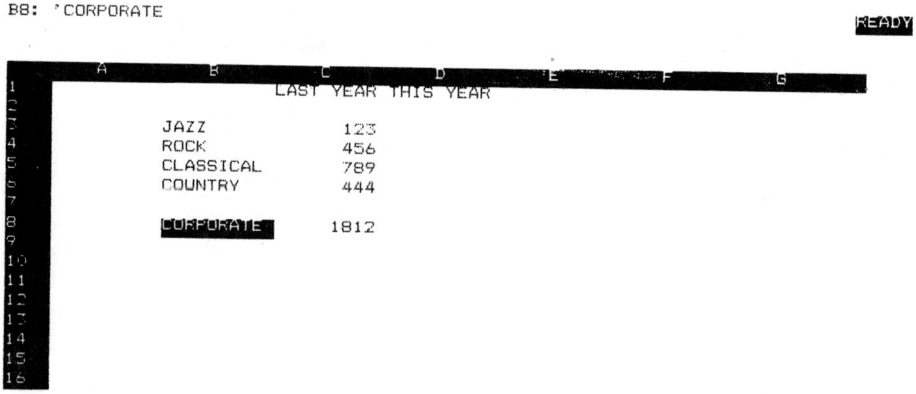

B8: 'CORPORATE

READY

	A	B	C	D	E	F	G
1			LAST YEAR	THIS YEAR			
2							
3		JAZZ	123				
4		ROCK	456				
5		CLASSICAL	789				
6		COUNTRY	444				
7							
8		CORPORATE	1812				
9							
10							
11							
12							
13							
14							
15							
16							

4. Formatting

Now enter the numbers for this year's sales. With the pointer on D3 type:

200[Down]

500[Down]

800[Down]

400[Down]

[Down]

Fig. 3.18   Profit Entries

Your pointer should now be on D8, where THIS YEAR's sum formula goes. See if you can build the formula yourself. (Hint: move your pointer to C8 to take a look at LAST YEAR's sum formula. Make sure the pointer is back on D8 when you start building the sum. If you have trouble, follow the third-formula steps you used to build the sum in section 2.)

Your worksheet should look like this:

Fig. 3.19   Second Sum

The labels you added make the spreadsheet easier to understand; however, the values are still somewhat unclear. It's impossible to tell whether the values represent dollar amounts or a number of units. To make it clear that these values represent dollar amounts, you must FORMAT the numbers.

1–2–3 has many options for formatting the values and labels in your spreadsheet. The value 1234.567, for example, could be displayed in any of these formats:

Fixed [with one decimal]	1234.6
Scientific	1.23E+03
Currency	$1,234.57
, [Comma] [with two decimals]	1,234.57
General	1234.567
+/−	**********
Percent [with two decimals]	123456.70%
Date	18–May–03 18–May May–03
Text	1234.567

We'll use some of these formats in the worksheet. If you want to learn others, read about formats in the *1–2–3 User's Manual* (see "Command Skills" under "/Worksheet Global Format" and "Range Format").

You could use the currency format to indicate dollar values, but you really don't need all those dollar signs on the spreadsheet. Instead, try the comma (,) format. You're going to define a default format for the entire worksheet. Later you'll override the default by formatting certain columns differently, but for now you can assume that all the numbers represent dollar values.

Select WORKSHEET GLOBAL FORMAT and type a Comma, [,], to select the comma format. Now 1–2–3 asks you how many decimal places it should display, and it suggests a default of two. You can accept the two-decimal default by typing [Enter]. As you see, 1–2–3 has quickly formatted all the values in your spreadsheet to display numbers with commas and two decimal places.

Fig. 3.20   Values Formatted

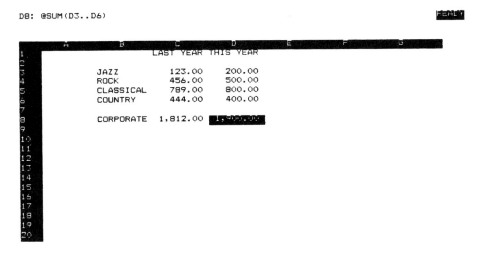

D8: @SUM(D3..D6)   READY

```
        A           B            C          D          E          F          G
 1                          LAST YEAR  THIS YEAR
 2
 3               JAZZ          123.00     200.00
 4               ROCK          456.00     500.00
 5               CLASSICAL     789.00     800.00
 6               COUNTRY       444.00     400.00
 7
 8               CORPORATE   1,812.00   1,900.00
 9
10
11
12
13
14
15
16
17
18
19
20
```

5. The COPY Command

Now that you have two years' sales figures in your spreadsheet, you can
build formulas with which to analyze this data. You'll analyze the figures
in two columns; one column will show dollar change in sales and the
other will show percent change in sales. First you'll build a formula for
JAZZ division, then you'll use the COPY command to copy the formula
down the column.

To build the formula to copy, move the pointer to E1 and type the
new column heading—CHANGE; then move the pointer to E3. The formula for computing dollar change in sales is

this year's sales minus last year's sales

or

200 – 123

or

+ D3–C3.

Build the formula by typing the symbols and pointing to the appropriate
cells. Type [+], point to cell D3, type [–], point to C3, and [Enter] the

6 3

formula. The dollar change for JAZZ division, 77.00, should appear in E3.

Fig. 3.21 CHANGE Formula

E3: +D3-C3   READY

	A	B	C	D	E	F	G
			LAST YEAR	THIS YEAR	CHANGE		
1							
2							
3		JAZZ	123.00	200.00	77.00		
4		ROCK	456.00	500.00			
5		CLASSICAL	789.00	800.00			
6		COUNTRY	444.00	400.00			
7							
8		CORPORATE	1,812.00	1,900.00			

We know that the same formula will work for each division. Rather than enter the formula four more times (for three divisions and one total), we'll use the COPY command to reproduce the formula in the range of cells from E4 to E8.

The COPY command has two parts:

the range you   and   the range you
are copying FROM   are copying TO

With the COPY command, you can copy the contents of one range into another range. A **range** can be one cell, a row of cells, a column of cells, or a block of cells.

Fig. 3.22 Ranges

These are ranges:

These are not:

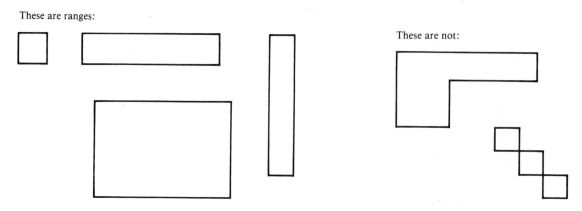

64

You defined a range when you used the RANGE ERASE command and when you built the @SUM function. To build columns E and F, you are going to COPY a formula from a one-cell range into a column-of-cells range.

Fig. 3.23   COPYing a Formula

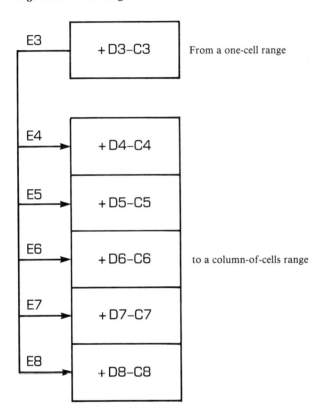

From a one-cell range

to a column-of-cells range

When you begin the COPY command sequence, your pointer should be on the cell (or the first of the range of cells) that you are copying *from*. With the pointer on E3, select COPY.

COPY does not have any sub-menus, but it does have a prompt line asking you to specify the ranges involved in the copy. First the prompt asks you what range to copy FROM. As you can see, 1–2–3 assumes that the range is one cell long (E3..E3) unless you specify otherwise.

Fig. 3.24   COPY Ranges

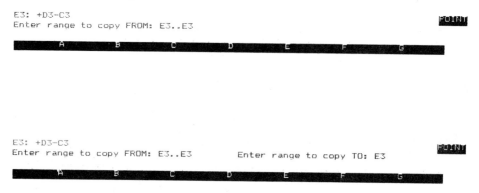

```
E3: +D3-C3
Enter range to copy FROM: E3..E3                                    POINT
```

```
E3: +D3-C3
Enter range to copy FROM: E3..E3        Enter range to copy TO: E3   POINT
```

Type [Enter] to accept the default, which sets the one-cell range to copy FROM as E3..E3.

Now 1–2–3 asks for the range to copy TO. Move the pointer to E4. As you did when you built the third sum formula, tack down the top of the range by typing a Period. Now move the pointer down to E8 to extend the range. The block pointer shows you the range that you have defined.

Fig. 3.25   Worksheet During COPY

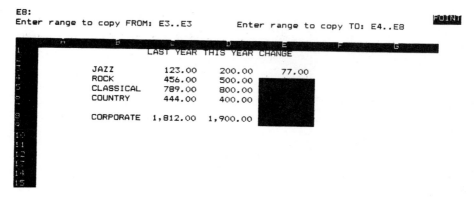

```
E8:
Enter range to copy FROM: E3..E3        Enter range to copy TO: E4..E8   POINT
```

Type [Enter] to set the range to copy TO as E4..E8, and 1–2–3 instantly copies the formula and calculates the values for the rest of column E.

Fig. 3.26   COPY Complete

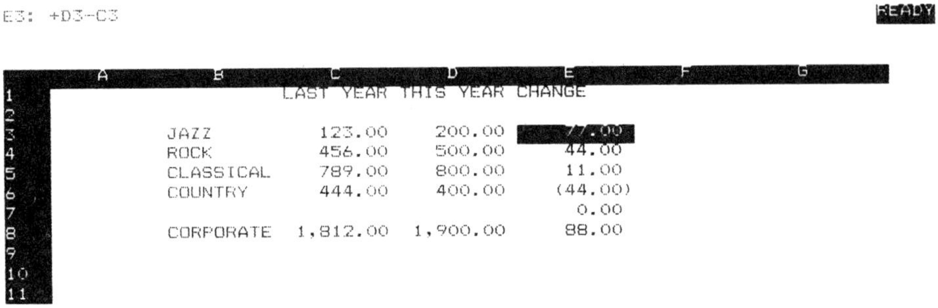

```
E3:  +D3-C3                                                              READY
```

```
       A           B            C           D           E          F          G
 1                            LAST YEAR  THIS YEAR  CHANGE
 2
 3              JAZZ         123.00     200.00      77.00
 4              ROCK         456.00     500.00      44.00
 5              CLASSICAL    789.00     800.00      11.00
 6              COUNTRY      444.00     400.00     (44.00)
 7                                                   0.00
 8              CORPORATE  1,812.00   1,900.00      88.00
 9
10
11
```

Though you may not have realized it, 1–2–3 made a convenient assumption about how you wanted the formulas to be copied. Take a close look at the formulas in column E: 1–2–3 adjusted the cell addresses in each formula relative to each row. That is,

> E3 = D3 – C3,
>
> E4 = D4 – C4,
>
> E5 = D5 – C5, and so on.

When we copy a formula into a range, 1–2–3 assumes that the cell addresses are to be adjusted. In the world of electronic spreadsheets this is called **relative adjustment.** There are other ways to copy formulas and we'll look at them later. For now, however, relative adjustment is just what we want.

You can build column F in much the same way you did column E. Enter the label % CHANGE in F1, and move the pointer to F3. The formula for percent change is

> change divided by last year's sales

or

> 77 / 123

or

> + E3/C3.

To build the formula in F3, type [+], point to E3, type [/], point to C3, and type [Enter]. Don't worry about how the answer looks right now; we'll make it cleaner-looking in a minute.

6 7

Fig. 3.27 %CHANGE Formula

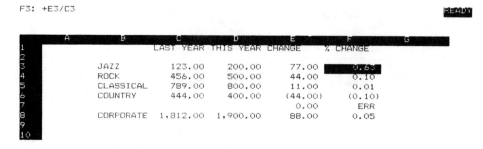

Before you refer to the step-by-step procedure in the next paragraph, see if you can copy the formula in F3 into the range F4 to F8 on your own. If you have trouble remembering the command sequence, reread this section. You'll find COPY to be one of the most useful commands for building spreadsheets, so it's worth taking some time to become proficient at it.

Here's how to copy the formula in F3 into the range F4 to F8:

1. Move the pointer to F3 and select COPY.
2. Type [Enter] to set the FROM range as F3..F3.
3. Move the pointer to F4, type a Period to tack down the range, and move the pointer to F8. This sets the TO range as F4..F8.
4. Type [Enter] to complete the COPY command.

Fig. 3.28 Second COPY Complete

F3: +E3/C3   READY

	A	B	C	D	E	F	G
			LAST YEAR	THIS YEAR	CHANGE	% CHANGE	
1							
2							
3		JAZZ	123.00	200.00	77.00	0.63	
4		ROCK	456.00	500.00	44.00	0.10	
5		CLASSICAL	789.00	800.00	11.00	0.01	
6		COUNTRY	444.00	400.00	(44.00)	(0.10)	
7					0.00	ERR	
8		CORPORATE	1,812.00	1,900.00	88.00	0.05	
9							
10							

1–2–3 displays the label ERR in F7 because the formula is trying to divide by zero (we'll erase it next).

6. Formatting a Single Column

Just three more command sequences and you'll have a completed spreadsheet! First, erase the formulas in E7 and F7. Move the pointer to F7 and select RANGE ERASE. Instead of typing [Enter], as you did to erase a single cell, extend the range to include E7.

Fig. 3.29   Erasing Two Entries

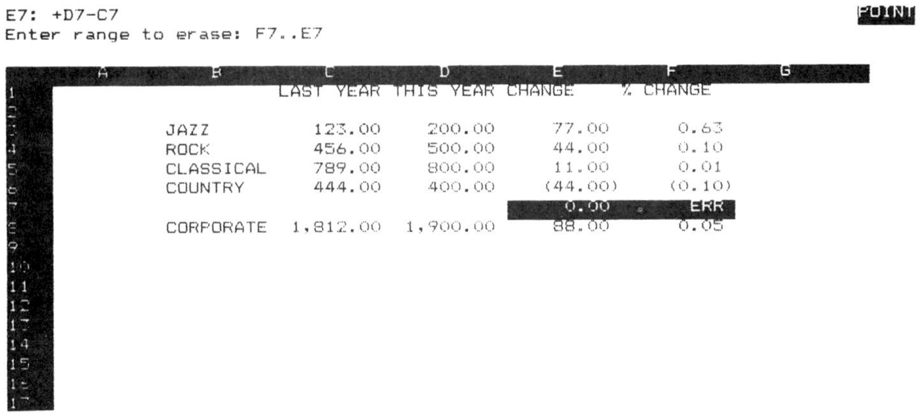

```
E7: +D7-C7                                                            POINT
Enter range to erase: F7..E7
```

	A	B	C	D	E	F	G
1			LAST YEAR	THIS YEAR	CHANGE	% CHANGE	
2							
3		JAZZ	123.00	200.00	77.00	0.63	
4		ROCK	456.00	500.00	44.00	0.10	
5		CLASSICAL	789.00	800.00	11.00	0.01	
6		COUNTRY	444.00	400.00	(44.00)	(0.10)	
7					0.00	ERR	
8		CORPORATE	1,812.00	1,900.00	88.00	0.05	

Type a Left Arrow, then [Enter]. Both cells should be cleared. Now move the pointer to F8. Probably you'd like to format this column in such a way that the numbers look more like percentages. But you can't use the GLOBAL formatting command you used before, because you don't want to set the whole worksheet to percent format.

In this situation you need another of the RANGE commands: RANGE FORMAT. Select RANGE FORMAT. You should now see a familiar list of formatting options. Select the PERCENT format, but instead of accepting the default number of decimals, type 0 (for no decimals), and [Enter] your selection.

Because you are formatting a single range and not the entire worksheet, 1–2–3 prompts you to define the range you want formatted. Type a Period to tack one end of the range at F8; then move your pointer up to F3 and type [Enter].

Fig. 3.30 Formatting Percent

```
F3:  +E3/C3                                                                    POINT
Enter range to format: F8..F3
```

```
         A          B           C          D          E          F        G
1                              LAST YEAR  THIS YEAR  CHANGE     % CHANGE
2
3                   JAZZ        123.00     200.00     77.00     0.63
4                   ROCK        456.00     500.00     44.00     0.10
5                   CLASSICAL   789.00     800.00     11.00     0.01
6                   COUNTRY     444.00     400.00    (44.00)   (0.10)
7
8                   CORPORATE  1,812.00  1,900.00     88.00     0.05
9
```

Notice that you can define ranges in any direction; you don't have to go left-to-right or top-to-bottom.

As a final beautifying measure, you can right-justify the column labels. To right-justify (or center) labels, you'll use another RANGE option: LABEL-PREFIX. Move the pointer to F1, select RANGE LABEL-PREFIX RIGHT, and enter the range F1..C1. The LABEL-PREFIX command inserts a prefix character at the beginning of each label. There are three LABEL-PREFIX options:

"   right-justifies the label

'   left-justifies the label

∧   centers the label

The LABEL-PREFIX command tells 1–2–3 how to display the label entry. (It's not necessary to use the LABEL-PREFIX command to justify a single label; simply type the prefix at the beginning of the label entry.) When you enter the label, 1–2–3 displays it with the justification indicated by the prefix. With the pointer in F1, look at the cell contents in the control panel. Notice in Fig. 3.31 that the label prefix, a double quote, is shown at the beginning of the label.

Fig. 3.31 LABEL-PREFIXES

```
F1:  "% CHANGE                                                                 READY
```

```
         A          B           C          D          E          F        G
1                              LAST YEAR  THIS YEAR  CHANGE     % CHANGE
2
3                   JAZZ        123.00     200.00     77.00        63%
4                   ROCK        456.00     500.00     44.00        10%
5                   CLASSICAL   789.00     800.00     11.00         1%
6                   COUNTRY     444.00     400.00    (44.00)      -10%
7
8                   CORPORATE  1,812.00  1,900.00     88.00         5%
9
```

Your completed spreadsheet should look like Fig. 3.32.

Fig. 3.32   THISYR Complete

F8: (PO) +E8/C8   READY

	A	B	C	D	E	F	G
1			LAST YEAR	THIS YEAR	CHANGE	% CHANGE	
2							
3		JAZZ	123.00	200.00	77.00	63%	
4		ROCK	456.00	500.00	44.00	10%	
5		CLASSICAL	789.00	800.00	11.00	1%	
6		COUNTRY	444.00	400.00	(44.00)	−10%	
7							
8		CORPORATE	1,812.00	1,900.00	88.00	5%	
9							
10							
11							
12							
13							
14							
15							
16							
17							
18							
19							
20							

CAPS

7. Saving Your Work

The final thing you must do before moving on to new work is *save your worksheet model.* Saving your worksheet on a disk is like filing your written work away in a folder. But remembering to do it is absolutely critical! If you don't save the worksheet, it will be erased as soon as you turn 1–2–3 or the computer off. (You'll have no chance to retrieve it from your wastebasket tomorrow.)

When you select the FILE SAVE command, 1–2–3 will display a list of the 1–2–3 worksheet files currently saved on your data disk. If you want to assign one of the names in the list to your new file, select that name with the menu pointer. Now 1–2–3 will ask whether you want to REPLACE the old file of the same name or CANCEL the save command. If you select REPLACE, the new file will be saved on the disk and the old file will be deleted.

If there are no worksheet files on your disk (hence no names in the list), or if you want to give the file-to-save a name different from any cur-

71

rently in the list, simply type the new name and enter it. When it finds a duplicate file name on the disk, 1–2–3 will always offer the REPLACE or CANCEL option; so if you inadvertently enter a duplicate name, select CANCEL and start the FILE SAVE command over again.

Now let's follow the four steps for saving your worksheet:

1. Make sure you have a formatted disk in the default drive.

2. Select FILE SAVE.

3. In response to the "File name" prompt, type THISYR (for "this-year profits") and enter it.

Fig. 3.33 Saving THISYR

```
F8:  (P0)  +E8/C8                                              EDIT
Enter save file name: THISYR
          A         B         C         D         E         F         G
 1                           LAST YEAR THIS YEAR  CHANGE   % CHANGE
 2
 3                 JAZZ       123.00    200.00     77.00       63%
 4                 ROCK       456.00    500.00     44.00       10%
 5                 CLASSICAL  789.00    800.00     11.00        1%
 6                 COUNTRY    444.00    400.00    (44.00)     -10%
 7
 8                 CORPORATE 1,812.00  1,900.00    88.00        5%
 9
10
11
12
13
14
```

4. Unless you have already saved a file called THISYR, 1–2–3 will save the file with no further prompts.

The REPLACE option gives you a chance to overwrite an old file by replacing it with an updated file. Often, though, you'll want to keep more than one version of a worksheet around. For example, you can save several THISYR files simply by calling them THISYR2, THISYR3, THISYR4, and so on.

Once you've saved your THISYR file, erase the worksheet with the WORKSHEET ERASE command.

When you want to work with your THISYR file again, you can reload it in the 1–2–3 worksheet. To reload the worksheet, select FILE RETRIEVE and either type in the file name to reload, or point to it in the list of available files that 1–2–3 displays. When you retrieve a file from the disk you are actually retrieving a *copy* of the file—the original file remains untouched on the disk until you erase it or overwrite it with the FILE-SAVE-REPLACE sequence.

Disk storage is *very* cheap when you compare its cost with that of your working time; so save your files regularly and don't hesitate to make backups of your data disks.

8.   Printing the Worksheet

You've already done a lot of work in this chapter, but before you go on, you might like to print a copy of your worksheet. Here's how it's done.

Move the pointer to B1 and select PRINT; 1-2-3 will ask whether you want to print to the printer or to a file. We'll print this worksheet directly to the printer, so select PRINTER.

Fig. 3.34   PRINTER Menu

The first option in the PRINTER menu, RANGE, lets you tell 1-2-3 what part of the worksheet to print. You can print all your work, or just a piece of it. LINE and PAGE are used to advance the paper in the printer by one line or one page, respectively. Other printing OPTIONS let you

- adjust margins, type size, and page length;
- add headers, footers, and borders;
- adjust the way the printed text is formatted.

We'll try some of the OPTIONS later in this section. CLEAR erases any previous print settings, ALIGN tells 1-2-3 where the top of the printer paper is, GO tells 1-2-3 to start printing, and QUIT exits the PRINT menu.

First, try printing the whole model using the original (out-of-the-box) OPTIONS settings. Make sure your paper is properly lined up with the printhead, then select ALIGN. Select RANGE to define the worksheet area that you want printed. To print the full worksheet, move the pointer to B1 and tack the range down by typing a Period, then extend the block pointer down and over to F8 and type [Enter].

Fig. 3.35 Print Range

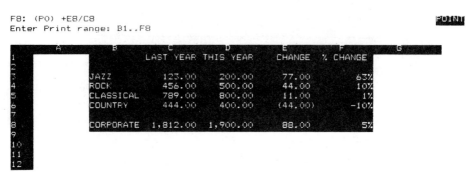

```
F8: (P0) +E8/C8                                                    POINT
Enter Print range: B1..F8
```

Select GO to start the printing. Your printed worksheet will look like this:

Fig. 3.36 THISYR Printed

```
           LAST YEAR THIS YEAR   CHANGE   % CHANGE

JAZZ         123.00    200.00     77.00      63%
ROCK         456.00    500.00     44.00      10%
CLASSICAL    789.00    800.00     11.00       1%
COUNTRY      444.00    400.00    (44.00)    -10%

CORPORATE  1,812.00  1,900.00     88.00       5%
```

When 1–2–3 finishes printing, select PAGE to advance the paper. Since 1–2–3 keeps track of how many lines were used for printing, it can calculate how many lines to advance to reach the next page.

Now let's add a header and a footer and print the worksheet again. You're still in the PRINT menu, so select OPTIONS. Select the first option, HEADER, and enter a one-line header:

MUSIC CORPORATION 1983

Next, select FOOTER and enter:

PAGE # ¦THISYR ¦@

The # (pound sign) tells 1–2–3 to number each page of printout starting with page 1. The ¦(vertical bars—Shift ╲, to the left of the Z) split the footer into sections. The first section is left-justified, the second section is centered, and the third section is right-justified. The @ (at sign) tells 1–2–3 to print today's date in the third section of the footer.

The final change is to reset the top and bottom margins. Select MARGINS TOP and enter 10, then select MARGINS BOTTOM and enter 10.

Fig. 3.37   Optional Print Settings

```
B1:                                                          EDIT
Enter Header Line: MUSIC CORPORATION
```

```
B1:                                                          EDIT
Enter Footer Line: PAGE #¦THISYR¦@
```

```
B1:                                                          EDIT
Enter Top Margin (0..10): 10
```

```
B1:                                                          EDIT
Enter Bottom Margin (0..10): 10
```

Select QUIT to return to the main PRINT menu; then, if your paper is properly aligned, select GO (1–2–3 will remember your previous range setting).

Fig. 3.38 THISYR with Print Options

```
MUSIC CORPORATION 1983


              LAST YEAR THIS YEAR      CHANGE   % CHANGE

JAZZ            123.00    200.00       77.00        63%
ROCK            456.00    500.00       44.00        10%
CLASSICAL       789.00    800.00       11.00         1%
COUNTRY         444.00    400.00      (44.00)      -10%

CORPORATE     1,812.00  1,900.00       88.00         5%
```

```
PAGE 1                      THISYR               04-May-83
```

1–2–3 will print the header and worksheet, but it won't print the footer until it reaches the end of the page. Select PAGE, and 1–2–3 will advance the paper and print the footer line. Try some of the other printing options on your own.

The BORDERS option lets you set a range of columns or rows to print at the left or top of every page. You can use it to print titles along with a section of your work that's farther down the worksheet. For example, to print the row of Corporate totals in THISYR under the column labels, select BORDER ~~COLUMNS~~ *Rows* and set the border range as B1..F1. The RANGE to print is the single row of Corporate data from B8..F8. When you select GO, the worksheet is printed like this:

Fig. 3.39   Border Printing

```
           LAST YEAR  THIS YEAR     CHANGE   % CHANGE
CORPORATE   1,812.00   1,900.00      88.00        5%
```

The SETUP option sends codes to your printer that tell it to activate a special print feature. For example, to activate compressed printing on an Epson MX80 printer, you would select SETUP and enter the code \015. (Codes and features vary among printers.) Through this code, 1–2–3 tells the Epson MX80 to turn on the compressed-printing feature. In compressed printing, THISYR looks like this:

Fig. 3.40   THISYR Compressed

```
           LAST YEAR THIS YEAR    CHANGE  % CHANGE

JAZZ          123.00    200.00     77.00       63%
ROCK          456.00    500.00     44.00       10%
CLASSICAL     789.00    800.00     11.00        1%
COUNTRY       444.00    400.00    (44.00)     -10%

CORPORATE   1,812.00  1,900.00     88.00        5%
```

PAGE-LENGTH lets you adjust the length of the page. The original page-length setting is 66 lines. OTHER lists four options that control how each entry is printed. It allows you to print the worksheet *formulas* rather than the displayed values.

When you've finished printing, select QUIT and 1–2–3 returns the worksheet to READY mode. The amount of worksheet data that you can print at one time is limited by the size of your printer. Your THISYR

77

worksheet fits easily on a printer that's 80 columns wide, but you may have to print larger worksheets in two or more pieces.

9. The Profit Model Summarized

You have covered a great deal of 1–2–3 in this chapter. In fact, you now know the basic commands that are necessary to build a simple worksheet model. You have learned how to

- enter labels and values,
- build formulas,
- sum a range of numbers,
- change the width of columns,
- FORMAT the way values are displayed,
- COPY an entry to a range of entries,
- SAVE your work, and
- PRINT a picture of your worksheet.

These commands and features are the building blocks for most spreadsheet work. Before you continue, make sure you are comfortable with them.

Chapter 3 Exercises

Now that you know the basic commands of 1–2–3, you're ready to try some exercises with the worksheet you just built. Following three of these, you'll find several exercises that introduce new models. Try building some of the new models for practice with what you have learned. If you have trouble with certain commands, read through the chapter again. Once you know how the commands work, your best teacher is practice!

THISYR Exercises

   A. Ask some what-if questions by trying different profit figures in the THIS YEAR column. COUNTRY seems to be in real trouble, but the other divisions may be able to push their figures up a bit. Try some reasonable profit increases to bring Corporate CHANGE up to 10 percent.

B. Try printing smaller pieces of the worksheet (just the LAST YEAR and THIS YEAR figures, for example) to learn about the PRINT command. Before you print, select OPTIONS and change the margins, or add a header or footer to your printout.

C. Build a table with THIS YEAR and LAST YEAR profits for your own division or group.

EVALUATE Exercise

Build the EVALUATE table using what you learned in Chapter 3. Start by entering the table's name, the date, and a line of documentation that describes what the program does. Next, enter the list of numbers in row 6 and the labels in column A. Finally, enter the formulas in column B. For additional help wth the model, consult notes 1–4.

1. The numbers in B6..F6 are straight values.

2. The labels are pushed to the right-hand side of the cell with the right-label-prefix character, a Double Quote ("). For example, E9 = "SUM:.

```
A1: 'EVALUATE


          A          B          C          D          E          F          G
 1   EVALUATE                 Date     April 20, 1983
 2
 3   Evaluate several characteristics of a list of numbers.
 4
 5
 6      THE LIST:        4         22         16         34          9
 7
 8
 9          SUM:        85
10      AVERAGE:        17
11      MAXIMUM:        34
12      MINIMUM:         4
13        COUNT:         5
14      STANDARD
15     DEVIATION:  10.46900
16      VARIANCE:     109.6
17
18
19
20
```

3. Column A is set to twelve characters wide to allow more room for the function titles. Use the WORKSHEET COLUMN SET command to expand the column.

4. The formulas in B9..B13 and B15..B16 use the 1–2–3 Statistical Functions to evaluate the list of numbers. All the formulas are entered in this form:

   @function [list]

   For example, the formula for *average* is

   @AVG [B6..F6]

   Enter the 1–2–3 function names like this:

   ```
   sum = @SUM
   average = @AVG
   maximum = @MAX
   minimum = @MIN
   count = @COUNT
   standard deviation = @STD
   variance = @VAR
   ```

Change the initial values and notice how quickly 1–2–3 recalculates the formulas. You could evaluate a progression of numbers by entering a formula in the list. For example, enter the formula +B6*2 in C6, then use the COPY command to copy the formula FROM C6 TO D6..F6. If you change the initial value (in B6), the rest of the list values and the @function values will change.

TABLE Exercise

Building TABLE is fairly easy with 1–2–3, and it solves a large class of problems that involve simple tables of numbers. A division manager could use TABLE to distribute project budgets over four quarters. A sales manager could use TABLE to set quarterly sales goals for various sales areas.

1. The table itself (B11..E15) is made up of straight values. The totals are calculated with the @SUM function. Enter the quarter sum formula in B17:

   B17 = @SUM [B10..B16]

```
A1:  'TABLE                                              READY

         A         B         C         D         E         F         G         H
1    TABLE              Date       April 20, 1983
2    @Copyright 1982 John M. Nevison Associates
3
4    Sum the rows and columns of a table of numbers.
5    The rows are projects and the columns are quarters.
6
7
8                              QUARTER              PROJECT
9    PROJECT        1         2         3         4      TOTALS
10
11        1        200       240       288       346      1074
12        2        400       600       900      1350      3250
13        3        700       770       847       932      3249
14        4        300       495       891      1604      3290
15        5        500       625       781       977      2883
16   QUARTER
17    TOTALS      2100      2730      3707      5209     13746
18
19
20
```

Put name in last Row of Worksheet

and COPY it across the row. For the project totals, enter the first sum formula in F11 and COPY it down the column.

2. The column sum formula totals a range two cells longer than the actual column of numbers (B10..B16 instead of B11..B15). This extra room gives you more flexibility in adding new rows to the table. So long as you add new rows inside the range to sum, the formulas are adjusted properly. If you add a row at one of the sum range boundaries (for example, B16), the sum ranges cannot be adjusted and 1–2–3 replaces the range with the error message: "ERR." Since the extra cells in the sum range are blank, they do not affect the totals.

SALES Exercise   *Due March 4 Tues*

1# PRINT OUT AS displayed
2# print out of cell formats

The SALES table compares budgeted and actual sales for five areas of a company. The table includes the name of the area, the budgeted and actual sales for the area, the difference between budgeted and actual sales, and the percent of budget that was sold. To build the SALES table, you'll do the following:

- Enter the documentation and labels in rows 1 to 9.
- Set the worksheet formats.

8 1

- Enter the labels and known values in columns A, B, and C.
- Build and copy the formulas in columns D and E.
- Build the Corporate totals in row 17.

```
A1:  'SALES                                                              READY

          A           B           C           D           E           F
 1   SALES       •                       Date    29-Apr-83
 2
 3   Compare budgeted vs. actual profits for a company's five
 4   sales areas. The table shows the difference in profit and
 5   calculates actual profits as a percent of budgeted profits.
 6
 7                                             Better/        Actual
 8                                             (Worse)        as a % of
 9   Area              Budget      Actual  Than Budget      Budget
10
11   Chicago            1,200        1185        (15)        98.8%
12   New York           3,000        1770     (1,230)        59.0%
13   Boston               600         760         160       126.7%
14   Dallas             2,400        1860       (540)        77.5%
15   Atlanta            1,800        1880          80       104.4%
16   ==============================================================
17   Corporate        $9,000      $7,455    ($1,545)        82.8%
18
19
20
                                                              CAPS
```

Use these notes for help as you build the SALES table.

1. The GLOBAL COLUMN-WIDTH is set to 11 to allow extra room for the labels.

2. The entire worksheet is formatted with the GLOBAL FORMAT , (Comma) option with no decimal places, so negative numbers are displayed in parentheses and large numbers include commas. The %-of-Budget column is formatted as PERCENT with one decimal, and the first three Corporate figures (in B17, C17, and D17) are formatted with the CURRENCY option with no decimal places.

3. The date in D1 is entered with the date function. To enter the date, move the pointer to D1 and enter the formula

    @DATE [83,4,29].

The format for dates is @DATE (Year, Month, Day). When you enter the formula, 1–2–3 will display a number that is the number of days since January 1, 1900, for your date. To format the entry to look like a date, select RANGE FORMAT DATE, type [Enter] to select the first date format option, and type [Enter] again to set the one-cell range.

4. Enter the Budget and Actual figures as straight values.

5. The underlines are entered with the Backslash (\ ) feature. Type a Backslash in front of a single character and the character repeats.

    \ = is displayed as ============

    You can enter the first underline in column A and then COPY it across the column.

6. The difference formula (column D) simply subtracts the Budget figure from the Actual figure. In row 11 the formula is:

    D11 = +C11–B11   difference = actual − budget

    Enter the formula once in D11; then COPY it down the column. You can copy the formula all the way to the Corporate line.

7. The %-of-Budget formula is the Actual profit divided by the Budgeted profit.

    E11 = +C11/B11   % of budget = actual / budget

    Again, enter the formula in E11 and then COPY it down the column.

83

Graphing THISYR

1. Graphing with 1–2–3

This chapter describes one of 1–2–3's most exciting features—its ability to produce graphs instantly. A number of 1–2–3's predecessors enable you to create graphs, but none are so easy to use in combination with a powerful worksheet program. Some earlier graphics programs can be linked to spreadsheet programs, but that link is clumsy and time-consuming. Usually you must save the spreadsheet file, leave the spreadsheet program, swap disks and start the graphics program, recall the saved file, and only then produce the desired graph.

Often you arrive at a graph only to find that you incorrectly defined some part of the spreadsheet. To correct even the slightest error, you must swap disks again, make your changes, and go through the whole process once more. Unless you have a lot of time on your hands, it's impractical to use such graphs for anything less than a formal presentation where they are absolutely necessary.

1–2–3 eliminates this lengthy procedure. A graph can be defined so easily and quickly that graphs become thinking tools, not just presentation tools. When it is easy to generate and easy to alter, a graph can give you a much better "feel" for what the numbers in your worksheet really mean. Let's look at what 1–2–3 graphs actually do:

- They work on the current worksheet. You need not save your worksheet in order to graph it.

- They use the same disk that you use to produce the worksheet. There is no need to swap disks when graphing on the screen.
- They can be defined a section at a time. In other words, you do not have to define the graph fully before you can take a look at it to see if it's what you really want.
- They appear very quickly. In less than a second, you see a picture of your data.

Your 1–2–3 program can produce five types of graphs that serve a wide range of purposes:

- **Line graphs** are often used to show a value, or several values, changing over time.
- **Bar charts** can be used to compare the same value for different entities.
- **Pie charts** show how the parts of a whole are distributed among several entities.
- **Stacked bar charts** compare one or more values for several entities.
- **X-Y graphs** show the interrelationships of two changing values.

Figure 4.1 shows samples of the five graphs generated by 1–2–3.

1–2–3 graphs are defined with the main menu's GRAPH command. The GRAPH command has seven sub-menus, some of which you'll use in this chapter to produce a bar graph from your worksheet of Chapter 3.

Fig. 4.1   Sample Graphs

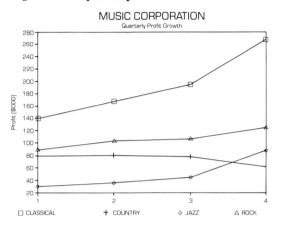

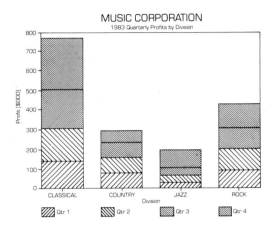

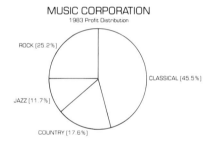

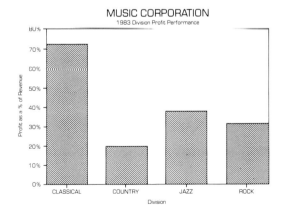

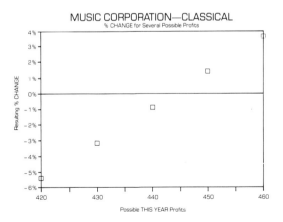

Fig. 4.2   Completed Graph of THISYR

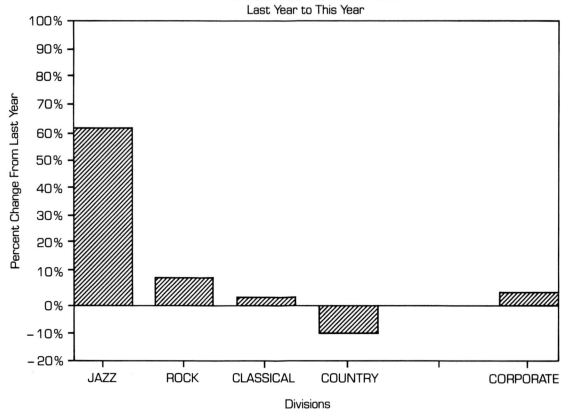

This bar graph is built from your THISYR file. It compares the percent change in sales for your worksheet's four divisions and Corporate total. The graph includes titles, and the y-axis numbers are shown in percent format. Load THISYR back into your worksheet with the FILE RETRIEVE command.

The graph illustrations in *1–2–3 Go!* were printed with the Lotus Graphprint program. They may look slightly different from the graphs pictured on your screen. Long labels, for example, may run together on your screen.

2. Defining What to Graph

Every graph is made up of an x-axis (the bottom boundary of the graph), a y-axis (the left boundary of the graph), and a series of numbers that make up the graph itself. 1–2–3 can plot up to six series of numbers in a single graph, and will automatically scale the axes to "fit" the numbers.

Select GRAPH and take a look at the graphing options.

Fig. 4.3   GRAPH Menu

To draw a graph, 1–2–3 needs at least one series of numbers, so you must define at least one of the graph ranges A, B, C, D, E, or F. By default, 1–2–3 draws a line graph, but you can also tell 1–2–3 to draw a bar chart, pie chart, x-y graph, or stacked bar chart with the TYPE option. (The stacked bar chart requires more than one set of data—that is, more than one set of bars to stack.) If you want to label the set of numbers being graphed, you can define an X range made up of numbers or labels. The X-range entries are displayed as x-axis labels.

The set of numbers in your graph is the percent change in sales values. Each number is shown as a bar and is labeled with a division name. Therefore each bar represents the percent change in sales for a division. Bar charts are often drawn from one set of numbers and one set of labels, whereas stacked bar charts are drawn from several sets of numbers and one set of labels.

You're ready to define your own graph now, so select TYPE, then select BAR to tell 1–2–3 you want to produce a bar graph. Your next step is to define the numbers and labels that make up the bars. You use entries stored in rows and columns of the worksheet to label the x-axis and define significant points in the graph.

Type X to tell 1–2–3 you are going to define the x-axis. The x-axis in your graph is the range of Division and Corporate labels from B3 to B8. Move the pointer to B3 and tack it down by typing a Period. Now, move the pointer down to include all the cells through B8 and [Enter] the range.

Fig. 4.4   X-Range Definition

```
B8: 'CORPORATE
Enter X-axis range: B3..B8
```

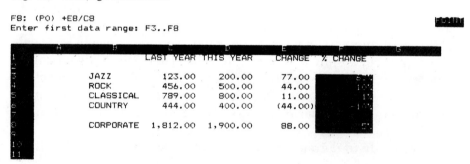

Your graph requires only one set of numbers: the percent-change values. Type A to define the A range, then move the pointer to F3, tack it down with a Period, extend the range to include all the cells through F8, and finally, [Enter] it.

Fig. 4.5   A-Range Definition

```
F8: (P0) +E8/C8
Enter first data range: F3..F8
```

Now that you've defined the graph's significant points, you can take a look at it. This early view of the graph gives you a chance to make sure you've defined the right numbers and are graphing something of interest. (Because 1–2–3 produces a graph so quickly, we'll look at it several times as we define it.) Type V to select the VIEW option. In less than a second 1–2–3 draws your graph:

Fig. 4.6   First Graph of THISYR

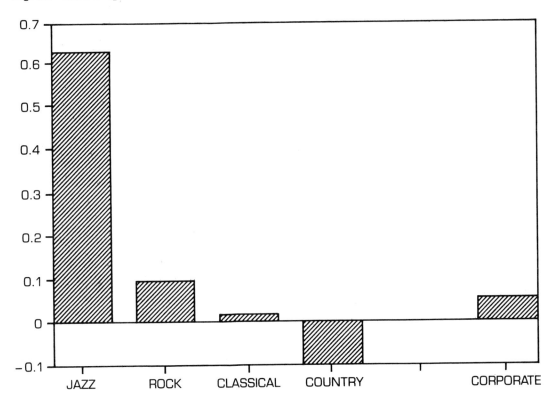

What you see on your screen will depend on your equipment:

If you have only a monochrome monitor,

1–2–3 cannot display the graph.

If you have only a graphics monitor (or a monochrome monitor with a special graphing card),

1–2–3 clears the worksheet and displays the graph. Hit any key to clear the graph and redisplay the worksheet.

If you have two monitors—one monochrome and one graphics,

1–2–3 displays the graph on the graphics monitor and the worksheet on the monochrome monitor. You do not have to clear the graph after viewing it.

3. Labels and Titles

Your first cut at the graph is pretty impressive. By defining just three options: TYPE, X-axis, and A range, you've produced a clear picture of how the four divisions did this year. If you're using graphs simply as thinking tools to check your worksheet and help verify that you've got the right numbers, you may not want to define this graph any further. You can go on to create other worksheets or perhaps define other graphs from the current worksheet.

You can even try another version of the same graph. If you have only a graphics monitor, hit any key to clear the graph and return to the worksheet. Now select TYPE LINE, then select the VIEW option again. With only two keystrokes you've created a new picture of your data. 1–2–3 graphs are so fast and so easy to modify that you can try several graph definitions in a very short time.

Before you go on, reset the graph to a bar chart. Select TYPE BAR, then VIEW the graph to make sure you're back to your initial bar graph.

If you're developing a graph for a presentation or report, you'll want to add labels and titles to make your graph's meaning clear to someone else. We'll continue to work on this graph until it has reached "presentation quality."

The commands for labeling graphs are in a third-level menu: the OPTIONS menu. If you have only a graphics monitor, hit any key to clear the graph and return to the worksheet. 1–2–3 returns you to the graph menu so you can define the graph further (or select the QUIT option to exit the menu). Select OPTIONS TITLES.

You can define four titles on a 1–2–3 graph—two of them label the graph itself (FIRST and SECOND) and two of them label the axes (X-AXIS and Y-AXIS). You must define the titles one at a time because 1–2–3 returns to the OPTIONS menu (where you must reselect TITLE) after each title is entered.

Type F to define the FIRST title; this is the primary title for the graph. 1–2–3 will prompt you to enter the title *exactly as you want to see it displayed*. Enter the first title as

PERCENT CHANGE

1–2–3 displays the title just as you enter it, including spaces, upper or lowercase letters, and so on. When you [Enter] the title, 1–2–3 returns you to the OPTIONS menu.

Fig. 4.7   Graph with Titles

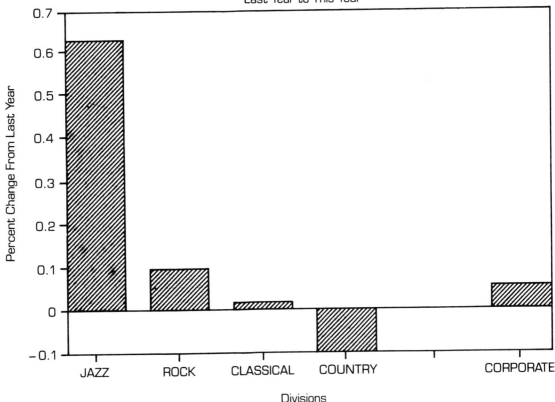

Define the other three titles on your own. Remember, if you run into trouble in one of the menus, you can "back out" of the command sequence by typing [Esc] until you are back to READY mode. 1–2–3 will remember the graph as far as you have defined it until you load another worksheet file, exit 1–2–3, turn the computer off, or RESET the graph specifications. If you enter one of the titles incorrectly, you can replace it by entering a new (correct) title.

Define the other titles like this:

SECOND   Last Year to This Year
X-AXIS   Divisions
Y-AXIS   Percent Change from Last Year

When you finish entering the titles, select QUIT to exit from the OPTIONS menu; then select VIEW to see the graph. Now that you've added labels, the graph is quite self-explanatory (Fig. 4.7).

You could stop here and consider this your finished product, but we're going to ask you to use another of the OPTIONS commands and make the graph a little more professional-looking.

4. Scaling

The x-axis labels are very helpful because they list the division that each bar represents. The y-axis labels, however, are much less specific; hence they're less clear. We're going to clarify the y-axis labels by formatting the numbers and adjusting the scale to allow for more space and a more common upper bound of 100 percent. Both functions are performed with the SCALE sub-menus, accessed through the OPTIONS menu.

If you have only a graphics monitor, hit any key to clear the graph from the screen. Select OPTIONS. Earlier you used this menu to set the TITLES, but this time we're going to use the SCALE option, so select SCALE.

Type Y to tell 1-2-3 you are going to set the y-axis scaling. The first way you can clarify the y-axis labels is by formatting the numbers, so select FORMAT. You're now looking at a familiar sub-menu that lets you choose from a variety of formats. Select PERCENT and type 0 [Enter] to define the scale as whole percents.

You should now be back at the SCALE menu, still defining the y-axis. Normally, scaling is done automatically by 1-2-3. Each time you view the graph, 1-2-3 scales the bars between the upper and lower limits of the y-axis range (or ranges). In this case, the low change is −.1 (COUNTRY division) and the high change is .7 (JAZZ division). We're going to define new lower and upper limits for the scale; we'll define the lower bound as −.2 (minus 20 percent) and the upper bound as 1 (100 percent). This will allow some space between the bars and the edges of the graph and will set the upper bound to a nice round limit of 100 percent.

To change the scale, you must do three things:

1. Define a new lower bound.
2. Define a new upper bound.
3. Tell 1–2–3 to use the settings you've defined to draw the graph.

Select LOWER and type –.2 [Enter] to set the lower bound to minus 20 percent. Select UPPER and type 1 [Enter] to set the upper bound to 100 percent. Finally, select MANUAL to tell 1–2–3 to use the manually defined bounds to draw the graph.

Your graph should be finished now, so let's take a look at the final version. Select QUIT to exit the SCALE menu, QUIT to exit the OPTIONS menu, and VIEW to see the final graph. Your completed graph should look like this:

Fig. 4.8   Completed Graph

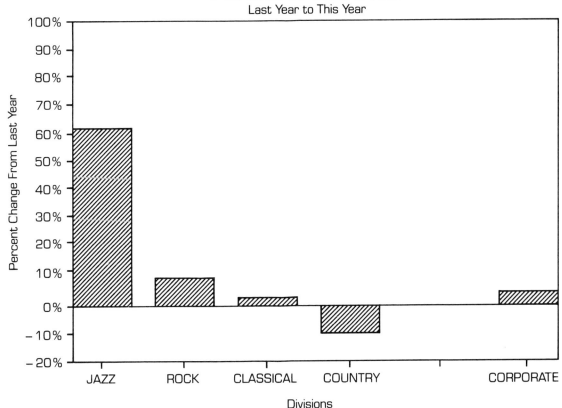

5. Naming the Graph

When you finished defining the worksheet, you SAVEd a copy of it on your disk for later use. The SAVE command in the GRAPH menu does something quite different. The SAVE in the GRAPH menu copies a *picture* of the graph onto your disk—it does *not* save your graph definition.

The graph definition—that is, the titles, axes, and other definitions that went into creating the graph—must be saved as part of the worksheet file. To save a graph definition, you must do two things:

1. QUIT the GRAPH menu.

2. SAVE the worksheet.

If you are going to define more than one graph for the worksheet, you must also NAME the graph. Then, whenever you load the worksheet file, all of its associated graph definitions are loaded with it.

Type any key to clear the graph; then select NAME CREATE to define a new graph name. 1–2–3 will display any graph names you have already defined for this worksheet. Since you haven't defined any graphs yet, no names are displayed. Type %CHANGE and [Enter] it as this graph's name.

Now you must resave the worksheet so that the specifications for your new graph, %CHANGE, will be saved with it. Select QUIT to exit the GRAPH menu; then select FILE SAVE, type [Enter], and select REPLACE to replace the old version of THISYR with the new version—THISYR with the graph %CHANGE. From now on (unless you delete the %CHANGE graph settings), the worksheet file THISYR will include a definition of the graph %CHANGE. (You won't see the definition, but 1–2–3 will.)

To look at the graph again, you need to type only one key—the Graph key. If you have many graphs defined for the worksheet, you can view a particular graph by selecting GRAPH NAME USE and pointing to the name of the graph you want to see. (If you have many graphs defined, the Graph key will display the graph you viewed last.)

To modify a graph, simply select it with the GRAPH NAME USE sequence and reenter any portion of the definition you want to change. Remember, though, that you must resave the *worksheet* to save the new graph definition.

6. What-If Graphing

Suppose you discover that COUNTRY division's sales this year were actually 500. How will you change the entry, adjust the percent-change numbers, and recreate the graph? Just follow two simple steps:

1. [Enter] 500 in D6.
2. Press the Graph key.

1–2–3 recalculates the percent change automatically and redraws the graph instantly. Once your graph is defined, it can give you a clear representation of any numbers you want to try in your spreadsheet. Your 1–2–3 graphs are powerful thinking tools; they provide graphic answers to what-if questions at the touch of a key.

Fig. 4.9   What-If %CHANGE Graph

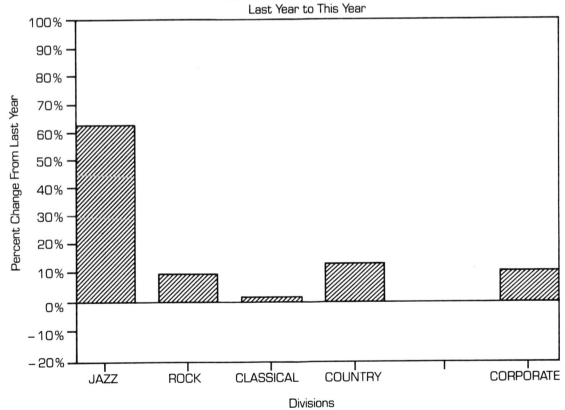

Chapter 4 Exercises

THISYR Exercise

You can build a second graph from your THISYR worksheet: a pie chart of THIS YEAR's sales. Graphs are easy to modify and correct, so don't worry about making a mistake in your definition. If you VIEW your graphs often as you build and modify them, you'll get a solid understanding of how 1–2–3 graphs work.

Before you begin building the new graph, clear the bar chart settings by selecting RESET GRAPH. The pie chart requires only five settings:

a TYPE	PIE
an X-axis range	the column of division names (not including Corporate)
an A range	the four THIS YEAR sales figures in column D
a FIRST title	MUSIC CORPORATION
a SECOND title	1983 Division Profits

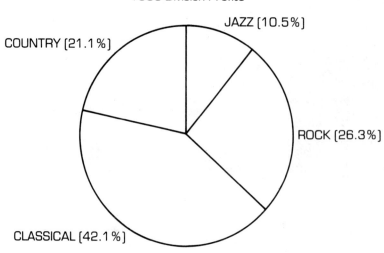

MUSIC CORPORATION
1983 Division Profits

JAZZ [10.5%]
COUNTRY [21.1%]
ROCK [26.3%]
CLASSICAL [42.1%]

Using the A-range figures, 1–2–3 draws the pie and then labels it with the x-axis division names. The percent figures are calculated and displayed automatically. After you build the graph, name it with the NAME command, then QUIT the graph menu and SAVE THISYR.

TABLE Exercise

The TABLE graph is a stacked bar chart of the yearly project budgets. Each bar represents a full year (four quarters) of a project budget. The first quarter is represented by the patterned area at the bottom of each bar, the second quarter is represented by the second pattern, and so on.

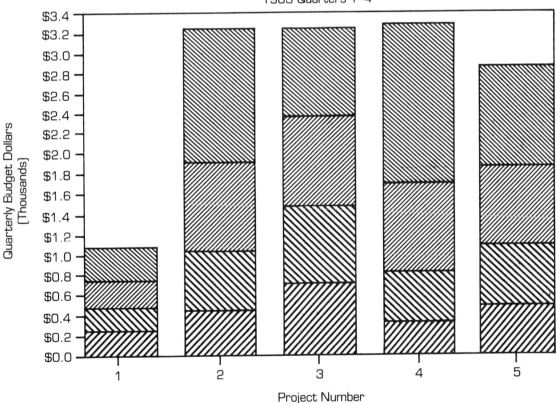

PROJECT BUDGETS
1983 Quarters 1–4

This exercise builds on the TABLE exercise at the end of Chapter 3. If you have already built TABLE, RETRIEVE it now and define the TABLE graph. If you haven't yet buit TABLE, do so now and then define the graph.

1. The A range is B11..B15, the first-quarter budgets. Define the B, C, and D ranges as the other quarter figures.

2. The y-scale is formatted as CURRENCY with one decimal place. To format the y-scale, select OPTIONS SCALE Y-SCALE FORMAT and set the format as CURRENCY with one decimal place.

3. Change the numbers to more evenly balance the total budget among the five projects. Use the Graph key to produce an instant graph reflecting the new numbers.

4. Change the project numbers to names of your own projects, products, or divisions, and enter some of your own numbers.

5. Try graphing some other numbers. Build a pie chart showing how profits are distributed among the five projects. Change the TYPE from PIE to BAR and you'll see the numbers pictured in a different way.

SALES Exercise

This exercise builds on the SALES exercise at the end of Chapter 3. Define a bar chart of the Actual as a % of Budget column. After defining the axis, format the y-scale as a percent and add titles to the graph. Set the four titles as shown:

FIRST	SALES PERFORMANCE
SECOND	1983 Actual Profit as a % of Budget
X-AXIS	Sales Area
Y-AXIS	Actual as a % of Budget

When the graph is complete NAME it, then QUIT the graph menu and SAVE your updated SALES file. Finally, select GRAPH RESET to prepare for new graph settings.

You can also define a paired bar chart of the Budget and Actual figures. The A range is the Budget column and the B range is the Actual column. The actual value is displayed above each bar with the DATA-LABELS option. To set the data labels, select OPTIONS DATA-LABELS

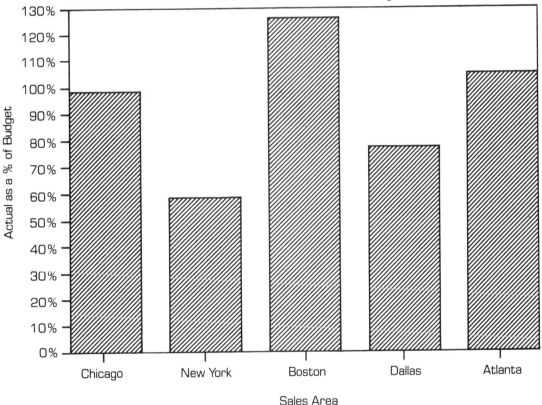

SALES PERFORMANCE
1983 Actual Profit as a % of Budget

A and enter the range of the Budget column (B11..B15), then select
ABOVE so 1–2–3 will display the labels above each bar. The second set
of labels, B, is the Actual range (C11..C15).

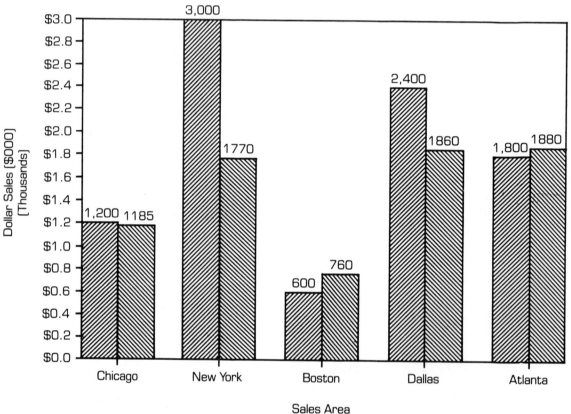

BUDGET vs. ACTUAL
1983 Sales

Updating the Spreadsheet

1. Inserting a Column

In Chapters 3 and 4, you learned how to build a worksheet, produce a graph of the worksheet's most significant numbers, and use both worksheet and graph to ask some simple what-if questions. In this chapter, you'll progress further with 1–2–3 by learning how to do the following things:

- Insert a new column and a new row in the worksheet.
- Build and copy a formula that includes a cell address that does not adjust.
- Delete a row and column from the worksheet.
- Build a table for keeping track of what-if values and their effect on worksheet values.

The expanded worksheet and the what-if table look like this:

	LAST YEAR	THIS YEAR	% TOTAL	CHANGE	% CHANGE
JAZZ	123.00	200.00	10%	77.00	63%
ROCK	456.00	500.00	24%	44.00	10%
CLASSICAL	789.00	800.00	38%	11.00	1%
FOLK	333.00	200.00	10%	(133.00)	-40%
COUNTRY	444.00	400.00	19%	(44.00)	-10%
CORPORATE	2,145.00	2,100.00	100%	(45.00)	-2%

	CHANGE	
COUNTRY	DIV %	CORP %
WHAT-IF?	-10%	-2%
420.00	-5%	6%
430.00	-3%	7%
440.00	-1%	7%
450.00	1%	8%
460.00	4%	8%

Fig. 5.1 Expanded THISYR and What-If Table

Suppose you want to know how much each division contributed to the total corporate sales of $1,900. You may be able to approximate the answer by doing a little fast calculation in your head. Immediately it's clear that JAZZ division contributed the least and CLASSICAL division contributed the most. But what is the actual percentage contribution for each division?

To answer this question, you must add a new column to the worksheet. The new column should calculate each division's sales as a percentage of the total corporate sales for this year. Where should the new column go? Well, you could easily put the new formula in the blank column G at the right of the worksheet . . . but actually this is not the best place for it. It would be better to add the new % TOTAL column between THIS YEAR and CHANGE (columns D and E). With the new column inserted there, the logical relationship between this year's sales figures and the percent-of-total figures is obvious.

Can you put the new column where you want to? Of course you can. Move your pointer to E1. You're going to insert a new column between D and E. Actually, 1–2–3 doesn't create a new column; it just moves the current columns over to make extra room. In other words, the CHANGE column will move to column F and the % CHANGE column will move to column G.

With the pointer in E1, select WORKSHEET INSERT COLUMN and type [Enter], because you want to insert only one column (rather than a range of columns). 1–2–3 moves the formulas in columns E and F over to column F and G, thereby "inserting" a blank column E.

Fig. 5.2 Inserted Column

E1:

		LAST YEAR	THIS YEAR		CHANGE	% CHANGE
JAZZ		123.00	200.00		77.00	63%
ROCK		456.00	500.00		44.00	10%
CLASSICAL		789.00	800.00		11.00	1%
COUNTRY		444.00	400.00		(44.00)	−10%
CORPORATE		1,812.00	1,900.00		88.00	5%

The pointer does not have to be in the first cell of the column for INSERT to work—it can be anywhere in column E. Just remember that 1–2–3 always inserts a column to the left of the current pointer position. (Rows are inserted *above* the pointer position.) Type the label % TOTAL in E1.

Fig. 5.3   Adjusted Formulas

G3:   (P0)   +F3/C3   READY

	B	C	D	E	F	G
		LAST YEAR	THIS YEAR	% TOTAL	CHANGE	% CHANGE
	JAZZ	123.00	200.00		77.00	5%
	ROCK	456.00	500.00		44.00	10%
	CLASSICAL	789.00	800.00		11.00	1%
	COUNTRY	444.00	400.00		(44.00)	-10%
	CORPORATE	1,812.00	1,900.00		88.00	5%

Notice that the formulas in the CHANGE and % CHANGE columns still point to the correct cells; 1–2–3 automatically adjusts formulas when a column or row is inserted. Move the pointer to G3, for example, and notice that it now contains the formula + F3/C3, instead of the original formula + E3/C3.

2. Absolute Cell Addresses

Move the pointer to E3, where you'll enter the new formula. At first glance the formula seems pretty simple:

$$\% \text{ TOTAL [for JAZZ division]} = \frac{\text{JAZZ this year sales}}{\text{CORPORATE this year sales}}$$

$$= 200 / 1900$$

$$= +D3/D8$$

$$= .11$$

This formula will work fine for JAZZ division, but you'll have a problem when you copy the formula down for the other divisions.

Remember when you first used the COPY command to duplicate the CHANGE and % CHANGE formulas? You found that 1–2–3 made a convenient assumption that all the cell addresses in the formulas should be adjusted for each new row. In those formulas you wanted the cell addresses adjusted. For the percent-of-total formula, however, only one cell address should be adjusted.

Think about this for a minute. If both cells in the formula were adjusted, our copied formulas would look like this:

```
E3 = +D3/D8
E4 = +D4/D9
E5 = +D5/D10, and so on.
```

Obviously, there is a problem when both cells in this formula are adjusted. In fact, we'd like to have 1–2–3 adjust the first cell (D3, D4, D5, D6, D7, D8), but leave the second cell unchanged (D8 in every case).

A cell address that doesn't change is called an **absolute.** The way to tell 1–2–3 that a cell is absolute is to put dollar signs, [$], in front of its row and column address. In other words, D8 will adjust, $D$8 will be absolute.

There are two ways to put the dollar signs into a formula. If you are typing the formula or editing a formula to add the absolute indicators, simply type Dollar Signs in the appropriate places. If you are building the formula by pointing, however, you can use the Absolute key. The Absolute key lets you set a cell address to one of four conditions:

a) $D$8   = absolute

b) D$8   = row does not adjust

c) $D8   = column does not adjust

d) D8   = adjusted

Options (b) and (c) simply set one part of the cell address as absolute and the other part as adjusted.

With the pointer in E3, type [+] to start the formula and point to D3. Continue the formula with a Slash, [/] (divided by), and move the pointer to D8. Now, type the Absolute key. You'll see the D8 cell address in the scratch area of the control panel change to read $D$8.

Fig. 5.4   Building an Absolute Formula

```
D8:  @SUM(D3..D6)                                          READY
+D3/$D$8
```

		LAST YEAR	THIS YEAR	% TOTAL	CHANGE	% CHANGE
JAZZ		123.00	200.00		77.00	63%
ROCK		456.00	500.00		44.00	10%
CLASSICAL		789.00	800.00		11.00	1%
COUNTRY		444.00	400.00		(44.00)	-10%
CORPORATE		1,812.00	1,900.00		88.00	5%

Continue typing the Absolute key slowly until you've looked at all the cell-address options and are back at $D$8. When your formula reads + D3/$D$8, [Enter] it.

Fig. 5.5   Absolute Formula Complete

```
E3:  +D3/$D$8                                              READY
```

		LAST YEAR	THIS YEAR	% TOTAL	CHANGE	% CHANGE
JAZZ		123.00	200.00	0.11	77.00	63%
ROCK		456.00	500.00		44.00	10%
CLASSICAL		789.00	800.00		11.00	1%
COUNTRY		444.00	400.00		(44.00)	-10%
CORPORATE		1,812.00	1,900.00		88.00	5%

Before you copy the formula you can use the FORMAT command to make the answer (.11) look better. To format E3, select RANGE FORMAT PERCENT and type 0 [Enter] [Enter]. This sequence formats the

107

one-cell range (E3..E3) as a percent with no decimal places. Notice that the control panel shows the format as (P0) in front of the formula for this cell. Now when you copy the formula, 1–2–3 will copy the format along with it.

Fig. 5.6 COPYing a Formatted Cell

```
E3: (P0) +D3/$D$8
```

	A	B	C	D	E	F	G
1			LAST YEAR	THIS YEAR	% TOTAL	CHANGE	% CHANGE
2							
3		JAZZ	123.00	200.00	11%	77.00	63%
4		ROCK	456.00	500.00		44.00	10%
5		CLASSICAL	789.00	800.00		11.00	1%
6		COUNTRY	444.00	400.00		(44.00)	-10%
7							
8		CORPORATE	1,812.00	1,900.00		88.00	5%
9							
10							
11							
12							

Copy the formula from E3 into the range of cells from E4 to E8. The range to copy FROM is E3..E3, and the range to copy TO is E4..E8. With the pointer on E3, select COPY and type [Enter] to specify the one-cell FROM range. Now move the pointer to E4, type a Period to tack down the range, and move the pointer down to E8 and type [Enter].

Fig. 5.7 COPY Complete

```
E3: (P0) +D3/$D$8                                                READY
```

		C	D	E	F	G
		LAST YEAR	THIS YEAR	% TOTAL	CHANGE	% CHANGE
	JAZZ	123.00	200.00	11%	77.00	63%
	ROCK	456.00	500.00	26%	44.00	10%
	CLASSICAL	789.00	800.00	42%	11.00	1%
	COUNTRY	444.00	400.00	21%	(44.00)	-10%
				0%		
	CORPORATE	1,812.00	1,900.00	100%	88.00	5%

Take a close look at the formulas in E4 to E8 to see how the absolute cell address worked with the COPY command. Notice that the percent format was also copied into the TO range. To erase the entry in E7, select RANGE ERASE and type E7 [Enter]. Here's a picture of your worksheet with the new column:

Fig. 5.8   THISYR with % TOTAL Column

E8:   (P0)   +D8/$D$8

	A	B	C	D	E	F	G
			LAST YEAR	THIS YEAR	% TOTAL	CHANGE	% CHANGE
1							
2							
3		JAZZ	123.00	200.00	11%	77.00	63%
4		ROCK	456.00	500.00	26%	44.00	10%
5		CLASSICAL	789.00	800.00	42%	11.00	1%
6		COUNTRY	444.00	400.00	21%	(44.00)	-10%
7							
8		CORPORATE	1,812.00	1,900.00	100%	88.00	5%
9							
10							
11							
12							

3. Adding a Division

Music Corporation is thinking about acquiring a new division. You have last year's and this year's sales figures for the new division and you would like to add them to the worksheet. Once again, you can use the INSERT command.

Move your pointer to B6, the label for COUNTRY division. We're going to add a new division before COUNTRY with this data:

FOLK   333   200

Before reading the steps that follow, see if you can figure out how to insert a row and add the new data. If you need help with the INSERT command, reread section 1 at the beginning of this chapter.

Here is the procedure for inserting the FOLK division:

1. Move the pointer to B6, select WORKSHEET INSERT ROW, and type [Enter].

2. Enter FOLK in B6.

3. Enter 333 in C6.

4. Enter 200 in D6.

109

Your worksheet should now look like this:

Fig. 5.9 THISYR with FOLK (B, C, D only)

D6: 200   READY

	LAST YEAR	THIS YEAR	% TOTAL	CHANGE	% CHANGE
JAZZ	123.00	200.00	10%	77.00	63%
ROCK	456.00	500.00	24%	44.00	10%
CLASSICAL	789.00	800.00	38%	11.00	1%
FOLK	333.00	200.00			
COUNTRY	444.00	400.00	19%	(44.00)	−10%
CORPORATE	2,145.00	2,100.00	100%	(45.00)	−2%

CAPS

As you can see in C9 and D9, the @SUM formulas for LAST YEAR and THIS YEAR adjusted to include the new figures. This illustrates a benefit of @SUM that was alluded to earlier. The range in an @SUM formula is elastic—it will stretch out to include new rows and will snap back when rows are deleted. (A sum across columns will stretch to accommodate inserted or deleted columns.)

You still have a problem, though, because the formulas in columns E, F, and G aren't in the new row. Fortunately, you can copy all three formulas with one COPY command.

Until now, you have copied from one cell to a range of cells. Now you're going to copy from a range of cells to another range of cells. 1–2–3 assumes that since you have a three-cell FROM range you'll be copying into at least three cells. You need only to tell 1–2–3 which single-cell "hook" (E6) to hang the FROM range on. Cells E7 and E8 make up the area connected to the hook.

To copy the range to your new row, select COPY, enter the FROM range, E5..G5, and enter the TO range, E6.

Fig. 5.10   COPY Ranges

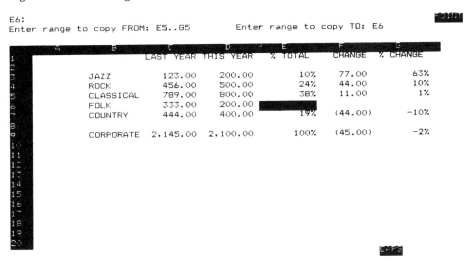

E6:
Enter range to copy FROM: E5..G5   Enter range to copy TO: E6

		LAST YEAR	THIS YEAR	% TOTAL	CHANGE	% CHANGE
JAZZ		123.00	200.00	10%	77.00	63%
ROCK		456.00	500.00	24%	44.00	10%
CLASSICAL		789.00	800.00	38%	11.00	1%
FOLK		333.00	200.00			
COUNTRY		444.00	400.00	19%	(44.00)	-10%
CORPORATE		2,145.00	2,100.00	100%	(45.00)	-2%

When you complete the copy your worksheet will look like this:

Fig. 5.11   THISYR With FOLK Division

D6: 200

		LAST YEAR	THIS YEAR	% TOTAL	CHANGE	% CHANGE
JAZZ		123.00	200.00	10%	77.00	63%
ROCK		456.00	500.00	24%	44.00	10%
CLASSICAL		789.00	800.00	38%	11.00	1%
FOLK		333.00	200.00	10%	(133.00)	40%
COUNTRY		444.00	400.00	19%	(44.00)	-10%
CORPORATE		2,145.00	2,100.00	100%	(45.00)	-2%

4. Deleting Rows and Columns

Your formulas look great, but FOLK doesn't seem like a profitable division to acquire, so you decide to cancel the deal. To delete FOLK division from the worksheet, put the pointer anywhere on row 6, select WORKSHEET DELETE ROW, and type [Enter]. Row 6 is deleted and, as you expected, the @SUM formula snaps back and adjusts to the four-division worksheet.

Fig. 5.12 FOLK Division Deleted

D8: @SUM(D3..D6)

	A	B	C	D	E	F	G
1			LAST YEAR	THIS YEAR	% TOTAL	CHANGE	% CHANGE
2							
3		JAZZ	123.00	200.00	11%	77.00	63%
4		ROCK	456.00	500.00	26%	44.00	10%
5		CLASSICAL	789.00	800.00	42%	11.00	1%
6		COUNTRY	444.00	400.00	21%	(44.00)	-10%
7							
8		CORPORATE	1,812.00	1,900.00	100%	88.00	5%
9							
10							
11							
12							
13							
14							
15							
16							
17							
18							
19							
20							

A column can be deleted just as easily. Before you read on, see if you can figure out how to delete column E, the % TOTAL column. Remember that the pointer should be in column E *before* you start the DELETE command sequence.

Deleting column E is a simple procedure:

Position the pointer anywhere in column E, select WORKSHEET DELETE COLUMN and type [Enter].

Your worksheet is back to its original state:

Fig. 5.13   THISYR After Deletes

F3:   (P0)   +E3/C3   READY

	LAST YEAR	THIS YEAR	CHANGE	% CHANGE
JAZZ	123.00	200.00	77.00	6 %
ROCK	456.00	500.00	44.00	10%
CLASSICAL	789.00	800.00	11.00	1%
COUNTRY	444.00	400.00	(44.00)	-10%
CORPORATE	1,812.00	1,900.00	88.00	5%

5. Building A What-If Table

You've already looked at one way of asking what-if questions about the numbers in your worksheet. In Chapter 3, you found that by simply entering a new value in place of one of your old assumptions you could see how dependent numbers were affected.

For example, you might try different values for COUNTRY division's this-year sales to see if you could raise COUNTRY's percent change figure to a positive number. By trying different values for COUNTRY you are asking, "What if COUNTRY could do X amount in this-year sales? How would the increase in sales affect the percent change for the division, and for the corporation?"

In fact, the THIS YEAR values were based on three quarters of actual sales figures and a fourth quarter of forecasted sales. By squeezing a little in the fourth quarter, COUNTRY division may be able to increase overall sales for the year. The manager of COUNTRY division thinks she may be able to bring this-year sales to somewhere in the range of 420 to 460 dollars. Your job is to test some numbers in this what-if range to determine what increase is needed to bring percent change up to a positive number.

113

One way to test the what-if range is to plug different numbers—420, 430, 440, and so on—into D6 (the cell for COUNTRY's THIS YEAR sales) to see their effect. Since 1–2–3 recalculates the change and percent-change numbers quickly, you will have your answer in a very short time.

But what if you want to track the effect on percent change for all the what-if values you intend to try? Each time you enter a new what-if number, you lose the previous number and its effect. Suppose you want to build a list showing each what-if value and its effect on percent change for the division and the corporation.

With the DATA TABLE command sequence, 1–2–3 can help you build this kind of list. In this book, we'll look at three of the many ways you can use data tables. Right now we're going to build a WHAT-IF data table below our THISYR worksheet. The new worksheet will look like this:

Fig. 5.14 THISYR with WHAT-IF Table

D12: 'COUNTRY   READY

		LAST YEAR	THIS YEAR	CHANGE	% CHANGE	
JAZZ		123.00	200.00	77.00	63%	
ROCK		456.00	500.00	44.00	10%	
CLASSICAL		789.00	800.00	11.00	1%	
COUNTRY		444.00	400.00	(44.00)	-10%	
CORPORATE		1,812.00	1,900.00	88.00	5%	
			CHANGE	TABLE		
		COUNTRY	DIV %	CORP %		
		WHAT-IF?	-10%	5%		
		420.00	-5%	6%		
		430.00	-3%	7%		
		440.00	-1%	7%		
		450.00	1%	8%		
		460.00	4%	8%		

CAPS

The WHAT-IF table lets you see how several alternative sales figures for COUNTRY division will affect COUNTRY's % CHANGE (DIV %) and the CORPORATE % CHANGE (CORP %). Before 1–2–3 will actually calculate and display the effect of the what-if values, you must enter some column labels and the what-if values you are testing.

The WHAT-IF table starts in D12 with a column of values in the what-if range. Each value will be substituted for the 400 sales figure in D6. Columns E and F show how the substituted values affect COUNTRY division's percent change and the CORPORATE percent change.

Start building the table by entering the labels in rows 11 and 12. Enter CHANGE TABLE in E11, COUNTRY in D12, DIV % in E12 and CORP % in F12. Now you can begin building the actual WHAT-IF table. Enter the label WHAT-IF? in D13. D13 is the top left-hand corner of the data table. This cell could be left blank (1–2–3 doesn't care), but the label helps clarify the table's purpose.

Fig. 5.15   Labeling the WHAT-IF Table

D13: 'WHAT-IF?   READY

	LAST YEAR	THIS YEAR	CHANGE	% CHANGE
JAZZ	123.00	200.00	77.00	63%
ROCK	456.00	500.00	44.00	10%
CLASSICAL	789.00	800.00	11.00	1%
COUNTRY	444.00	400.00	(44.00)	-10%
CORPORATE	1,812.00	1,900.00	88.00	5%

CHANGE TABLE
COUNTRY   DIV %   CORP %
WHAT-IF?

CAPS

Cell E13 shows COUNTRY's percent change in the current THIS-YR worksheet, –10%. Actually, the cell contains a simple formula that equals the entry in F6, where COUNTRY's percent change is computed. Move the pointer to E13 and type +F6 [Enter]. (You can also build the formula by pointing—type + then move the pointer to F6 and type

115

[Enter]). Whichever way you build it, 1–2–3 will use this formula to determine which values to include in column 2 of the WHAT-IF table.

Fig. 5.16   First Table Formula

E13: +F6

		LAST YEAR	THIS YEAR	CHANGE	% CHANGE
	JAZZ	123.00	200.00	77.00	63%
	ROCK	456.00	500.00	44.00	10%
	CLASSICAL	789.00	800.00	11.00	1%
	COUNTRY	444.00	400.00	(44.00)	-10%
	CORPORATE	1,812.00	1,900.00	88.00	5%

CHANGE TABLE
COUNTRY DIV %   CORP %
WHAT-IF?   (0.10)

The third column of the table (F12 to F18) shows how each what-if value affects the CORPORATE percent-change figure. It also contains a simple formula pointing to a cell in the main worksheet. In this case the formula equals the entry in F8, the cell where CORPORATE percent change is computed. Enter + F8 in F13 to complete the table headings.

Fig. 5.17   Second Table Formula

F13: +F8

		LAST YEAR	THIS YEAR	CHANGE	% CHANGE
	JAZZ	123.00	200.00	77.00	63%
	ROCK	456.00	500.00	44.00	10%
	CLASSICAL	789.00	800.00	11.00	1%
	COUNTRY	444.00	400.00	(44.00)	-10%
	CORPORATE	1,812.00	1,900.00	88.00	5%

CHANGE TABLE
COUNTRY DIV %   CORP %
WHAT-IF?   (0.10)   0.05

The last step before you invoke the table-building sequence is to enter the what-if values you want 1–2–3 to try. Enter these values in column D:

D14 = 420
D15 = 430
D16 = 440
D17 = 450
D18 = 460

Fig. 5.18   What-If Values

D18: 460   READY

	A	B	C	D	E	F	G
				LAST YEAR	THIS YEAR	CHANGE	% CHANGE
1							
2			JAZZ	123.00	200.00	77.00	63%
3			ROCK	456.00	500.00	44.00	10%
4			CLASSICAL	789.00	800.00	11.00	1%
5			COUNTRY	444.00	400.00	(44.00)	-10%
6							
7			CORPORATE	1,812.00	1,900.00	88.00	5%
8							
9						CHANGE TABLE	
10				COUNTRY	DIV %	CORP %	
11				WHAT-IF?	(0.10)	0.05	
12				420.00			
13				430.00			
14				440.00			
15				450.00			
16				460.00			

When you invoke the DATA TABLE command sequence, 1–2–3 asks for two things: the **Table range** and the **Input cell.** The Table range includes the rectangle where 1–2–3 builds the table (E13..F18), the what-if values (D13..D18), and the table formula headings (D12..F12). The Input cell is the cell into which you want 1–2–3 to put the what-if values. In your worksheet the Input cell is D6, because you want 1–2–3 to try each what-if value in place of the value (400) now in D6.

You won't actually see 1–2–3 testing each what-if value, but you will see a completed WHAT-IF table listing each value, its associated COUNTRY division percent change, and its associated CORPORATE percent change.

117

Move the pointer to D13 and select DATA TABLE. 1–2–3 will ask you whether the table has one or two Input cells. In this case there is only one Input cell, D6, so type 1.

Now 1–2–3 asks you to define the Table range. Type a Period to tack the pointer down on D13, and move the pointer down and over to F18. Your screen should show a block pointer, from D13 to F18, that looks like this:

Fig. 5.19   Block Pointer for Table Range

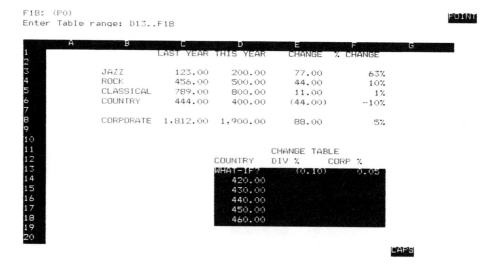

Check the scratch area in the control panel to make sure it lists the Table range as D13..F18. If the scratch area does not list this block, type the Backspace Delete key and try defining the range again. Once the range is properly defined, [Enter] it.

Finally, 1–2–3 asks you to define the Input cell where the what-if values will be substituted. You can either point to D6 and [Enter], or simply type D6 [Enter]. Now 1–2–3 quickly completes the table showing how each what-if value would affect the division and corporate percent change.

Fig. 5.20   Completed WHAT-IF Table

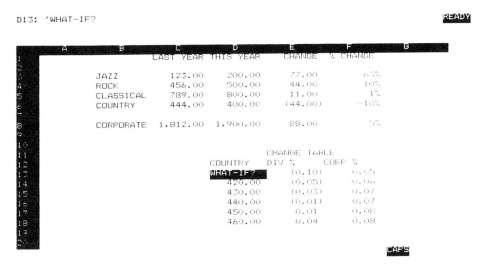

You should probably format the numbers in the table as whole percents so they'll be easier to read. Move the pointer to E13 and select RANGE FORMAT PERCENT, type 0 [Enter], then move your pointer down five and right one to specify the range from E13..F18, and [Enter] it.

Fig. 5.21   Formatted Table

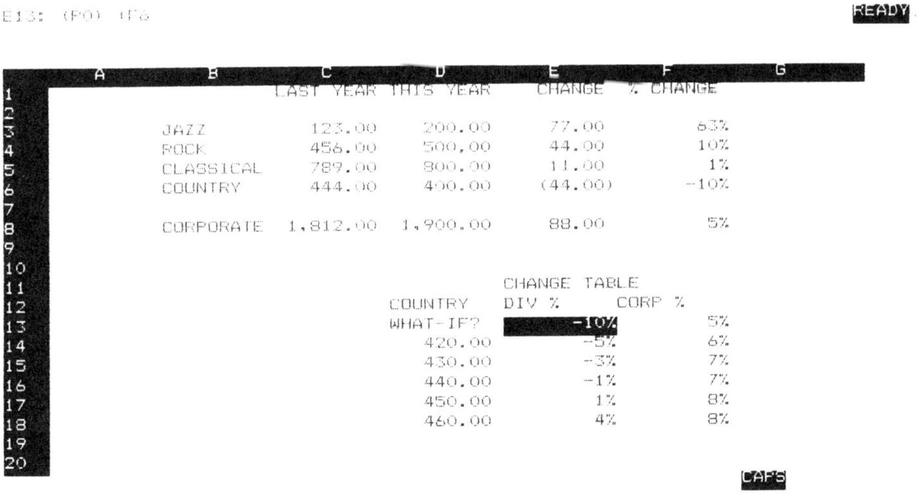

119

Now that you've enhanced your worksheet, you want to save it on the disk. You could save this worksheet under the old name, THISYR, but that would mean overwriting the old file. Instead, assign this worksheet a new file name, such as WHATIF. Each time you alter a worksheet and want to save both it and your orginal, you can simply give it a different file name. To save the file, select FILE SAVE and type WHATIF [Enter].

You now have a handy table listing some possible values for COUNTRY's this-year sales and showing how each would affect percent change for the division and the corporation. If you were showing your table to someone else, you might leave the initial forecast of 400 in the main worksheet table, but include the WHAT-IF table to show how higher sales would affect your figures.

In three steps you can generate a new table for COUNTRY, using different what-if values:

1. Enter the new what-if values in D14 to D18.

2. Type the Table function key, and 1–2–3 will generate a new table based on the new figures.

3. FORMAT the table to PERCENT with one decimal place, so the results of the new values will be clearer.

Fig. 5.22   New WHAT-IF Values

D14: 442   READY

	A	B	C	D	E	F	G
1			LAST YEAR	THIS YEAR	CHANGE	% CHANGE	
2							
3		JAZZ	123.00	200.00	77.00	63%	
4		ROCK	456.00	500.00	44.00	10%	
5		CLASSICAL	789.00	800.00	11.00	1%	
6		COUNTRY	444.00	400.00	(44.00)	-10%	
7							
8		CORPORATE	1,812.00	1,900.00	88.00	5%	
9							
10							
11				CHANGE TABLE			
12			COUNTRY	DIV %	CORP %		
13			WHAT-IF?	-10%	5%		
14			442.00	-0.5%	7%		
15			444.00	0.0%	7%		
16			446.00	0.5%	7%		
17			448.00	0.9%	8%		
18			450.00	1.4%	8%		
19							
20							

CAPS

In this table, the DIV % column (E14..E18) is formatted as percent with one decimal. The new WHAT-IF values pinpoint the sales that will bring COUNTRY above 0%. If you try more or fewer what-if values, you'll have to redefine the Table range with the DATA TABLE command sequence.

To track what-if values for another division—CLASSICAL, for example—you need to make only three changes:

1. Enter in D14 to D18 the what-if values you want to try for CLASSICAL.

2. Change the formula in E13 so it points to CLASSICAL division's percent change (E13 = +F5).

3. Regenerate the table with the DATA TABLE 1 command sequence, only define the Input cell as D5 (rather than D6), CLASSICAL division's THIS YEAR figure.

Fig. 5.23   CLASSICAL Division's WHAT-IF

D13: 'WHAT-IF?   READY

	A	B	C	D	E	F	G
1			LAST YEAR	THIS YEAR	CHANGE	% CHANGE	
2							
3		JAZZ	123.00	200.00	77.00	63%	
4		ROCK	456.00	500.00	44.00	10%	
5		CLASSICAL	789.00	800.00	11.00	1%	
6		COUNTRY	444.00	400.00	(44.00)	−10%	
7							
8		CORPORATE	1,812.00	1,900.00	88.00	5%	
9							
10					CHANGE	TABLE	
11				CLASSICAL	DIV %	CORP %	
12							
13				WHAT-IF?	1%	5%	
14				805.00	2%	5%	
15				810.00	3%	5%	
16				815.00	3%	6%	
17				820.00	4%	6%	
18				825.00	5%	6%	
19							
20							

CAPS

Though you need the formulas in E13 and F13 to build the table, the values there are really quite distracting. You can't label them clearly or separate them from the table without disrupting the TABLE command setup, but you can suppress the value display by formatting the entries with the +/− option. To format the cells:

1. Move the pointer to E13.
2. Select RANGE FORMAT +/−.
3. Type a Right Arrow to extend the range and type [Enter] to complete the command.

The new formats give you a table like Fig. 5.24, with periods displayed instead of values.

Fig. 5.24 Table with Formatted Formulas

```
E13: (+) +F5                                                    READY
```

	A	B	C	D	E	F	G
1			LAST YEAR	THIS YEAR	CHANGE	% CHANGE	
3		JAZZ	123.00	200.00	77.00	63%	
4		ROCK	456.00	500.00	44.00	10%	
5		CLASSICAL	789.00	800.00	11.00	1%	
6		COUNTRY	444.00	400.00	(44.00)	−10%	
8		CORPORATE	1,812.00	1,900.00	88.00	5%	
11				CHANGE TABLE			
12				CLASSICAL	DIV %	CORP %	
13				WHAT−IF?			
14				805.00	2%	5%	
15				810.00	3%	5%	
16				815.00	3%	6%	
17				820.00	4%	6%	
18				825.00	5%	6%	

Chapter 5 Exercises

THISYR Exercise

Practice what you've learned in this chapter by trying the following procedures:

1. Change the division names and THIS YEAR and LAST YEAR figures to reflect your own company. If you have to insert new rows, make sure you add them between existing divisions so the @SUM formulas will be adjusted properly.

2. Try another series of numbers in the WHAT-IF table. How much would CLASSICAL have to increase THIS YEAR profits to raise its %CHANGE to 10%?

3. Change the column formulas at the top of the WHAT-IF table (E13 and F13) so they show how the numbers affect CHANGE (instead of %CHANGE).

4. Add a couple of rows at the top and change the labels and headings to make the table look like the CHANGE SUMMARY in Chapter 1. (Don't worry about the different ordering of divisions.) Once you've set up the report headings, print a copy of the table.

5. Insert two or three rows at the top of the table and enter the file's name, the date, and a short description of the model. This information clarifies the model's purpose and helps you keep track of your work.

INTEREST Exercise

The INTEREST table compares a sum of money earning interest at three different rates over a period of ten years. The table is constructed so you can easily try different initial sums of money, or different rates, and see their effect on the final savings.

1. The worksheet is formatted with the GLOBAL FORMAT FIXED option with 2 decimal places.

2. The first YEAR number (in A8) is entered as a straight value. A9 contains a formula,

$$A9 = + A8 + 1 = 1,$$

which is entered once in A9 and copied into the range A10..A18.

3. The rates are entered as decimals (.10, .12, .15) and formatted with the PERCENT option with no decimal places.

4. The initial sum is entered as a straight value (100) in B8, then is copied into the range C8..D8.

5. B9..D9 contain formulas:

$$B9 = (1 + B\$6) *B8$$
$$C9 = (1 + C\$6) *C8$$
$$D9 = (1 + D\$6) *D8$$

the new sum = (1 + the interest rate) * the previous sum
= (1 + .10)*100 = 110

6. You can enter the formula once, in B9, then copy it into C9..D9. The $ sign freezes only the row part of the cell address. The column part is not frozen, so it adjusts (to C and D) when you copy the formula.

7. Once you've entered the first row of formulas, COPY them into the other rows. Remember that when the range to copy FROM is a row of cells, the range to copy TO is a column of hooks on which to hang the FROM range.

```
A1:  'INTEREST                                                           READY

        A       B        C        D      E       F       G       H
1    INTEREST          Date     April 20, 1983
2
3    Computes a sum growing at three
4    different interest rates.
5
6    RATE >        10%       12%       15%
7    YEAR     SUM       SUM       SUM
8       0    100.00    100.00    100.00
9       1    110.00    112.00    115.00
10      2    121.00    125.44    132.25
11      3    133.10    140.49    152.09
12      4    146.41    157.35    174.90
13      5    161.05    176.23    201.14
14      6    177.16    197.38    231.31
15      7    194.87    221.07    266.00
16      8    214.36    247.60    305.90
17      9    235.79    277.31    351.79
18     10    259.37    310.58    404.56
19
20
                                                        CAPS
```

When you finish building INTEREST, save a copy of it on your disk. Then try some new what-if values in the starting sums and rates in rows 6 and 8. If the starting sum is $800 and the interest rate is 7.5%, what will the sum be after 10 years? Extend the table to see what the sum will be after 20 years. You might also want to change the initial values to see how different sums would grow at the same interest rate. Date the table by entering an actual year number, such as 1983, instead of the 0 in A8.

TIMELY Exercise

You can use TIMELY to estimate the length of a project. The project is divided into several tasks and each task is assigned a low, a likely, and a high completion time. This is a fairly simple table but it includes a long equation to compute the expected completion time for each task.

1. The EXPECTED time is the average of twice the LIKELY time plus half of the sum of the LOW and HIGH times. That is:

$$E9 = (2*C9) \quad \text{twice the LIKELY time}$$
$$+ (B9+D9)/2 \quad \text{plus half of the sum of the LOW and HIGH estimates}$$
$$/3 \quad \text{divided by 3 to get the average.}$$

$$E9 = ((2*C9) + ((B9+D9)/2))/3$$

The extra parentheses tell 1–2–3 the order in which to calculate each part of the equation; the operations in the innermost parentheses are performed first. You can enter the equation once, in E9, then COPY it down the rest of the column.

```
A1:  'TIMELY                                                          READY

           A              B       C        D        E      F      G
1   TIMELY                    April 21, 1983
2   @Copyright 1982 John M. Nevison Associates
3
4   Compute the expected completion times for a table of tasks.
5   Each task is given a low, likely and high time estimate.
6
7
8   TASK                 LOW    LIKELY      HIGH EXPECTED
9   Plan                 1.5        3         4     2.92
10  Design                 2        2         5     2.50
11  Outline                1      1.5         2     1.50
12  Write First Draft      5        7        13     7.67
13  Revise                 2        3         5     3.17
14  Write Final Draft      3        5        10     5.50
15
16                   Total project time:     23.25 days
17
18
19
20
                                                    CAPS
```

125

2. The low, likely, and high estimates are entered as straight values; they can represent hours, days, or some other measure of time, depending on the length of the project. In this table, the times are estimated in days.

3. Column A is set to 17 characters wide—the width of the longest task name.

4. The expected times in column E are formatted using the FIXED option with two decimal places.

5. Use the @SUM function to total the expected times.

PROJECT Exercise

This table shows a breakdown of the tasks in the TIMELY exercise table. In this table, the time estimates are divided among three employees. All three employees are scheduled to work 8 hours on Task 1, Plan. For Task 4, Write First Draft, jpf will work 40 hours and meb will work 24 hours. All three employees work at a standard rate of $35.00 per hour.

1. The TASK, TASK #, EMP, and HOUR entries are all straight figures or labels. The EMP column entries are right-justified with the RANGE LABEL RIGHT command.

2. The CHARGES are calcualted by multiplying each HOUR entry by the standard RATE in C11. When you build the first CHARGES formula, use the Absolute key to set the rate address as absolute. The absolute address won't adjust when you COPY the formula.

    E14 = +D14*$C$11   [charge = hour * rate]

   Once you have entered the first CHARGES formula, COPY it down the column.

3. In the TOTALS line, row 28, enter the total number of tasks and employees as straight values. If you add or subtract tasks or employees, you'll have to change these entries by hand. Use the @SUM function to calculate the total hours and charges.

4. The Total Project Time is given in days.

$$C8 = +D28/8 \quad [\text{total days} = \text{total hours} / 8]$$

5. The Total Project Cost is equal to the sum of the CHARGE entries.

$$C9 = +E28 \quad [\text{total cost} = \text{total charges}]$$

The cost is formatted with the CURRENCY format with no decimals. The RATE in C11 is also formatted CURRENCY with no decimals.

```
A1: 'PROJEST                                                    READY


          A          B        C         D        E       F      G
1    PROJEST                  Date    April 30, 1983
2
3    Compute total project time and cost estimates at a standard hourly
4    rate. The project is divided into tasks, some of which include more
5    than one employee. This project is estimated in hours and summarized
6    in days.
7
8    Project Completion Time:        23.5 days
9    Project Cost:           $6,580
10
11   Rate:                   $35.00 hour
12
13   TASK              TASK #     EMP     HOURS   CHARGES
14   Plan                 1       wrb       8       280
15                        1       jpf       8       280
16                        1       meb       8       280
17   Design               2       jpf      20       700
18   Outline              3       wrb       6       210
19                        3       jpf       6       210
20   Write First Draft    4       jpf      40      1400
21                        4       meb      24       840
22   Revise               5       wrb       8       280
23                        5       jpf       8       280
24                        5       meb       8       280
25   Write Final Draft    6       jpf      36      1260
26                        6       meb       8       280
27   --------------------------------------------------------
28   Totals               6        3      188     $6,580
29
```

127

Data Management

---

1. The FINANCE Database

The central item in a data management system is the collection of data itself. This collection is generally called a **database.** The data in a database is organized by rows (called **records**) and by columns (called **fields**).

- A *record* is a row that describes a particular entity. The records in the database you will use describe a division's quarterly financial data.

- A *field* is a column that describes some characteristic of the entity. In your database each field describes some part of a division's financial data. Under each column title (called a **field name**) is a list of field values. For example, under the field name DIVISION are the values ROCK, CLASSICAL, JAZZ, and COUNTRY.

Figure 6.1 shows Music Corporation's FINANCE database as you will enter it in the 1–2–3 worksheet. The database includes the four divisions, with three quarters of revenue and cost figures for each. (Fourth-quarter figures aren't in yet.)

As Fig. 6.1 shows, 1–2–3 field values are stored in columns, and records are stored in rows. There are twelve records in the FINANCE database and each record includes values for four fields: DIVISION, QTR (quarter), REVENUE, and COST.

Fig. 6.1 FINANCE Database

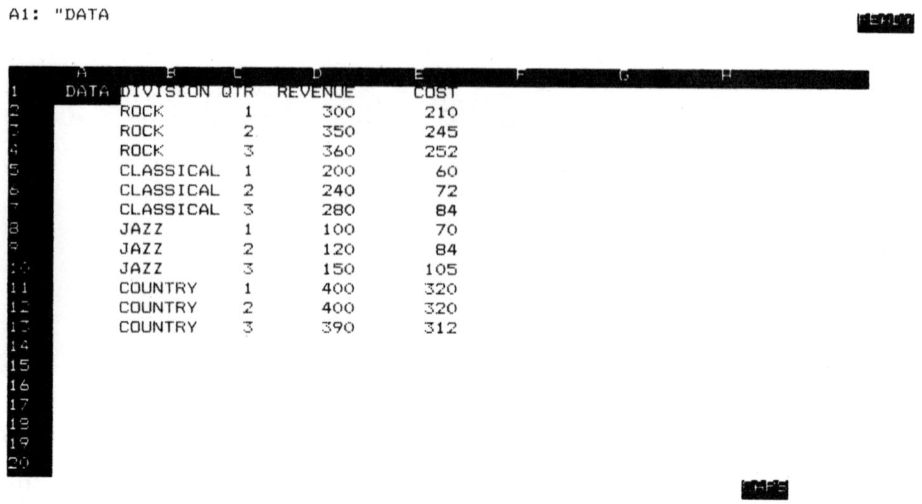

A1: "DATA

```
      A         B        C       D          E         F       G        H
1    DATA   DIVISION   QTR    REVENUE      COST
2            ROCK       1       300         210
3            ROCK       2       350         245
4            ROCK       3       360         252
5            CLASSICAL  1       200          60
6            CLASSICAL  2       240          72
7            CLASSICAL  3       280          84
8            JAZZ       1       100          70
9            JAZZ       2       120          84
10           JAZZ       3       150         105
11           COUNTRY    1       400         320
12           COUNTRY    2       400         320
13           COUNTRY    3       390         312
14
15
16
17
18
19
20
```

You'll be required to do a little extra typing in this chapter, since you must enter a collection of data to manipulate. Please enter the exact data in the same cells shown in Fig. 6.1. The quarter, revenue, and cost figures are all straight values; there are no formulas in the database. Column A is adjusted to 6 characters wide and column C is 4 characters wide. Set the widths by moving to the column, selecting WORKSHEET COLUMN SET, and typing the column width number and [Enter]. When you've finished entering the data, SAVE a copy of the worksheet on your disk—select FILE SAVE and enter the name FINANCE.

In this chapter, you'll use the DATA commands to

1. order the data by quarter (SORT),
2. locate specific records in the database (FIND),
3. create a list of records that match certain criteria (EXTRACT), and
4. summarize the data by quarter (TABLE).

2. Numbering the Rows

Before you sort (reorder) your data, we're going to suggest a trick to keep track of each record's original position. The trick is to use the DATA FILL command to create a sequence of numbers in column A. By sorting the column-A sequence along with the database, you'll be able to keep track of the data's original order.

Move the pointer to A2 and select DATA FILL. 1–2–3 prompts you to define the range to fill. Type a Period to tack the pointer down, extend the range down to A13 (the last record in the database), and type [Enter]. The second prompt asks you for the start value of your number sequence. Type 1 [Enter] to set the first number to 1.

Next, 1–2–3 prompts you for a **step** value. A step is simply an increment; it tells 1–2–3 whether to increase each number in the sequence by 1, 8, 100, or whatever you choose. Type [Enter] to accept the default step value of 1.

Fig. 6.2   Defining the Fill Range

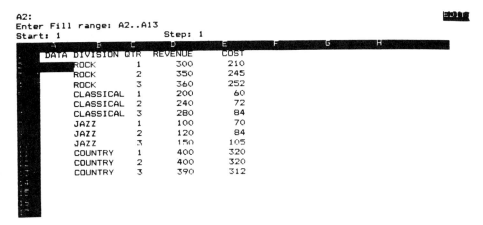

Finally, 1–2–3 prompts you for the stop value in the sequence. Since you defined a range to fill that's exactly the length of the database, you don't need to specify the last number in the sequence. 1–2–3 will fill numbers only into the range you defined, no further. Type [Enter]

131

instead of a stop value and the range is immediately filled with a sequence of numbers.

Fig. 6.3 FINANCE with Sequence Numbers

A2: 1

READY

	A	B	C	D	E	F	G	H
1	DATA	DIVISION	QTR	REVENUE	COST			
2	1	ROCK	1	300	210			
3	2	ROCK	2	350	245			
4	3	ROCK	3	360	252			
5	4	CLASSICAL	1	200	60			
6	5	CLASSICAL	2	240	72			
7	6	CLASSICAL	3	280	84			
8	7	JAZZ	1	100	70			
9	8	JAZZ	2	120	84			
10	9	JAZZ	3	150	105			
11	10	COUNTRY	1	400	320			
12	11	COUNTRY	2	400	320			
13	12	COUNTRY	3	390	312			
14								
15								
16								
17								
18								
19								
20								

CAPS

3. Sorting the Data

In computer terms, putting a collection of data in order is called **sorting.** A sort reorders each row in the database based on the value of one of its fields. You'll sort the rows by quarter: first-quarter figures together, second-quarter figures together, and so on. 1–2–3 sorts are easy to define and *very* fast.

To perform the sort, you must tell 1–2–3 two things: which records to sort and what order to put them in. The **Data range** is the range of data that must be sorted (*all* the rows and *all* the columns) and the **Primary key** is the field that determines the record's order. In this case, C2 (the first-quarter figure) is the Primary key, because you want each record sorted by quarter.

Before you sort the data, be sure to save a copy of your worksheet. Then, if you make an error sorting, you can retrieve the saved file and try again. To save the file, select FILE SAVE and type [Enter] R to replace the old FINANCE file with your updated worksheet.

With the pointer on A2, select DATA SORT. The first part of the SORT command is the DATA-RANGE: the range of records that you want sorted. You'll want to sort five columns and twelve rows of data; the range A2..E13. Don't include the field names (row 1) in the range or they will be sorted in with the actual data. You *do* want the sequence numbers in column A sorted along with each record. Select DATA-RANGE and type A2..E13, or build the range by pointing, and type [Enter].

Fig. 6.4 Defining the Data Range for Sorting

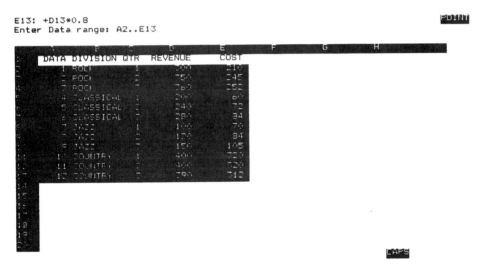

The next step is to define the Primary key. A key is a field whose values determine the order in which the records are sorted. Select PRI-MARY-KEY, move the pointer to C2, and type [Enter]. C2 is the Primary key because you want the data sorted by quarter. (Actually, to define the key, you can put the pointer anywhere in the column.) You can sort records in either ascending (low-to-high) or descending (high-to-low) order. Type A to set the order as Ascending.

133

Select GO, and in less than a second 1–2–3 sorts the data. Notice that each record (or row) is now listed in order of quarter number.

Fig. 6.5   FINANCE Sorted by Quarter

A2: 7   READY

	A	B	C	D	E	F	G	H
1	DATA	DIVISION	QTR	REVENUE	COST			
2	7	JAZZ	1	100	70			
3	1	ROCK	1	300	210			
4	10	COUNTRY	1	400	320			
5	4	CLASSICAL	1	200	60			
6	8	JAZZ	2	120	84			
7	5	CLASSICAL	2	240	72			
8	2	ROCK	2	350	245			
9	11	COUNTRY	2	400	320			
10	9	JAZZ	3	150	105			
11	6	CLASSICAL	3	280	84			
12	3	ROCK	3	360	252			
13	12	COUNTRY	3	390	312			
14								
15								
16								
17								
18								
19								
20								

CAPS

You can also define a **Secondary key**. The Secondary key determines the order of records that share a common Primary key. (For example, a telephone directory is a list sorted on the basis of surname as Primary key and first name as Secondary key. Entries appear alphabetically by surname, and multiple surname entries appear alphabetically by first name.) You can sort the records by quarter and by division name within quarters. The Primary key is quarter and the Secondary key is division. It's very easy to resort the data because 1–2–3 remembers the sort as you have defined it so far. You need to define only one more option—SECONDARY-KEY. Select DATA SORT SECONDARY-KEY, move the pointer to B2 (the first division entry), and type [Enter] A. Select GO and you'll see the records resorted first by quarter and then by division. Your sorted database should look like Fig. 6.6.

Notice that each record is still associated with its original sequence number. If you wished to return the data to its original order, you would simply resort, using A2 as the primary (and only) key.

Fig. 6.6   FINANCE Sorted by Quarter and Division

A2: 4   READY

```
        A      B        C       D         E       F       G       H
   1  DATA DIVISION QTR   REVENUE     COST
   2       4 CLASSICAL  1       200       60
   3      10 COUNTRY    1       400      320
   4       7 JAZZ       1       100       70
   5       1 ROCK       1       300      210
   6       5 CLASSICAL  2       240       72
   7      11 COUNTRY    2       400      320
   8       8 JAZZ       2       120       84
   9       2 ROCK       2       350      245
  10       6 CLASSICAL  3       280       84
  11      12 COUNTRY    3       390      312
  12       9 JAZZ       3       150      105
  13       3 ROCK       3       360      252
```

CAPS

4. Locating Significant Items

A common task for someone working with a large collection of data is to locate a particular item, or a number of items, that meet some criteria. Suppose, for example, that you want to find all the records for JAZZ division. In a database this small the manual task is fairly simple—you run your finger down the DIVISION column until you find a JAZZ entry. If you want to find subsequent JAZZ entries, you continue running your finger down the list checking division names against your criteria: JAZZ.

What if you want to find records with revenues less than $300? Again, the task is quite simple. This time you run your finger down the REVENUE column, starting at the top so you don't miss any entries, until you find a revenue that is less than $300.

Now imagine that the FINANCE database were much larger—instead of four divisions, let's say thirty divisions. That would mean ninety records in the database. Obviously it would be much more difficult to locate a particular record, or a group of records that meet some criteria, in a database of that size. For these types of jobs, 1–2–3's DATA

135

QUERY FIND command automates the task and 1–2–3 does the searching for you.

Fig. 6.7   QUERY Menu

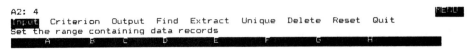

```
A2: 4                                                                    MENU
Input  Criterion  Output  Find  Extract  Unique  Delete  Reset  Quit
Set the range containing data records
     A        B       C       D      E        F       G        H
```

Select DATA QUERY and look at the nine options in the QUERY sub-menu. INPUT, CRITERION, and OUTPUT are used to define areas of the worksheet in preparation for a query. These are similar to the GRAPH sub-menu options that let you define the graph in preparation for viewing, naming, or saving it. Unlike GRAPH definitions, however, all the pieces of a database must be defined before a query can be executed.

FIND, EXTRACT, UNIQUE, and DELETE are all used to query the database. That is, based on certain criteria, they perform operations on particular rows of the database. RESET clears the current query definitions. QUIT leaves the QUERY menu and returns to READY mode.

Before you can perform a query, you must define two or three areas of the worksheet as the **Input range**, the **Criterion range** and the **Output range.** The DATA FIND command, which we'll use first, requires only Input and Criterion ranges.

- *The Input range* is the range of your database, including the row of field names and the data you are querying. The FINANCE Input range goes from B1 to E13. (The sequence numbers in A are used only for resorting the data.)

- *The Criterion range* is the area where you enter the basis for your query. It includes a row of labels made up of some or all of the field names and some entries telling 1–2–3 which records you want to find, extract, or delete. You'll build a Criterion area in rows 15 and 16.

Figure 6.8 is a picture of the worksheet showing the Input and Criterion areas.

Fig. 6.8   FINANCE with Input and Criterion Areas

A15: 'CRIT   READY

```
      A      B        C      D          E        F      G      H      I
1   DATA DIVISION   QTR   REVENUE     COST
2      4 CLASSICAL   1      200         60
3     10 COUNTRY     1      400        320
4      7 JAZZ        1      100         70
5      1 ROCK        1      300        210
6      5 CLASSICAL   2      240         72
7     11 COUNTRY     2      400        320
8      8 JAZZ        2      120         84
9      2 ROCK        2      350        245
10     6 CLASSICAL   3      280         84
11    12 COUNTRY     3      390        312
12     9 JAZZ        3      150        105
13     3 ROCK        3      360        252
14
15   CRIT  DIVISION QTR    REVENUE     COST
16
17
18
19
20
```

CAPS

The best way to enter the labels for the Criterion range is to COPY the row of field names from the database. That way, you are sure the labels exactly match the field names. The labels must look exactly like the field names (same spelling, case, and label-prefix) or 1–2–3 won't know which fields the labels refer to.

With the pointer on B1, select COPY; type three Right Arrows (to set the FROM range as B1..E1), and type [Enter]. Move the pointer to B15 (the TO-range "hook") and type [Enter]. You can add the label CRIT in A15 to label this as the criterion area, though 1–2–3 doesn't require any label at all. Your worksheet should look like the one in Fig. 6.8.

Now that you've set up the criterion labels, you're ready to define the database for queries. Move the pointer to B1 and select DATA QUERY INPUT. The Input range is the database including the field names in row 1. Type a Period to tack down the beginning of the range. A fast way to get to the end of a column or row of entries is with the [End] key. If the pointer is starting on an entry, [End] and an Arrow will move the pointer to the last entry before a space occurs. If the pointer starts on a space, it will move to the next cell that contains an entry. In either case, if there are no more entries in the arrow direction, the

137

pointer will move to the edge of the worksheet. Type [End] Down Arrow, [End] Right Arrow.

Fig. 6.9   Pointer Movement with the [End] Key

```
        ┌─  DIVISION QTR    REVENUE        COST
END     │   CLASSICAL   1        200          60
        │   COUNTRY     1        400         320
   ↓    │   JAZZ        1        100          70
        │   ROCK        1        300         210
        │   CLASSICAL   2        240          72
        │   COUNTRY     2        400         320
        │   JAZZ        2        120          84
        │   ROCK        2        350         245
        │   CLASSICAL   3        280          84
        │   COUNTRY     3        390         312
        │   JAZZ        3        150         105
        └─► ROCK        3        360         252
            └───────────────────────────────┐
                                             ↑
          END ───►
```

Your Input range should be listed in the scratch area as B1..E13. If the scratch area lists something different, or if you want to try using the [End] key again, type a Backspace [←—]. The pointer will return to B1, the block pointer will clear, and you can begin defining the range again. When the Input range is listed as B1..E13, type [Enter].

Fig. 6.10   Defining the Input Range

```
E13: 252
Enter Input range: B1..E13

        A      B         C      D          E       F      G      H      I
1    DATA DIVISION QTR    REVENUE      COST
2       4 CLASSICAL   1        200          60
3      10 COUNTRY     1        400         320
4       7 JAZZ        1        100          70
5       1 ROCK        1        300         210
6       5 CLASSICAL   2        240          72
7      11 COUNTRY     2        400         320
8       8 JAZZ        2        120          84
9       2 ROCK        2        350         245
10      6 CLASSICAL   3        280          84
11     12 COUNTRY     3        390         312
12      9 JAZZ        3        150         105
13      3 ROCK        3        360         252
14
15   CRIT DIVISION QTR    REVENUE      COST
16
17
```

138

The Criterion range is only two rows long. It includes the row of labels starting in B15 and the blank area in row 16. (Later we'll expand the range to handle more complicated criteria.) Select CRITERION, move the pointer to B15, and enter the range B15..E16 by pointing or typing.

Fig. 6.11   Defining the Criterion Range

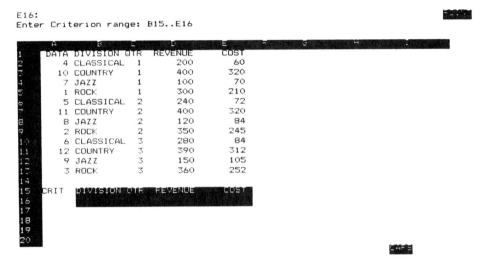

You're almost ready to select the FIND command. FIND locates records in the Input range based on entries in the Criterion range. When you execute FIND, 1–2–3 positions the pointer on the first record matching the criteria. The Down Arrow will move the pointer to the next record that matches the criteria. If no records are found, the computer will beep. If you try to move past the last "found" record, the computer will beep then, too.

Before you can actually FIND a record, however, you must tell 1–2–3 the criteria for the search. You'll need to make an entry in the Criterion range, so select QUIT to return to READY mode.

Move the pointer to row 16, the blank row in your Criterion range. 1–2–3 uses the entries you make in this row to FIND particular records in the database. To have 1–2–3 find all the JAZZ records, enter JAZZ in B16 and select DATA QUERY again. You've already defined INPUT and CRITERION (1–2–3 remembers them until you clear them), so just select

FIND. Now 1–2–3 positions the pointer on the first record that matches the criteria—in this case the first record for JAZZ division.

Fig. 6.12   The First-Found JAZZ Record

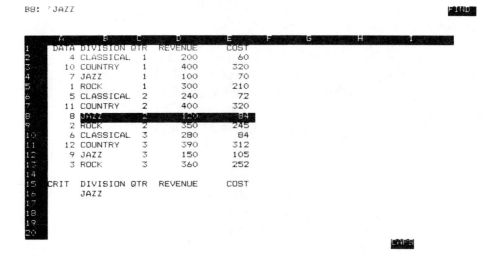

Type a Down Arrow and the pointer jumps to the next JAZZ record.

Fig. 6.13   The Second-Found JAZZ Record

B8: 'JAZZ   FIND

	A	B	C	D	E	F	G	H	I
1	DATA	DIVISION	QTR	REVENUE	COST				
2	4	CLASSICAL	1	200	60				
3	10	COUNTRY	1	400	320				
4	7	JAZZ	1	100	70				
5	1	ROCK	1	300	210				
6	5	CLASSICAL	2	240	72				
7	11	COUNTRY	2	400	320				
8	8	JAZZ	2	120	84				
9	2	ROCK	2	350	245				
10	6	CLASSICAL	3	280	84				
11	12	COUNTRY	3	390	312				
12	9	JAZZ	3	150	105				
13	3	ROCK	3	360	252				
14									
15	CRIT	DIVISION	QTR	REVENUE	COST				
16		JAZZ							
17									
18									
19									
20									

CAPS

Two more Down Arrows will move the pointer to the last JAZZ record and then cause the computer to beep. The beep tells you that there are no more JAZZ records in the database. Up Arrows will move the pointer back up through the found records. You can also use the Right and Left Arrows to look at different fields within a record. When you've finished looking at the records, type [Enter] or [Esc] to return to the QUERY menu.

You can also locate records based on numeric criteria. For example, you can FIND all records whose COST is less than $100. To do this, first QUIT the QUERY menu, then erase JAZZ from B16 using the RANGE ERASE command. Move the pointer to E16 and enter +E2<100. The formula points to the first cost entry, E2, to tell 1–2–3 where to start looking for records that match the criteria. When you enter the formula, 1–2–3 evaluates it as true or false. If the formula is true (E2 *is* less than $100), 1–2–3 displays a 1 in E16; if the formula is false, 1–2–3 displays a 0 in E16. Since the cost in E2 is 60, E16 contains a 1 (true).

Fig. 6.14   COST Criteria

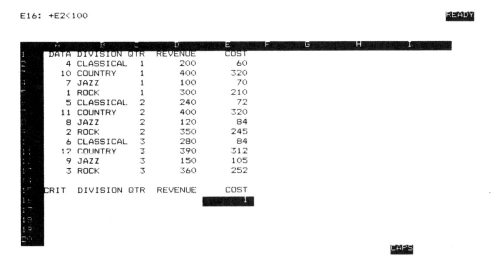

E16: +E2<100   READY

	A	B	C	D	E	F	G	H	I
1	DATA	DIVISION	QTR	REVENUE	COST				
2	4	CLASSICAL	1	200	60				
3	10	COUNTRY	1	400	320				
4	7	JAZZ	1	100	70				
5	1	ROCK	1	300	210				
6	5	CLASSICAL	2	240	72				
7	11	COUNTRY	2	400	320				
8	8	JAZZ	2	120	84				
9	2	ROCK	2	350	245				
10	6	CLASSICAL	3	280	84				
11	12	COUNTRY	3	390	312				
12	9	JAZZ	3	150	105				
13	3	ROCK	3	360	252				
14									
15	CRIT	DIVISION	QTR	REVENUE	COST				
16					1				

CAPS

You can make this entry easier to understand by formatting it as text. The TEXT format will display the formula rather than the true-false value. With the pointer on E16, select RANGE FORMAT TEXT and type [Enter]. The formatted cell displays the formula +E2<100.

Fig. 6.15 Formatted Criteria

E16: (T) +E2<100   READY

	A	B	C	D	E	F	G	H	I
1	DATA	DIVISION	QTR	REVENUE	COST				
2	4	CLASSICAL	1	200	60				
3	10	COUNTRY	1	400	320				
4	7	JAZZ	1	100	70				
5	1	ROCK	1	300	210				
6	5	CLASSICAL	2	240	72				
7	11	COUNTRY	2	400	320				
8	8	JAZZ	2	120	84				
9	2	ROCK	2	350	245				
10	6	CLASSICAL	3	280	84				
11	12	COUNTRY	3	390	312				
12	9	JAZZ	3	150	105				
13	3	ROCK	3	360	252				
14									
15	CRIT	DIVISION	QTR	REVENUE	COST				
16					+E2<100				
17									
18									

Once you've entered the new criteria, you can tell 1–2–3 to FIND the new records by simply typing the QUERY function key. 1–2–3 finds the first record with a cost less than $100 and lets you move, as before, to subsequent "found" records.

Fig. 6.16 First COST Record Found

B2: 'CLASSICAL   FIND

	A	B	C	D	E	F	G	H	I
1	DATA	DIVISION	QTR	REVENUE	COST				
2	4	CLASSICAL	1	200	60				
3	10	COUNTRY	1	400	320				
4	7	JAZZ	1	100	70				
5	1	ROCK	1	300	210				
6	5	CLASSICAL	2	240	72				
7	11	COUNTRY	2	400	320				
8	8	JAZZ	2	120	84				
9	2	ROCK	2	350	245				
10	6	CLASSICAL	3	280	84				
11	12	COUNTRY	3	390	312				
12	9	JAZZ	3	150	105				
13	3	ROCK	3	360	252				
14									
15	CRIT	DIVISION	QTR	REVENUE	COST				
16					+E2<100				
17									
18									

It's easy to try different queries because you don't have to reissue the DATA commands—you simply change the criteria and type the Query key.

You can even find records on the basis of "fuzzy" (or unspecific) criteria. Suppose you want to find all records for divisions that begin with the letter C. Erase the formula from E16 and enter the new criteria—a C followed by an asterisk—in B16 (C*). The asterisk is a "wild card"; the criteria tells 1–2–3 to look for any record whose division name begins with a C. Press the Query key, and 1–2–3 finds all the COUNTRY and CLASSICAL records.

You can combine criteria by making more than one entry in the blank row of the Criterion range (row 16). To find each record bearing a division name that starts with C *and* a revenue less than $400, simply add the revenue criteria in D16. Move the pointer to D16 and enter the formula +D2<400. Since C* is still entered in B16, 1–2–3 now checks each record against two criteria before finding a record. Press the Query key and move the pointer through the found records. Notice that only one COUNTRY record (row 11) is found, because the other two COUNTRY records have revenues greater than $400.

Fig. 6.17   AND Criteria

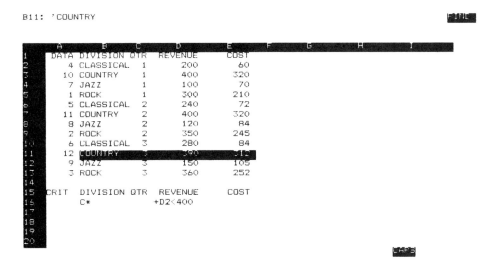

143

To find records based on either one or another criteria you must extend the Criterion range. Criteria entered on different lines are treated as "or" conditions—that is, found records match one condition or the other. A three-line criteria like that shown in Fig. 6.18 tells 1–2–3 to find records with revenues greater than $300 or with a division name starting with the letter C.

Fig. 6.18   FINANCE with Three Criteria Lines

```
E17:                                                                      POINT
Enter Criterion range: B15..E17

         A      B        C       D          E       F      G      H      I
1      DATA  DIVISION  QTR   REVENUE      COST
2         4  CLASSICAL   1       200         60
3        10  COUNTRY     1       400        320
4         7  JAZZ        1       100         70
5         1  ROCK        1       300        210
6         5  CLASSICAL   2       240         72
7        11  COUNTRY     2       400        320
8         8  JAZZ        2       120         84
9         2  ROCK        2       350        245
10        6  CLASSICAL   3       280         84
11       12  COUNTRY     3       390        312
12        9  JAZZ        3       150        105
13        3  ROCK        3       360        252
14
15    CRIT  DIVISION  QTR   REVENUE      COST
16          C*
17                           +D2>300
18
19
20
                                                                          CAPS
```

Before issuing the FIND command, you must expand the Criterion range to cover the new row containing the "or" criteria. Fig. 6.18 shows a three-line Criterion range made up of the labels and two rows for criterion entries. When FIND is issued, 1–2–3 finds all the COUNTRY and CLASSICAL records because their division names start with C, as well as two ROCK records whose revenues are greater than $300.

Fig. 6.19   OR Criteria

B9: 'ROCK   FIND

	A	B	C	D	E	F	G	H	I
1	DATA	DIVISION	QTR	REVENUE	COST				
2	4	CLASSICAL	1	200	60				
3	10	COUNTRY	1	400	320				
4	7	JAZZ	1	100	70				
5	1	ROCK	1	300	210				
6	5	CLASSICAL	2	240	72				
7	11	COUNTRY	2	400	320				
8	8	JAZZ	2	120	84				
9	2	ROCK	2	350	245				
10	6	CLASSICAL	3	280	84				
11	12	COUNTRY	3	390	312				
12	9	JAZZ	3	150	105				
13	3	ROCK	3	360	252				
14									
15	CRIT	DIVISION	QTR	REVENUE	COST				
16		C*							
17				+D2>300					
18									
19									
20									

CAPS

Obviously the FIND command is more impressive when you're working with a large database. A 1000-file Rolodex, for example, would call for frequent FINDs. By using FIND and a so-called wild card (*), you can locate the record of someone whose name or company you only partially remember. The Criterion range's ability to handle "and/or" conditions gives you the power to do searches based on complicated criteria.

5. Extracting Significant Records

Often, when you locate some important entries, you want to distinguish or list them apart from your database. You don't want to move these entries *out* of the database, you simply want to copy them into another area of the worksheet. To create such a list manually, you proceed as you did when you were first locating the records—that is, by moving your finger along the list until you find an entry that matches your criteria. Each time you find a matching entry, you copy it (and possibly its associated entries) into your separate list. It's a time-consuming task.

145

Once again, 1–2–3 can automate your work, this time with the DATA QUERY EXTRACT command. The EXTRACT command finds the records that match your criteria and copies all or part of the matching records into another area of the worksheet. The area where the extracted records are listed is called the **Output range**.

- *The Output range* may include one row or a block of rows. In either case, the first row in the Output range must be made up of labels that match one or more of the field names in the database. 1–2–3 uses the labels to determine which fields to list and where to put them. If the Output range is defined as a block of rows, it is made up of the top row of labels and several rows in which the extracted records can be listed. If the Output range is defined as the single row of labels, 1–2–3 assumes the entire worksheet area below those labels is available for listing extracted records.

When you invoke the EXTRACT command, 1–2–3 locates the records to list, clears the range below the output labels, and displays the list in the cleared area. Let's start by entering a single-row Output range in row 18, below both database and criteria.

Fig. 6.20 FINANCE with Output Range

A18: 'OUT   READY

	DATA	DIVISION	QTR	REVENUE	COST
	4	CLASSICAL	1	200	60
	10	COUNTRY	1	400	320
	7	JAZZ	1	100	70
	1	ROCK	1	300	210
	5	CLASSICAL	2	240	72
	11	COUNTRY	2	400	320
	8	JAZZ	2	120	84
	2	ROCK	2	350	245
	6	CLASSICAL	3	280	84
	12	COUNTRY	3	390	312
	9	JAZZ	3	150	105
	3	ROCK	3	360	252
	CRIT	DIVISION	QTR	REVENUE	COST
	OUT	DIVISION	QTR	REVENUE	COST

CAPS

Enter the output labels as you did the criterion labels—using the COPY command. You can copy the labels from either row 1 or row 15; they're identical. To make the purpose of the Output area clear, enter the new label OUT in A18. (As you know, 1–2–3 doesn't *require* any label, but a label makes the worksheet easier to understand.)

First, you'll extract all the records for the ROCK division. The criteria for extracts work just like the criteria for finds. Remember to ERASE existing entries in the Criterion range when you want to try different criteria. You must also select CRITERION and adjust the range if you want to add or subtract criterion rows. A blank row included in the Criterion range tells 1–2–3 to select *every* record in the database.

Redefine your Criterion range now so that it includes only rows 15 and 16—the labels and a row for entries. ERASE any entries currently in rows 16 and 17 and enter ROCK in B16. Your worksheet should look like Fig. 6.21.

Fig. 6.21   Criteria for Extract

B16: 'ROCK

	A	B	C	D	E	F	G	H	I
1	DATA	DIVISION	QTR	REVENUE	COST			
2		4 CLASSICAL	1	200	60			
3		10 COUNTRY	1	400	320			
4		7 JAZZ	1	100	70			
5		1 ROCK	1	300	210			
6		5 CLASSICAL	2	240	72			
7		11 COUNTRY	2	400	320			
8		8 JAZZ	2	120	84			
9		2 ROCK	2	350	245			
10		6 CLASSICAL	3	280	84			
11		12 COUNTRY	3	390	312			
12		9 JAZZ	3	150	105			
13		3 ROCK	3	360	252			
14							
15	CRIT	DIVISION	QTR	REVENUE	COST			
16		ROCK						
17							
18	OUT	DIVISION	QTR	REVENUE	COST			
19							
20							

Before you can perform an extract, you must define the Output range. You can define the Output range as either a single row of labels or a block including the row of labels and several blank rows. If you define

147

a block range, only the entries that will fit in the block can be extracted. If the extracted entries won't fit in the Output range, 1–2–3 will display an error message: the computer will beep, and the EXTRACT command will be canceled.

If you define the Output range as a single row of labels, 1–2–3 clears all the rows below the range *to the bottom of the worksheet* and then displays the extracted records. If you do use a single-row Output range, be sure you make no entries below the output row, as they will be erased during extracts.

To define the range, select DATA QUERY OUTPUT. The Output range is the single row of labels from B18 to E18. Enter the range B18..E18 and select EXTRACT. You'll see two records appear below the output labels. Select QUIT to leave the menu, and move the pointer down to row 21. As you can see, there are actually three entries in the Output area: the three records whose division is ROCK.

Fig. 6.22   Extracted Records for ROCK

B21: 'ROCK   READY

		B		D	E	F	G	H	I
	4	CLASSICAL	1	200	60				
	10	COUNTRY	1	400	320				
	7	JAZZ	1	100	70				
	1	ROCK	1	300	210				
	5	CLASSICAL	2	240	72				
	11	COUNTRY	2	400	320				
	8	JAZZ	2	120	84				
	2	ROCK	2	350	245				
	6	CLASSICAL	3	280	84				
	12	COUNTRY	3	390	312				
	9	JAZZ	3	150	105				
	3	ROCK	3	360	252				
	CRIT	DIVISION	QTR	REVENUE	COST				
		ROCK							
	OUT	DIVISION	QTR	REVENUE	COST				
		ROCK	1	300	210				
		ROCK	2	350	245				
		ROCK	3	360	252				

CAPS

To perform another extract, simply enter the new criteria and press the Query key. For example, to list all second-quarter records, erase ROCK from B16, enter 2 in C16, and press the Query key. 1–2–3 instantly extracts the four records with second-quarter data (Fig. 6.23).

Fig. 6.23   Extracted Records for Quarter 2

C22: 2   READY

	A	B	C	D	E	F	G	H	I
3		10 COUNTRY	1	400	320				
4		7 JAZZ	1	100	70				
5		1 ROCK	1	300	210				
6		5 CLASSICAL	2	240	72				
7		11 COUNTRY	2	400	320				
8		8 JAZZ	2	120	84				
9		2 ROCK	2	350	245				
10		6 CLASSICAL	3	280	84				
11		12 COUNTRY	3	390	312				
12		9 JAZZ	3	150	105				
13		3 ROCK	3	360	252				
14									
15	CRIT	DIVISION QTR		REVENUE	COST				
16		2							
17									
18	OUT	DIVISION QTR		REVENUE	COST				
19		CLASSICAL	2	240	72				
20		COUNTRY	2	400	320				
21		JAZZ	2	120	84				
22		ROCK	2	350	245				

CAPS

It's very easy to change the contents and order of your output labels. Suppose you want to produce a report on the second quarter. You want to include the division name and revenue and cost figures, but eliminate the quarter number from the body of the report.

To erase the QTR heading, move the pointer to C18, select RANGE ERASE, and type [Enter]. Press the Query key to extract, and you'll get a new listing with no quarter entries displayed.

Fig. 6.24   Limiting Output

C18:   READY

	A	B	C	D	E	F	G	H	I
3		10 COUNTRY	1	400	320				
4		7 JAZZ	1	100	70				
5		1 ROCK	1	300	210				
6		5 CLASSICAL	2	240	72				
7		11 COUNTRY	2	400	320				
8		8 JAZZ	2	120	84				
9		2 ROCK	2	350	245				
10		6 CLASSICAL	3	280	84				
11		12 COUNTRY	3	390	312				
12		9 JAZZ	3	150	105				
13		3 ROCK	3	360	252				
14									
15	CRIT	DIVISION QTR		REVENUE	COST				
16		2							
17									
18	OUT	DIVISION		REVENUE	COST				
19		CLASSICAL		240	72				
20		COUNTRY		400	320				
21		JAZZ		120	84				
22		ROCK		350	245				

CAPS

149

You could now type a temporary report heading "QUARTER 2, 1983" in B17, insert a blank row in 18, and PRINT the range from B17..E23. Your printed report would look like Fig. 6.25.

Fig. 6.25   Quarter 2 Report

```
QUARTER 2, 1983

DIVISION        REVENUE        COST
CLASSICAL           240          72
COUNTRY             400         320
JAZZ                120          84
ROCK                350         245
```

To produce the same report for the third quarter:

1. Retype the heading in B17.
2. Change the criteria (C16 = 3).
3. Press the Query key to get the new list.
4. Print the report range (B17..E23).

Fig. 6.26   Quarter 3 Report

```
QUARTER 3, 1983

DIVISION        REVENUE        COST
CLASSICAL           280          84
COUNTRY             390         312
JAZZ                150         105
ROCK                360         252
```

As you can see, database queries take some extra setting up. Once you've created and defined the Query ranges, however, you're able to perform different queries very easily. By adjusting the labels in the Output range, you can produce some simple reports on portions of the database. With the FIND command, you can quickly locate a record or group of records, even when you're not sure of the field value you're searching for. The 1–2–3 QUERY command gives you a fast and easy way to query collections of data and extract portions of it. The extracted lists can be the basis for reports and graphs, and they adjust easily to new data and new criteria.

Chapter 6 Exercises

FINANCE Exercise

Practice what you've learned in Chapter 6 by doing the following things with your FINANCE database.

1. Add a new column to the Output area that calculates profit as REVENUE minus COST. Enter a column heading, PROFIT, in F18, and the first profit formula in F19:

   F19 = +D19–E19.

   Then COPY the profit formula down the column. Change the DIVISION criteria and check on another division's profits.

2. Change the criteria to look at a particular quarter rather than a division. Since there are four entries for each quarter, you'll have to extend the profit formula down a row.

3. Define a graph that draws a bar or pie chart of the PROFIT figures. When you change the criteria, you have to press only two keys, the Query key and the Graph key, to extract and graph the new data.

4. Build a small database of your own and add a criteria and output section for queries. A good first database is a small Rolodex. Include a name, phone number, city and state in each row. Try to enter some duplicates in the city and state columns so you can extract lists based on these entries. Use the FIND command to locate particular entries.

PROJDATA Exercise

PROJDATA is an expanded version of the model PROJEST, described at the end of Chapter 5. If you haven't yet built PROJEST, do so now. PROJDATA includes Criterion and Output ranges for extracting pieces of the project estimate data.

151

```
A1:  'PROJDATA                                                    READY

          A          B          C         D        E         F        G
 1   PROJDATA                  Date      April 30, 1983
 2
 3   Compute total project time and cost estimates at a standard hourly
 4   rate. The project is divided into tasks, some of which include more
 5   than one employee. This project is estimated in hours and summarized
 6   in days.
 7
 8   Project Completion Time:        23.5 days
 9   Project Cost:              $6,580
10
11   Rate:                      $35.00 hour
12
13   TASK                TASK #       EMP     HOURS   CHARGES
14   Plan                  1          wrb        8       280
15   Plan                  1          jpf        8       280
16   Plan                  1          meb        8       280
17   Design                2          jpf       20       700
18   Outline               3          wrb        6       210
19   Outline               3          jpf        6       210
20   Write First Draft     4          jpf       40      1400
21   Write First Draft     4          meb       24       840
22   Revise                5          wrb        8       280
23   Revise                5          jpf        8       280
24   Revise                5          meb        8       280
25   Write Final Draft     6          jpf       36      1260
26   Write Final Draft     6          meb        8       280
27   --------------------------------------------------------------
28   Totals                6          3        188    $6,580
29
30
31   CRITERION AREA
32   TASK                TASK #       EMP     HOURS   CHARGES
33                                    jpf
34
35   OUTPUT AREA                    TOTALS:     118      4130       63%
36
37   TASK                TASK #       EMP     HOURS   CHARGES  % OF TOTAL
38   Plan                  1          jpf        8       280       7%
39   Design                2          jpf       20       700      17%
40   Outline               3          jpf        6       210       5%
41   Write First Draft     4          jpf       40      1400      34%
42   Revise                5          jpf        8       280       7%
43   Write Final Draft     6          jpf       36      1260      31%
44                                                                 0%
```

1. Enter the criterion labels in row 32 by COPYing the raw data labels from row 13, then COPY the labels into row 37—the output row.

2. The two TOTALS entries in D35 and E35 are sums of the extracted entries. Since the number of extracted entries varies, set the Sum range to the maximum number of entries you ever expect to extract. For example:

D35 = @SUM [D38..D50] = total extracted hours

If the extracted entries don't fill the Sum range, 1–2–3 will simply add zeros to the sum.

3. The %TOTAL column divides each CHARGES entry by the total charges in E35. That is:

$$F38 = +E38/\$E\$35 = \text{charge 1 / total charges,}$$
$$F39 = +E39/\$E\$35 = \text{charge 2 / total charges,}$$

and so on. If you use the Absolute key to freeze the total cell, you can enter the formula once in F38 and then COPY it down the column. COPY the formula down to row 51, the last row that might contain extracted entries, and format the column as PERCENTs. Extra percent formulas will be calculated as 0%.

4. Use this formula to calculate the total % TOTAL:

$$F35 = +E25/E28 = \text{total extracted charges / total charges.}$$

5. The TASK names are copied into any blank lines in column A of the database so that all extracted records will have a TASK entry.

Once you've built the areas and defined them with the DATA QUERY command, try a few EXTRACTS; the EMP (employee) column is a good category for extracts, but you might also try a formula in the HOURS or CHARGES column. If you do enter a formula, format the entry as TEXT so it will be easy to read. Remember to enter the employee initials in lowercase (unless they are in uppercase in your database), or 1–2–3 won't be able to match the criteria to the entries. You don't have to precede the criterion initials with the label-prefix character ("), though.

STOREDATA Exercise

The STOREDATA exercise is a breakdown of the sales figures introduced in the SALES exercise at the end of Chapter 3. This table shows the budgeted and actual sales for the stores in five sales areas.

1. Build the database and query section for the store data. The database contains only value entries (no formulas).

```
A1:  'STOREDATA                                                              READY

      A       B        C        D        E        F        G        H
 1  STOREDATA
 2
 3  Raw sales' figures ($000) for stores in five areas. The
 4  data lists each store's area, category, and budgeted and
 5  actual revenues. Some stores sell only women's shoes
 6  (W), some sell only men's shoes (M), and some sell both
 7  men's and women's (B).
 8
 9  DATA AREA          CAT      BUDGET    ACTUAL
10      CHICAGO        M           150       150
11      CHICAGO        W           200       240
12      CHICAGO        B           450       350
13      CHICAGO        W           100       160
14      CHICAGO        B           300       285
15      NEW YORK       W           800       250
16      NEW YORK       B           500       600
17      NEW YORK       B         1,700       920
18      BOSTON         B           600       760
19      DALLAS         W           300       220
20      DALLAS         W           750       825
21      DALLAS         M           400       295
22      DALLAS         B           950       520
23      ATLANTA        B           500       470
24      ATLANTA        M         1,300     1,410
25
26  CRIT AREA          CAT      BUDGET    ACTUAL
27                     W
28
29                                                  INCREASE/
30  OUT  AREA          CAT      BUDGET    ACTUAL  (DECREASE)
31       CHICAGO       W           200       240         40
32       CHICAGO       W           100       160         60
33       NEW YORK      W           800       250      (550)
34       DALLAS        W           300       220       (80)
35       DALLAS        W           750       825         75
36
37
38
39
40
```

2. The OUT area includes a formula, in column F, that calculates the difference between actual and budgeted sales.

   increase = +E30–D30 = actual – budget

   Build the formula in F30, then COPY it down the column.

3. Define the QUERY ranges and try some extracts.

4. SORT the database (B8..E23) by CATegory or by AREA. Remember to enter a column of original sequence numbers before you perform the sort.

Summarizing Database Contents

1. Database Functions

You have learned how to find and extract particular database entries. By extracting portions of the data—all records for ROCK division, for example—you can begin to summarize the data for each division. Once you extract the ROCK data, you might add up all the revenue entries to get a total revenue figure for ROCK.

But why not let 1–2–3 do the work for you? Just as you used the EXTRACT command to automate the two-step process of finding and listing particular records, you can use the 1–2–3 database functions, or @D functions, to automate the two-step process of extracting and summarizing particular entries.

The @D functions are like regular 1–2–3 functions (such as SUM) except they work on a database. There are seven @D functions:

@DCOUNT	count
@DSUM	sum
@DAVG	average
@DMIN	minimum
@DMAX	maximum
@DSTD	standard deviation
@DVAR	variance

155

Like other functions, @D functions are treated as formulas by 1–2–3. (We'll call them @D formulas.) An @D formula summarizes the entries in a particular database column according to some criteria. The summarizing criteria work just like the query criteria: entries made below the criteria labels determine which data is included in the summary.

Suppose you want to total all the revenues for ROCK division. With the @DSUM function, 1–2–3 can build the total. Think of 1–2–3 as producing the sum just as you might produce it with pencil and paper: First, you scan the DIVISION column for entries that match the criteria. Each time you find a matching entry, you look across to the REVENUE column and copy that figure onto your list of values to sum. When you finish checking for matching division entries, you add the figures on your list and you have your total sum.

In your pencil-and paper-summary, three things are important: the range of entries that make up the database, the column whose entries are included in the sum, and the criteria for selecting records. The same three things are important to 1–2–3: **Input range, Offset value,** and **Criterion range.** The 1–2–3 @D formulas are entered in this form:

@Dfunction (Input range, Offset, Criterion range)

- *The Input range* is the area of the database. It includes all the fields in the database, not just the one being summarized. The Input range in FINANCE is B1..E13.

- *The Offset value* tells 1–2–3 which column contains the entries being summarized. Offset columns are counted starting with zero (that is, no offset), so the offset for FINANCE's DIVISION field is 0, for QTR is 1, and so on.

- *The Criterion range* contains the criteria for determining which records to include in the summary (just as the criterion for QUERY commands indicates which records to include in an extracted list).

You first @D formula will use the @DCOUNT function to count the number of records in the database for one division or for the whole company (depending on the criteria). Before you can build the @D formula, you must create a new Criterion area for the summary formulas and tables. It may be possible to use the CRIT area you already created in rows 15 and 16, but the worksheet will be easier to use and understand if you keep the summary area separate from the query area.

Move the pointer to F1. Column F should be left as a blank column to separate the summary area from the database, but you can make it thinner to give yourself more worksheet room on the screen. Select WORKSHEET COLUMN SET and type 5 [Enter] to set the width of column F to 5. As you see, the thinner column F made room for another column, I, on the screen. In order to keep the database and summary area on the same screen, we'll start the summary in column G. You'll probably want to leave more space between areas when you're building your own worksheets.

You're going to build a summary area in columns G, H, and I that looks like Fig. 7.1.

Fig. 7.1   FINANCE with Summary Area

G2: 'ROCK   READY

	DIVISION	QTR	REVENUE	COST		DIVISION	QTR	
DATA								
4	CLASSICAL	1	200	60		ROCK		
10	COUNTRY	1	400	320				
7	JAZZ	1	100	70		SUMMARY		
1	ROCK	1	300	210		ENTRIES	REVENUE	COST
5	CLASSICAL	2	240	72		3	1010	707
11	COUNTRY	2	400	320				
8	JAZZ	2	120	84				
2	ROCK	2	350	245				
6	CLASSICAL	3	280	84				
12	COUNTRY	3	390	312				
9	JAZZ	3	150	105				
3	ROCK	3	360	252				
CRIT	DIVISION	QTR	REVENUE	COST				
	ROCK							
OUT	DIVISION	QTR	REVENUE	COST				
	ROCK	1	300	210				
	ROCK	2	350	245				

CAPS

The summary shows the number of entries, total revenues, and total costs for records matching the criteria. Enter these labels in col-

157

umns G, H, and I:

G1 = DIVISION

H1 = "QTR

G2 = ROCK

G4 = SUMMARY

G5 = ENTRIES

H5 = REVENUE

I5 = COST

Fig. 7.2 Summary Area Labels

I5: "COST

`READY`

	A	B	C	D	E	F	G	H	I
1	DATA	DIVISION	QTR	REVENUE	COST		DIVISION	QTR	
2	4	CLASSICAL	1	200	60		ROCK		
3	10	COUNTRY	1	400	320				
4	7	JAZZ	1	100	70		SUMMARY		
5	1	ROCK	1	300	210		ENTRIES	REVENUE	COST
6	5	CLASSICAL	2	240	72				
7	11	COUNTRY	2	400	320				
8	8	JAZZ	2	120	84				
9	2	ROCK	2	350	245				
10	6	CLASSICAL	3	280	84				
11	12	COUNTRY	3	390	312				
12	9	JAZZ	3	150	105				
13	3	ROCK	3	360	252				
14									
15	CRIT	DIVISION	QTR	REVENUE	COST				
16		ROCK							
17									
18	OUT	DIVISION	QTR	REVENUE	COST				
19		ROCK	1	300	210				
20		ROCK	2	350	245				

`CAPS`

The area from G1 to H2 is the Criterion range for the @D formulas. The labels from G5 to I5 are headings for the @D formulas; the labels aren't required, but they make the worksheet easier to understand.

Move the pointer to G6, and type @DCOUNT(to start the formula. You can enter the first part of the formula—the Input range—by pointing. Move the pointer to B1, type a Period to tack the start of the range down, move the pointer right and down to E13, and—instead of typing [Enter]—type a Comma [,]. The comma closes off the first part of the formula (Input range) and returns the pointer to G6.

Fig. 7.3   Building an @D Function

```
G6:                                                                    VALUE
@DCOUNT(B1..E13,
```

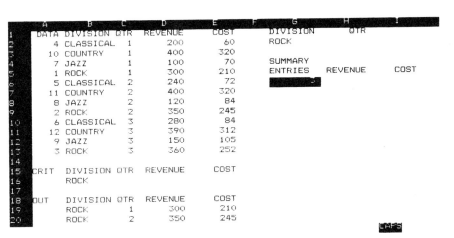

Now enter the offset, 0, and type a Comma to close the second part of the formula. The offset is 0 because the DIVISION column, B, is the first column in the Input range, hence it has no offset. The last part of the formula is the Criterion range—in this case, G1..H2. Type in the Criterion range and close the whole formula with a right parentheses,). The formula tells 1–2–3 to count entries in the DIVISION column that match the criteria. Type [Enter] and 1–2–3 calculates and displays the number of DIVISION entries that match ROCK: 3.

Fig. 7.4   The @DCOUNT Formula

```
G6:  @DCOUNT(DATA,0,DCRIT)                                             READY
```

The @D formula isn't difficult to build, but pointing out the range is time-consuming. You can omit some of your typing and pointing by making use of a particularly handy 1–2–3 feature—the **named range**. Once you've given any worksheet range a name, you can refer to it by its name rather than its cell addresses. To name the database, move the pointer to B1 and select RANGE NAME CREATE; then enter the name, DATA, and the range to name, B1..E13.

Fig. 7.5 Naming a Range

```
E13: 252                                                                    POINT
Enter name: DATA                        Enter range: B1..E13

       A      B        C       D          E      F      G          H         I
1    DATA  DIVISION  QTR    REVENUE     COST          DIVISION    QTR
2       4  CLASSICAL   1       200         60          ROCK
3      10  COUNTRY     1       400        320
4       7  JAZZ        1       100         70          SUMMARY
5       1  ROCK        1       300        210          ENTRIES    REVENUE    COST
6       5  CLASSICAL   2       240         72                 3
7      11  COUNTRY     2       400        320
8       8  JAZZ        2       120         84
9       2  ROCK        2       350        245
10      6  CLASSICAL   3       280         84
11     12  COUNTRY     3       390        312
12      9  JAZZ        3       150        105
13      3  ROCK        3       360        252
14
15   CRIT  DIVISION  QTR    REVENUE     COST
16         ROCK
17
18   OUT   DIVISION  QTR    REVENUE     COST
19         ROCK        1       300        210
20         ROCK        2       350        245
                                                                            CAPS
```

Before you enter the next @D formula, move the pointer to G6 and look at the formula listed in the control panel. Notice that the Input range is no longer listed by its coordinates; it's listed with the name DATA instead. Range names are easier both to enter and to read, so using them makes sense. And while you're at it, you can name the Criterion range as well. Name the G1..H2 area DCRIT, using the RANGE NAME command.

Fig. 7.6   Range Names in Formulas

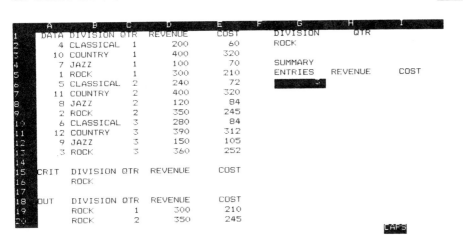

```
G6:  @DCOUNT(DATA,0,DCRIT)                                          READY
```

	A	B	C	D	E	F	G	H	I
1	DATA	DIVISION	QTR	REVENUE	COST		DIVISION	QTR	
2		4	CLASSICAL	1	200	60	ROCK		
3		10	COUNTRY	1	400	320			
4		7	JAZZ	1	100	70	SUMMARY		
5		1	ROCK	1	300	210	ENTRIES	REVENUE	COST
6		5	CLASSICAL	2	240	72			
7		11	COUNTRY	2	400	320			
8		8	JAZZ	2	120	84			
9		2	ROCK	2	350	245			
10		6	CLASSICAL	3	280	84			
11		12	COUNTRY	3	390	312			
12		9	JAZZ	3	150	105			
13		3	ROCK	3	360	252			
14									
15	CRIT	DIVISION	QTR	REVENUE	COST				
16		ROCK							
17									
18	OUT	DIVISION	QTR	REVENUE	COST				
19		ROCK	1	300	210				
20		ROCK	2	350	245				

CAPS

Now you're ready to enter the next @D formula in H6. This formula tells 1–2–3 to sum all REVENUE column entries under the division name of ROCK. Move the pointer to H6 and enter the revenue-summing formula:

@DSUM[DATA,2,DCRIT]

Notice how much easier it is to enter range names than to move the pointer around or try to remember what the range coordinates are. The offset in this formula is 2, because DIVISION is counted as the 0th column, making REVENUE the second column. When you enter the formula, 1–2–3 displays total revenues for ROCK division—$1010.

161

Fig. 7.7   Revenue @DSUM

H6: @DSUM(DATA,2,DCRIT)   READY

	A	B	C	D	E	F	G	H	I
1	DATA	DIVISION	QTR	REVENUE	COST		DIVISION	QTR	
2	4	CLASSICAL	1	200	60		ROCK		
3	10	COUNTRY	1	400	320				
4	7	JAZZ	1	100	70		SUMMARY		
5	1	ROCK	1	300	210		ENTRIES	REVENUE	COST
6	5	CLASSICAL	2	240	72		3	1010	
7	11	COUNTRY	2	400	320				
8	8	JAZZ	2	120	84				
9	2	ROCK	2	350	245				
10	6	CLASSICAL	3	280	84				
11	12	COUNTRY	3	390	312				
12	9	JAZZ	3	150	105				
13	3	ROCK	3	360	252				
14									
15	CRIT	DIVISION	QTR	REVENUE	COST				
16		ROCK							
17									
18	OUT	DIVISION	QTR	REVENUE	COST				
19		ROCK	1	300	210				
20		ROCK	2	350	245				

CAPS

In I6, enter a similar formula:

@DSUM[DATA,3,DCRIT]

to summarize total costs for the division. Your final summary area should look like Fig. 7.8.

Fig. 7.8   FINANCE Summary for ROCK

I6: @DSUM(DATA,3,DCRIT)   READY

	A	B	C	D	E	F	G	H	I
1	DATA	DIVISION	QTR	REVENUE	COST		DIVISION	QTR	
2	4	CLASSICAL	1	200	60		ROCK		
3	10	COUNTRY	1	400	320				
4	7	JAZZ	1	100	70		SUMMARY		
5	1	ROCK	1	300	210		ENTRIES	REVENUE	COST
6	5	CLASSICAL	2	240	72		3	1010	707
7	11	COUNTRY	2	400	320				
8	8	JAZZ	2	120	84				
9	2	ROCK	2	350	245				
10	6	CLASSICAL	3	280	84				
11	12	COUNTRY	3	390	312				
12	9	JAZZ	3	150	105				
13	3	ROCK	3	360	252				
14									
15	CRIT	DIVISION	QTR	REVENUE	COST				
16		ROCK							
17									
18	OUT	DIVISION	QTR	REVENUE	COST				
19		ROCK	1	300	210				
20		ROCK	2	350	245				

CAPS

Now that you've created the summary area, you can easily look at other summaries based on other criteria. Enter JAZZ in G2 and 1–2–3 quickly recalculates the number of entries, total revenue, and cost for JAZZ division.

Fig. 7.9   FINANCE Summary for JAZZ

G2: 'JAZZ   READY

	A	B	C	D	E	F	G	H	I
1	DATA	DIVISION	QTR	REVENUE	COST		DIVISION		QTR
2		4 CLASSICAL	1	200	60		JAZZ		
3		10 COUNTRY	1	400	320				
4		7 JAZZ	1	100	70		SUMMARY		
5		1 ROCK	1	300	210		ENTRIES	REVENUE	COST
6		5 CLASSICAL	2	240	72		3	370	259
7		11 COUNTRY	2	400	320				
8		8 JAZZ	2	120	84				
9		2 ROCK	2	350	245				
10		6 CLASSICAL	3	280	84				
11		12 COUNTRY	3	390	312				
12		9 JAZZ	3	150	105				
13		3 ROCK	3	360	252				
14									
15	CRIT	DIVISION	QTR	REVENUE	COST				
16		ROCK							
17									
18	OUT	DIVISION	QTR	REVENUE	COST				
19		ROCK	1	300	210				
20		ROCK	2	350	245				

CAPS

Use the RANGE ERASE command to clear G2, enter 3 in H2, and you'll get the entries, revenue, and cost for the third quarter.

Fig. 7.10   FINANCE Summary for Quarter 3

H2: 3   READY

	A	B	C	D	E	F	G	H	I
1	DATA	DIVISION	QTR	REVENUE	COST		DIVISION	QTR	
2		4 CLASSICAL	1	200	60			3	
3		10 COUNTRY	1	400	320				
4		7 JAZZ	1	100	70		SUMMARY		
5		1 ROCK	1	300	210		ENTRIES	REVENUE	COST
6		5 CLASSICAL	2	240	72		4	1180	753
7		11 COUNTRY	2	400	320				
8		8 JAZZ	2	120	84				
9		2 ROCK	2	350	245				
10		6 CLASSICAL	3	280	84				
11		12 COUNTRY	3	390	312				
12		9 JAZZ	3	150	105				
13		3 ROCK	3	360	252				
14									
15	CRIT	DIVISION	QTR	REVENUE	COST				
16		ROCK							
17									
18	OUT	DIVISION	QTR	REVENUE	COST				
19		ROCK	1	300	210				
20		ROCK	2	350	245				

CAPS

You could build a larger Criterion range including the REVENUE and COST labels, though it's less likely you'd want to summarize based on these fields. If you do increase the Criterion range, you'll have to redefine the DCRIT name, and reenter the @D formulas.

You may want to try some of the other @D functions listed at the beginning of this section. Change the @DSUM in H6 to @DAVG and 1–2–3 will compute the average revenue for the third quarter.

Fig. 7.11 Revenue Average

H6: @DAVG(DATA,2,DCRIT)   READY

DATA	DIVISION	QTR	REVENUE	COST		DIVISION	QTR	
4	CLASSICAL	1	200	60			3	
10	COUNTRY	1	400	320				
7	JAZZ	1	100	70		SUMMARY		
1	ROCK	1	300	210		ENTRIES	REVENUE	COST
5	CLASSICAL	2	240	72		4	295	753
11	COUNTRY	2	400	320				
8	JAZZ	2	120	84				
2	ROCK	2	350	245				
6	CLASSICAL	3	280	84				
12	COUNTRY	3	390	312				
9	JAZZ	3	150	105				
3	ROCK	3	360	252				
CRIT	DIVISION	QTR	REVENUE	COST				
	ROCK							
OUT	DIVISION	QTR	REVENUE	COST				
	ROCK	1	300	210				
	ROCK	2	350	245				

CAPS

@DMAX will give the largest third-quarter revenue and @DMIN will give the smallest. You can try different functions and criteria in the summary area, but keep a copy like the one in Fig. 7.12 to use in the next section, where you'll be learning about data tables.

Before you move on to tables, change the criteria so that the @D formulas summarize the entire database. The criteria for the whole database is either an asterisk (*) in G2 and a blank in H2, or blanks in both G2 and H2. We prefer to include the asterisk in G2 to highlight the fact that this criteria includes all database records. Your final FINANCE worksheet should look like Fig. 7.12.

Fig. 7.12 FINANCE with Summary for Entire Database

H6: @DSUM(DATA,2,DCRIT)   READY

```
        A       B       C       D         E       F       G         H         I
1    DATA  DIVISION QTR   REVENUE    COST        DIVISION      QTR
2        4 CLASSICAL.  1     200       60        *
3       10 COUNTRY     1     400      320
4        7 JAZZ        1     100       70        SUMMARY
5        1 ROCK        1     300      210        ENTRIES    REVENUE       COST
6        5 CLASSICAL.  2     240       72            12        3290        2134
7       11 COUNTRY     2     400      320
8        8 JAZZ        2     120       84
9        2 ROCK        2     350      245
10       6 CLASSICAL.  3     280       84
11      12 COUNTRY     3     390      312
12       9 JAZZ        3     150      105
13       3 ROCK        3     360      252
14
15    CRIT  DIVISION QTR   REVENUE    COST
16          ROCK.
17
18     OUT  DIVISION QTR   REVENUE    COST
19          ROCK        1     300      210
20          ROCK        2     350      245
```

                                                                          CAPS

---

2. Data Tables

In Chapter 5, you built a data table to summarize the effects of various what-if values. Each what-if number was plugged into a cell of the worksheet, its effect on dependent formulas calculated, and the calculation results displayed in the WHAT-IF table. In this section, you're going to build a data table that summarizes the database.

With the @D formulas in row 6, you can look at summaries of individual criteria (JAZZ division, quarter 3, etc.), but you can see only one summary at a time. To see revenue and cost summarized for all divisions at once, you'll need a data table like that shown in Fig. 7.13.

H9 and I9 contain column labels. Row 10, the top row of the table, includes a column heading and two formulas that use @D functions to sum revenue and cost figures. The @D functions are formatted with the $+/-$ option. The division labels in G11 through G14 tell 1–2–3 which revenue entries to add together.

Again, 1–2–3 produces the table in somewhat the same way as you would by hand. If you wanted to know total revenues for each division,

165

Fig. 7.13   FINANCE with Data Table

G9:   READY

	A	B	C	D	E	F	G	H	I
1	DATA	DIVISION	QTR	REVENUE	COST		DIVISION	QTR	
2		4 CLASSICAL	1	200	60		*		
3		10 COUNTRY	1	400	320				
4		7 JAZZ	1	100	70		SUMMARY		
5		1 ROCK	1	300	210		ENTRIES	REVENUE	COST
6		5 CLASSICAL	2	240	72		12	3290	2134
7		11 COUNTRY	2	400	320				
8		8 JAZZ	2	120	84				
9		2 ROCK	2	350	245			REVENUE	COST
10		6 CLASSICAL	3	280	84		DIVISION	*****************	
11		12 COUNTRY	3	390	312		CLASSICAL	720	216
12		9 JAZZ	3	150	105		COUNTRY	1190	952
13		3 ROCK	3	360	252		JAZZ	370	259
14							ROCK	1010	707
15	CRIT	DIVISION	QTR	REVENUE	COST				
16		ROCK							
17									
18	OUT	DIVISION	QTR	REVENUE	COST				
19		ROCK	1	300	210				
20		ROCK	2	350	245				

                                                                                             CAPS

you'd probably make a list of the division names, find the entries for the first division, and add them up. Then you'd find and total the next division's entries, and so on. 1–2–3 does the same kind of thing with its DATA TABLE command. This command requires two definitions:

- The **Table range** includes the formulas and division names for building the table, as well as the area where 1–2–3 will enter the sums it produces. The Table range in FINANCE is G10..I14.

- The **Input cell** is a cell in the Criterion area where 1–2–3 plugs in the name of the division it's currently working on. The Input cell in FINANCE is G2.

When you invoke the DATA TABLE command and define these two areas, 1–2–3 plugs the first division name into the Input cell and checks the whole database for matching entries. Once the first sum is computed, 1–2–3 plugs the second division name into the Input cell and repeats the search through the database for matching entries. As you can see, 1–2–3 works something like you would, only much faster and with guaranteed accuracy. (You won't see 1–2–3 at work, you'll see only the results.)

Enter the label, DIVISION, in G10. Since you have only four divisions in your database, it would be pretty easy to just type them in. But instead of typing you can use another of the DATA QUERY commands to enter the names. With the pointer on G10, select DATA QUERY. First you must define the new Input, Criterion, and Output ranges. These ranges will already have definitions from the last time you tried a query, so select RESET to clear the old definitions. Select INPUT and enter DATA in response to the Input range prompt. (Remember that DATA is the name you gave to the database range B1..E13.) Next, select CRITE-RION and enter the name DCRIT. Finally, select OUTPUT and enter the one-cell range G10.

Fig. 7.14   Defining New Query Ranges

Make sure you have an asterisk in G2 as the only criteria entry. (If not, QUIT the command, change the entry, and reselect DATA QUERY). Select UNIQUE, and 1–2–3 produces a list of all the division names in

167

the database. The UNIQUE command tells 1–2–3 to produce a list of column entries, ignoring duplicates. This is a particularly useful command for building data tables in conjunction with a large database. In a database with 50 or 100 divisions and duplicate entries, the UNIQUE command is a real time-saver.

Fig. 7.15 UNIQUE Queries

```
G10: 'DIVISION                                                    MENU
Input  Criterion  Output  Find  Extract  Unique  Delete  Reset  Quit
Copy all records that match criteria to Output range, eliminating duplicates
      A       B      C      D         E        F     G          H        I
1    DATA DIVISION QTR   REVENUE    COST         DIVISION       QTR
2        4 CLASSICAL  1     200       60         *
3       10 COUNTRY    1     400      320
4        7 JAZZ       1     100       70         SUMMARY
5        1 ROCK       1     300      210         ENTRIES    REVENUE     COST
6        5 CLASSICAL  2     240       72             12      3290      2134
7       11 COUNTRY    2     400      320
8        8 JAZZ       2     120       84
9        2 ROCK       2     350      245
10       6 CLASSICAL  3     280       84         DIVISION
11      12 COUNTRY    3     390      312         CLASSICAL
12       9 JAZZ       3     150      105         COUNTRY
13       3 ROCK       3     360      252         JAZZ
14                                               ROCK
15   CRIT  DIVISION QTR  REVENUE    COST
16         ROCK
17
18   OUT   DIVISION QTR  REVENUE    COST
19         ROCK      1     300      210
20         ROCK      2     350      245
                                                              CAPS
```

Now, in H10 and I10, you must enter the same two totaling formulas that you used to sum revenues and costs in the preceding section. With the formula in H10, 1–2–3 will produce the first column of the table: total revenues for each division. With the formula in I10, 1–2–3 will total the costs for each division.

The criteria should also be the same, so we'll use the summary criteria area (G1..H2) to produce the table.

Select QUIT to leave the QUERY menu, and move the pointer to H10. Enter the two totaling formulas in H10 and I10:

    H10 = @DSUM[DATA,2,DCRIT]
    I10 = @DSUM[DATA,3,DCRIT]

Enter two labels in H9 and I9:

    H9 = "REVENUE
    I9 = "COST

Fig. 7.16 Table Formulas and Labels

```
I9: "COST                                                              READY

       A      B      C        D         E     F      G         H         I
1     DATA DIVISION QTR   REVENUE     COST       DIVISION      QTR
2        4 CLASSICAL  1      200        60    *
3       10 COUNTRY    1      400       320
4        7 JAZZ       1      100        70    SUMMARY
5        1 ROCK       1      300       210    ENTRIES    REVENUE     COST
6        5 CLASSICAL  2      240        72        12      3290       2134
7       11 COUNTRY    2      400       320
8        8 JAZZ       2      120        84
9        2 ROCK       2      350       245                  REVENUE     COST
10       6 CLASSICAL  3      280        84    DIVISION       3290      2134
11      12 COUNTRY    3      390       312    CLASSICAL
12       9 JAZZ       3      150       105    COUNTRY
13       3 ROCK       3      360       252    JAZZ
14                                            ROCK
15    CRIT DIVISION QTR   REVENUE     COST
16         ROCK
17
18    OUT  DIVISION QTR   REVENUE     COST
19         ROCK       1      300       210
20         ROCK       2      350       245
                                                              CAPS
```

The quote marks align the labels against the right-hand side of the cell. Finally, format the two DSUM formulas as +/− so the values there won't be distracting.

Fig. 7.17 Formatted Table Formulas

```
I10: (+) @DSUM(DATA,3,DCRIT)                                          READY

       A      B      C        D         E     F      G         H         I
1     DATA DIVISION QTR   REVENUE     COST       DIVISION      QTR
2        4 CLASSICAL  1      200        60    *
3       10 COUNTRY    1      400       320
4        7 JAZZ       1      100        70    SUMMARY
5        1 ROCK       1      300       210    ENTRIES    REVENUE     COST
6        5 CLASSICAL  2      240        72        12      3290       2134
7       11 COUNTRY    2      400       320
8        8 JAZZ       2      120        84
9        2 ROCK       2      350       245                  REVENUE     COST
10       6 CLASSICAL  3      280        84    DIVISION ********** **********
11      12 COUNTRY    3      390       312    CLASSICAL
12       9 JAZZ       3      150       105    COUNTRY
13       3 ROCK       3      360       252    JAZZ
14                                            ROCK
15    CRIT DIVISION QTR   REVENUE     COST
16         ROCK
17
18    OUT  DIVISION QTR   REVENUE     COST
19         ROCK       1      300       210
20         ROCK       2      350       245
                                                              CAPS
```

169

Now you're ready to invoke the DATA TABLE command. With the pointer on G10 (the upper left-hand corner of the table), select DATA TABLE. The first prompt asks whether there are one or two Input cells in the table. (RESET clears previous table settings.) Your table has only one Input cell, G2, where each division name is plugged in for comparison against the database. Select 1, and 1–2–3 asks for the Table range. Type a Period to tack down the start of the range, then move the pointer to the right twice and down four times to I14. The block pointer shows the labels and formulas used to produce the table and displays the blank area that 1–2–3 will fill in (G10..I14).

Fig. 7.18 Defining the Table Range

```
I14:
Enter Table range: G10..I14
```

	A	B	C	D	E	F	G	H	I
1	DATA	DIVISION	QTR	REVENUE	COST		DIVISION	QTR	
2	4	CLASSICAL	1	200	60		*		
3	10	COUNTRY	1	400	320				
4	7	JAZZ	1	100	70		SUMMARY		
5	1	ROCK	1	300	210		ENTRIES	REVENUE	COST
6	5	CLASSICAL	2	240	72		12	3290	2134
7	11	COUNTRY	2	400	320				
8	8	JAZZ	2	120	84				
9	2	ROCK	2	350	245			REVENUE	COST
10	6	CLASSICAL	3	280	84		DIVISION	*****************	
11	12	COUNTRY	3	390	312		CLASSICAL		
12	9	JAZZ	3	150	105		COUNTRY		
13	3	ROCK	3	360	252		JAZZ		
14							ROCK		
15	CRIT	DIVISION	QTR	REVENUE	COST				
16		ROCK							
17									
18	OUT	DIVISION	QTR	REVENUE	COST				
19		ROCK	1	300	210				
20		ROCK	2	350	245				

Type [Enter] and 1–2–3 asks for the Input cell. Type G2 [Enter] and 1–2–3 produces the table listing total revenues and costs for each division.

Fig. 7.19   The Completed Data Table

G10: 'DIVISION   `READY`

```
         A       B        C      D         E       F      G         H        I
    1  DATA  DIVISION  QTR  REVENUE    COST         DIVISION     QTR
    2       4 CLASSICAL  1      200        60        *
    3      10 COUNTRY    1      400       320
    4       7 JAZZ       1      100        70        SUMMARY
    5       1 ROCK       1      300       210        ENTRIES   REVENUE    COST
    6       5 CLASSICAL  2      240        72            12      3290     2134
    7      11 COUNTRY    2      400       320
    8       8 JAZZ       2      120        84
    9       2 ROCK       2      350       245                  REVENUE    COST
   10       6 CLASSICAL  3      280        84       DIVISION ****************
   11      12 COUNTRY    3      390       312       CLASSICAL    720      216
   12       9 JAZZ       3      150       105       COUNTRY     1190      952
   13       3 ROCK       3      360       252       JAZZ         370      259
   14                                               ROCK        1010      707
   15  CRIT  DIVISION  QTR  REVENUE    COST
   16       ROCK
   17
   18  OUT   DIVISION  QTR  REVENUE    COST
   19       ROCK       1      300       210
   20       ROCK       2      350       245
```
                                                                                    `CAPS`

Before you move on to modifying the table, save a copy of the FINANCE file now. You'll need the current file to build on in the next section. To save the file, type / F S [Enter] R. If you don't want to overwrite your last version of FINANCE, give the new file a different name.

To generate a new table summing revenue and cost for each quarter, follow these steps:

1. Change the DIVISION label in G10 to QTR. (Actually, this label doesn't affect the table values—it just makes the meaning of the G column clearer.)

2. Enter the quarter values in column G: G11 = 1, G12 = 2, G13 = 3.

3. Erase the fourth-row ROCK figures from the worksheet (using the RANGE ERASE command).

4. Select DATA TABLE 1 and shorten the Table range by typing an Up Arrow and [Enter]. The new Table range is G10..I13.

5. Change the Input cell to H2 (by typing or pointing) and enter it.

171

Fig. 7.20 Quarterly Data Table

G10: 'QTR   READY

	A	B	C	D	E	F	G	H	I
1	DATA	DIVISION	QTR	REVENUE	COST		DIVISION	QTR	
2		4 CLASSICAL	1	200	60		*		
3		10 COUNTRY	1	400	320				
4		7 JAZZ	1	100	70		SUMMARY		
5		1 ROCK	1	300	210		ENTRIES	REVENUE	COST
6		5 CLASSICAL	2	240	72		12	3290	2134
7		11 COUNTRY	2	400	320				
8		8 JAZZ	2	120	84				
9		2 ROCK	2	350	245			REVENUE	COST
10		6 CLASSICAL	3	280	84		QTR	*****************	
11		12 COUNTRY	3	390	312		1	1000	660
12		9 JAZZ	3	150	105		2	1110	721
13		3 ROCK	3	360	252		3	1180	753
14									
15	CRIT	DIVISION	QTR	REVENUE	COST				
16		ROCK							
17									
18	OUT	DIVISION	QTR	REVENUE	COST				
19		ROCK	1	300	210				
20		ROCK	2	350	245				

CAPS

Now 1–2–3 generates a new table of sums showing total revenue and cost for each quarter. As before, a change to the database is reflected in the table when you type the [F8] Table key.

If you change the criteria entries and type [F8], the table sums will reflect the new criteria. For example, enter JAZZ in G2 (the DIVISION criteria) and type the [F8] key. The new table shows a quarterly breakdown of revenue and cost for JAZZ.

Fig. 7.21 FINANCE Summary by Quarter for JAZZ

G2: 'JAZZ   READY

	A	B	C	D	E	F	G	H	I
1	DATA	DIVISION	QTR	REVENUE	COST		DIVISION	QTR	
2		4 CLASSICAL	1	200	60		JAZZ		
3		10 COUNTRY	1	400	320				
4		7 JAZZ	1	100	70		SUMMARY		
5		1 ROCK	1	300	210		ENTRIES	REVENUE	COST
6		5 CLASSICAL	2	240	72		3	370	259
7		11 COUNTRY	2	400	320				
8		8 JAZZ	2	120	84				
9		2 ROCK	2	350	245			REVENUE	COST
10		6 CLASSICAL	3	280	84		QTR	*****************	
11		12 COUNTRY	3	390	312		1	100	70
12		9 JAZZ	3	150	105		2	120	84
13		3 ROCK	3	360	252		3	150	105
14									
15	CRIT	DIVISION	QTR	REVENUE	COST				
16		ROCK							
17									
18	OUT	DIVISION	QTR	REVENUE	COST				
19		ROCK	1	300	210				
20		ROCK	2	350	245				

CAPS

Try some variations in your summary to get a better feel for the DATA TABLE command. You'll find it essential when you begin building your own databases in the 1–2–3 worksheet.

3. Tables with Two Input Cells

The table you created in section 2 used one Input cell (G2) and two formulas (the @DSUMS in H10 and I10) to produce summaries of revenues and costs for each division. In this section, you will build a table that uses two Input cells and one formula to summarize revenues in tabular form.

Fig. 7.22   Two-Cell Data Table

*********	1	2	3
CLASSICAL	200	240	280
COUNTRY	400	400	390
JAZZ	100	120	150
ROCK	300	350	360

The table lists revenues for each division *and* quarter. Each cell in the table shows the revenue figure for one division in one quarter.

Why produce such a table? First, the table is easier to read than the database listing. It's very easy to find a particular revenue, or to see how revenues are distributed among divisions and quarters. It's something like having the revenues sorted by both division and quarter.

Second, the tabular format is better suited to reporting than the full database listings are. With the addition of some labels and blank lines you could easily turn the table into a summary report on revenues. You could even add simple @SUM formulas at the bottom and right to show total revenues by division and quarter.

The third advantage of this table isn't illustrated by the simple FINANCE database: This is the fact that when more than one record matches both criteria, their revenues are summed together. (FINANCE includes no duplicate criteria entries.) Suppose Music Corporation received revenue and cost figures every month, but reported on them only by quarter. Assuming that six months' reports are in, a partial database listing would look like this:

CLASSICAL	1	100	20
CLASSICAL	1	50	20
CLASSICAL	1	50	20
CLASSICAL	2	80	25
CLASSICAL	2	80	22
CLASSICAL	2	80	25
JAZZ	1	25	20
JAZZ	1	30	25
JAZZ	1	45	25

There is no month column, but there are three entries for every quarter (one for every month), or three records for each division-quarter pair. The data table in Fig. 7.22 would sum the duplicate figures, giving you a single revenue for each division-quarter combination. Later you can test this by adding some new records to your database; for now, however, build the table using the current data.

If you made alterations to the worksheet at the end of the last section, recall your saved file now. (Save this file first if you want to keep your modified table.) You'll need the division summary table to build the two-cell data table in this section. The summary area now on your worksheet should look like Fig. 7.23.

The new table will have to run slightly off the screen into column J. Fortunately, you'll lose only a column of labels and resequencing numbers in A when you move into J, so you'll still be able to see the whole database as you work on your table.

The two-cell data table is produced like the one-cell table with a few differences:

1. The upper left-hand corner of the table holds the single @D formula used to produce the whole table.

Fig. 7.23 FINANCE with Division Summary

G16:   READY

	A	B	C	D	E	F	G	H	I
1	DATA	DIVISION	QTR	REVENUE	COST		DIVISION	QTR	
2	4	CLASSICAL	1	200	60		*		
3	10	COUNTRY	1	400	320				
4	7	JAZZ	1	100	70		SUMMARY		
5	1	ROCK	1	300	210		ENTRIES	REVENUE	COST
6	5	CLASSICAL	2	240	72		12	3290	2134
7	11	COUNTRY	2	400	320				
8	8	JAZZ	2	120	84				
9	2	ROCK	2	350	245			REVENUE	COST
10	6	CLASSICAL	3	280	84		DIVISION	*****************	
11	12	COUNTRY	3	390	312		CLASSICAL	720	216
12	9	JAZZ	3	150	105		COUNTRY	1190	952
13	3	ROCK	3	360	252		JAZZ	370	259
14							ROCK	1010	707
15	CRIT	DIVISION	QTR	REVENUE	COST				
16		ROCK							
17									
18	OUT	DIVISION	QTR	REVENUE	COST				
19		ROCK	1	300	210				
20		ROCK	2	350	245				

CAPS

2. The left-hand column and top row of the table lists the entries that will be plugged into the criteria (Input) cells.

3. There are two Input cells in the table, because 1–2–3 checks against two criteria at a time.

When you invoke the DATA TABLE command, 1–2–3 checks each combination of division name and quarter number in turn (i.e., CLASSI-CAL-1, CLASSICAL-2, CLASSICAL-3, COUNTRY-1, etc.). Since you included both DIVISION and QTR labels in the DCRIT area, you can use that area for the criteria just as you did for the other summaries. You're summarizing for every division and quarter, so your criteria should still be an asterisk in G2 and an empty cell in H2.

Start building the table by copying the division labels FROM G11..G14 TO G17. Enter the three quarter numbers 1, 2, and 3 in cells H16, I16, and J16, respectively. Notice that when you enter the 3 in column J the screen shifts a column to the right. Conveniently, you can still see the whole database. Enter the @DSUM formula @DSUM (DATA,2,DCRIT) in G16, and format the entry with the +/– option. Your new screen should look like Fig. 7.24.

Fig. 7.24   Building a Two-Cell Data Table

G16: (+) @DSUM(DATA,2,DCRIT)   READY

	B	C	D	E	F	G	H	I	J
1	DIVISION	QTR	REVENUE	COST		DIVISION		QTR	
2	CLASSICAL	1	200	60		*			
3	COUNTRY	1	400	320					
4	JAZZ	1	100	70		SUMMARY			
5	ROCK	1	300	210		ENTRIES		REVENUE		COST
6	CLASSICAL	2	240	72		12		3290		2134
7	COUNTRY	2	400	320					
8	JAZZ	2	120	84					
9	ROCK	2	350	245			REVENUE		COST
10	CLASSICAL	3	280	84		DIVISION	****************
11	COUNTRY	3	390	312		CLASSICAL	720	216
12	JAZZ	3	150	105		COUNTRY	1190	952
13	ROCK	3	360	252		JAZZ	370	259
14							ROCK	1010	707
15	DIVISION	QTR	REVENUE	COST					
16	ROCK					*********		1	2	3
17						CLASSICAL			
18	DIVISION	QTR	REVENUE	COST		COUNTRY			
19	ROCK	1	300	210		JAZZ			
20	ROCK	2	350	245		ROCK			

With the pointer on G16, select DATA TABLE and type 2. Now 1–2–3 positions the block pointer on the previously defined Table range. Cancel that range and return the pointer to G16 by typing the Backspace-Delete arrow. ([Esc] will cancel the range, but it won't return the pointer to G16.) Type a Period to tack the range down, then type [End] [Down] to move to G20 and three Right Arrows to define the Table range as G16..J20.

Fig. 7.25   Defining the Two-Cell Table Range

J20:   POINT
Enter Table range: G16..J20

	B	C	D	E	F	G	H	I	J
1	DIVISION	QTR	REVENUE	COST		DIVISION		QTR	
2	CLASSICAL	1	200	60		*			
3	COUNTRY	1	400	320					
4	JAZZ	1	100	70		SUMMARY			
5	ROCK	1	300	210		ENTRIES		REVENUE		COST
6	CLASSICAL	2	240	72		12		3290		2134
7	COUNTRY	2	400	320					
8	JAZZ	2	120	84					
9	ROCK	2	350	245			REVENUE		COST
10	CLASSICAL	3	280	84		DIVISION	****************
11	COUNTRY	3	390	312		CLASSICAL	720	216
12	JAZZ	3	150	105		COUNTRY	1190	952
13	ROCK	3	360	252		JAZZ	370	259
14							ROCK	1010	707
15	DIVISION	QTR	REVENUE	COST					
16	ROCK					*********	1	2	3
17						CLASSICAL			
18	DIVISION	QTR	REVENUE	COST		COUNTRY			
19	ROCK	1	300	210		JAZZ			
20	ROCK	2	350	245		ROCK			

CAPS

When you type [Enter], 1–2–3 asks for the first Input cell and positions the pointer on the previously defined Input cell, G2. You want to use G2 as the first Input cell (where 1–2–3 will plug in each division), so type [Enter]. Finally, 1–2–3 asks for the second Input cell, the criteria cell where each quarter number is plugged in. Type H2 [Enter] and in a few seconds 1–2–3 produces a full table of revenue figures broken out by both division and quarter. Notice that the mode indicator flashes "WAIT" while 1–2–3 works on the table.

Fig. 7.26   The Completed Two-Cell Table

G16: (+) @DSUM(DATA,2,DCRIT)   READY

	B	C	D	E	F	G	H	I	J
1	DIVISION	QTR	REVENUE	COST		DIVISION	QTR		
2	CLASSICAL	1	200	60		*			
3	COUNTRY	1	400	320					
4	JAZZ	1	100	70		SUMMARY			
5	ROCK	1	300	210		ENTRIES	REVENUE	COST	
6	CLASSICAL	2	240	72		12	3290	2134	
7	COUNTRY	2	400	320					
8	JAZZ	2	120	84					
9	ROCK	2	350	245			REVENUE	COST	
10	CLASSICAL	3	280	84		DIVISION ******************			
11	COUNTRY	3	390	312		CLASSICAL	720	216	
12	JAZZ	3	150	105		COUNTRY	1190	952	
13	ROCK	3	360	252		JAZZ	370	259	
14						ROCK	1010	707	
15	DIVISION	QTR	REVENUE	COST					
16	ROCK					*********	1	2	3
17						CLASSICAL	200	240	280
18	DIVISION	QTR	REVENUE	COST		COUNTRY	400	400	390
19	ROCK	1	300	210		JAZZ	100	120	150
20	ROCK	2	350	245		ROCK	300	350	360

A final reason for summarizing data in this kind of table now becomes apparent—it's easier to graph. You now have some ranges clearly laid out for producing two useful types of graphs:

1. Bar graphs, comparing revenues for all the divisions in any quarter or all the quarters for any division.

2. Stacked bar graphs, comparing revenues for all divisions in all quarters.

Fig. 7.27   Graphs of Data Table

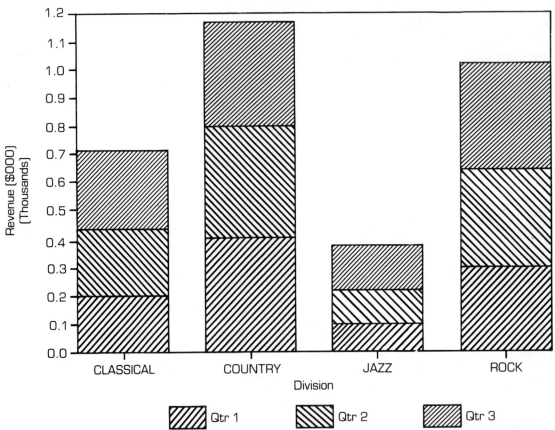

If you add @SUM formulas at the bottom and to the right of the table, you can compute and graph total revenues by division or quarter. If you then add appropriate headings and labels, your table and graphs will be of presentation quality.

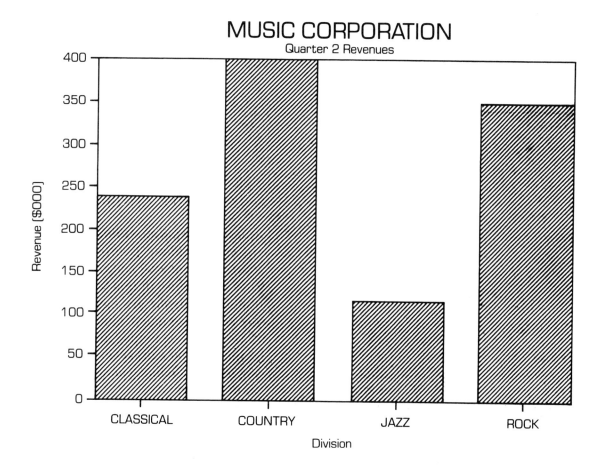

4. Counting Frequency of Distribution

The final DATA command, DISTRIBUTION, counts the frequency of numeric data occurring within certain bounds. For example, you can use it to determine how the revenues are distributed over a series of upper and lower bounds that you set: revenues less than or equal to $100, greater than $100 but less than or equal to $200, greater than $200 but less than or equal to $300 and so on.

179

The command has two parts:

- The **Values range** is the list of values whose distribution is being determined. The Values range in this example is the list of revenues from D2 to D13.
- The **Bin range** is the list of bounds over which the revenues are distributed. Your Bin range will include four values: 100, 200, 300, and 400.

The completed distribution table for revenues looks like Fig. 7.28.

Fig. 7.28   Revenue Distribution

J1:   "RANGES   READY

	D	E	F	G	H	I	J	K
1	REVENUE	COST		DIVISION	QTR		RANGES	DISTRIB
2	200	60		*			100	1
3	400	320					200	3
4	100	70		SUMMARY			300	3
5	300	210		ENTRIES	REVENUE	COST	400	5
6	240	72		12	3290	2134		0
7	400	320						
8	120	84						
9	350	245			REVENUE	COST		
10	280	84		DIVISION	*****************			
11	390	312		CLASSICAL	720	216		
12	150	105		COUNTRY	1190	952		
13	360	252		JAZZ	370	259		
14				ROCK	1010	707		
15	REVENUE	COST						
16				*********	1	2	3	
17				CLASSICAL	200	240	280	
18	REVENUE	COST		COUNTRY	400	400	390	
19	300	210		JAZZ	100	120	150	
20	350	245		ROCK	300	350	360	

CAPS

The values in column J make up the Bin range. Each revenue is compared against the bin values to determine where it should be distributed. For example, the first revenue, 200, falls in the second bin because it is less than or equal to the second-bin value (200), but greater than the first-bin value (100). The last revenue, 360, falls in the fourth bin because it is less than or equal to 400, but greater than 300. Each entry in the Values range is compared against the entries in the Bin range to determine where it should be distributed. The number of revenues in each bin are counted and the total is displayed to the right of the bin value.

The final distribution value (0 in this case) is the number of revenues greater than the largest bin value. Since the largest revenue is 400, no entries are greater than the last-bin value of 400. 1–2–3 always displays one more value than the number of bin values, so be sure to leave room at the bottom of the list.

You'll build the distribution list up against the summary area so you can see the REVENUE database column as you work. In future worksheets you should clearly label and separate different functional areas from one another.

Enter two labels in row 1: ''RANGES in J1 and ''DISTRIB in K1. You can enter the bin values with the DATA FILL command or by just typing them in. If you use DATA FILL , define the range to fill as J2..J5, the start value as 100, the step value as 100, and just type [Enter] for the stop value.

Fig. 7.29 Building the Values Range with FILL

```
J2:
Enter Fill range: J2..J5
Start: 100              Step: 100              Stop: 2047
       D        E       F       G       H       I       J       K
```

```
J2: 100
```

	D	E	F	G	H	I	J	K
1	REVENUE	COST		DIVISION	QTR		RANGES	DISTRIB
2	200	60		*			100	
3	400	320					200	
4	100	70		SUMMARY			300	
5	300	210		ENTRIES	REVENUE	COST	400	
6	240	72		12	3290	2134		
7	400	320						
8	120	84						
9	350	245			REVENUE	COST		
10	280	84		DIVISION	*****************			
11	390	312		CLASSICAL	720	216		
12	150	105		COUNTRY	1190	952		
13	360	252		JAZZ	370	259		
14				ROCK	1010	707		
15	REVENUE	COST						
16				*********	1	2	3	
17				CLASSICAL	200	240	280	
18	REVENUE	COST		COUNTRY	400	400	390	
19	300	210		JAZZ	100	120	150	
20	350	245		ROCK	300	350	360	

With the pointer on J2, select DATA DISTRIBUTION and enter D2..D13 in response to the Values-range prompt. Enter J2..J5 as the Bin range and 1–2–3 produces the distribution list. As you can see, all but one of the revenues are between 100 and 400, with the greatest number falling between 300 and 400.

Fig. 7.30   The Completed Distribution List

J2: 100   READY

	D	E	F	G	H	I	J	K
1	REVENUE	COST	DIVISION	QTR			RANGES	DISTRIB
2	200	60	*				100	1
3	400	320					200	3
4	100	70	SUMMARY				300	3
5	300	210	ENTRIES	REVENUE		COST	400	5
6	240	72	12	3290		2134		0
7	400	320						
8	120	84						
9	350	245		REVENUE		COST		
10	280	84	DIVISION	******************				
11	390	312	CLASSICAL	720		216		
12	150	105	COUNTRY	1190		952		
13	360	252	JAZZ	370		259		
14			ROCK	1010		707		
15	REVENUE	COST						
16			********	1	2	3		
17			CLASSICAL	200	240	280		
18	REVENUE	COST	COUNTRY	400	400	390		
19	300	210	JAZZ	100	120	150		
20	350	245	ROCK	300	350	360		

CAPS

You can easily turn a distribution list into a histogram—a pictorial representation of the numbers as horizontal bars—with the RANGE FORMAT +/− command. You've already used the +/− format to mask distracting numbers in the data tables. Here you'll use the +/− format to display the integer part of each distribution value as a series of formatted symbols:

+ for positive integers
− for negative integers
. for zero

Move the pointer to the first entry in the list (J2) and select RANGE FORMAT +/−. Type a Period to tack down the range, extend the block pointer to J5, and type [Enter]. The distribution values are now displayed as shown in Fig. 7.31.

Fig. 7.31   Revenue Distribution Histogram

K2: (+) 1   READY

	D	E	F	G	H	I	J	K
1	REVENUE	COST		DIVISION	QTR		RANGES	DISTRIB
2	200	60		*			100	+
3	400	320					200	+++
4	100	70		SUMMARY			300	+++
5	300	210		ENTRIES	REVENUE	COST	400	+++++
6	240	72		12	3290	2134		
7	400	320						
8	120	84						
9	350	245			REVENUE	COST		
10	280	84		DIVISION	*****************			
11	390	312		CLASSICAL	720	216		
12	150	105		COUNTRY	1190	952		
13	360	252		JAZZ	370	259		
14				ROCK	1010	707		
15	REVENUE	COST						
16				*********	1	2	3	
17				CLASSICAL	200	240	280	
18	REVENUE	COST		COUNTRY	400	400	390	
19	300	210		JAZZ	100	120	150	
20	350	245		ROCK	300	350	360	

CAPS

You might also graph the distribution values in a bar or pie chart.

Chapter 7 Exercises

FINANCE Exercise

Practice what you learned in Chapter 7 by doing the following:

1. Change some of the original data and regenerate the summary and distribution tables.

2. Enter your own division or company data and build extract and summary areas with which to analyze it.

3. Add fourth-quarter data and regenerate the tables. Enter the new rows between existing records so the @DSUMs will adjust properly. Remember to redefine the database range, DATA.

STORESUM Exercise

STORESUM summarizes the data in STOREDATA (a Chapter 6 exercise). There are two summary tables: one summarizes profits by sales area and the other summarizes profits by category.

```
A1:  'STORESUM                                                          READY

        A       B       C       D       E       F       G       H       I
1    STORESUM
2
3    Raw sales' figures ($000) for stores in five areas. The data lists
4    each store's area, category, and budgeted and actual revenues.
5    Some stores sell only women's shoes (W), some sell only men's
6    shoes (M), and some sell both men's and women's (B).
7
8    DATA AREA       CAT     BUDGET  ACTUAL  AREA    SUMMARY BY AREA
9         CHICAGO    M          150     150  *
10        CHICAGO    W          200     240          BUDGET   ACTUAL
11        CHICAGO    B          450     350  AREA       9000     7455
12        CHICAGO    W          100     160  CHICAGO    1200     1185
13        CHICAGO    B          300     285  NEW YORK   3000     1770
14        NEW YORK   W          800     250  BOSTON      600      760
15        NEW YORK   B          500     600  DALLAS     2400     1860
16        NEW YORK   B         1700     920  ATLANTA    1800     1880
17        BOSTON     B          600     760
18        DALLAS     W          300     220  CAT     SUMMARY BY CATEGORY
19        DALLAS     W          750     825  *
20        DALLAS     M          400     295          BUDGET   ACTUAL
21        DALLAS     B          950     520  CAT        9000     7455
22        ATLANTA    B          500     470  M          1850     1855
23        ATLANTA    M         1300    1410  W          2150     1695
24                                           B          5000     3905
```

1. Each table uses its own criteria-named area:

   ACRIT [G8..G9]   for the AREA summary
   CCRIT [G18..G19]   for the CATegory summary

   and its own named Table range:

   ATABLE [G11..I16]   for the AREA summary
   CTABLE [G21..I24]   for the CATegory summary

   The named ranges make it easier to recalculate the table when changes are made to the raw data. The database (B8..E23) is named DATA.

2. Several column widths are adjusted to allow more room on the screen and to make the table easy to read.

3. You could also build a two-input-cell DATA TABLE to get a breakdown of total profits for all sales areas by category. List the areas down the side and the categories across the top. The first input cell is the AREA criteria in G9, and the second input cell is the CATegory criteria in G19.

4. All three summary tables give you a good basis for producing reports and graphs.

PROJSUM Exercise

This table is a summary of the data in the PROJEST and PROJDATA files. If you haven't built either file yet, do so now. PROJEST is the basic spreadsheet file, and it's described in an exercise at the end of Chapter 5. PROJDATA is an embellishment of PROJEST that includes an area for extracting portions of the data, and it's described in an exercise at the end of Chapter 6.

```
H1:                                                              READY


       H          I          J         K         L        M        N        O
 1                          SUMMARY AREA
 2
 3                          EMP
 4                           *
 5
 6                                     HOURS  CHARGES   % TOTAL
 7                              EMP      188    6580      100%
 8                              wrb       22     770       12%
 9                              jpf      118    4130       63%
10                              meb       48    1680       26%
11
12
13
14
15
16
17
18
19
20
```

1. J3..J4 is the Criterion range for the DATA TABLE. Name the range SCRIT (for Summary CRITeria) to make the data-table formulas easier to build.

2. Name the raw data range in A13..E26 DATA.

185

3. You can enter the employee initials with the help of the UNIQUE command, or by just typing them in. If you type them, make sure you use the same case (either uppper or lower) that you used for the entries in DATA.

4. The HOURS formula sums the hours for each employee:

    K7 = @DSUM[DATA,3,SCRIT] = total hours for employee.

   The CHARGES formula is similar, but it requires a different off-set value.

5. Once you've entered the employee initials and the two @ DSUM formulas, you can create the summary table. If you have any trouble with the DATA TABLE command, reread section 2 of this chapter.

6. The formulas in column M compute each employee's percent of total charges. Enter the formula in M7, then COPY it down the column.

    M7 = +L7/$L$7 = charge 1 / total charges
    M8 = +L8/$L$7 = charge2 / total charges

   The first formula looks a little strange because it's dividing by itself, but it is correctly calculated as 100%—that is, the total is 100% of itself.

CHAPTER **8**

Text Handling

1. Creating a Simple Memo

Although 1–2–3's text-handling features are less expansive than those of
a full word processor, they offer a convenient means of writing memos,
outlines, and other short documents on the 1–2–3 worksheet. The text
features are particularly useful for adding documentation to a spreadsheet, or for combining a spreadsheet into a document. In this chapter,
you'll create a short memo summarizing profit and profit as a percent of
revenue for the four divisions. The basis of the memo is the revenue/cost
summary table that you built in G9..I14 of the FINANCE worksheet.
You'll write the memo starting in M1, still on the FINANCE worksheet.
The completed memo includes two short paragraphs and a small table
summarizing Music Corporation's finances.

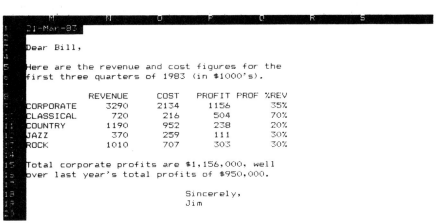

**Fig. 8.1
FINANCE
with Memo**

```
M1:  (D1) 30396                                                    READY

       M          N        O        P        Q        R        S
1    21-Mar-83
2
3    Dear Bill,
4
5    Here are the revenue and cost figures for the
6    first three quarters of 1983 (in $1000's).
7
8                  REVENUE     COST    PROFIT PROF %REV
9    CORPORATE       3290      2134      1156        35%
10   CLASSICAL        720       216       504        70%
11   COUNTRY         1190       952       238        20%
12   JAZZ             370       259       111        30%
13   ROCK            1010       707       303        30%
14
15   Total corporate profits are $1,156,000, well
16   over last year's total profits of $950,000.
17
18                           Sincerely,
19                           Jim
20
```

187

Move to a clean area of the worksheet by pressing the [Goto] key and typing M1. As you learned in Chapter 2, the [Goto] key gives you a fast way of moving around the worksheet.

Fig. 8.2   Clean Worksheet Area

2. The @DATE Function

Start the memo with a date entered with the 1–2–3 @DATE function. Dates are entered in the order year, month, day, and in the format @DATE(YY,MM,DD). With the pointer on M1, type @DATE(83,3,21) for March 21, 1983, and enter it. (This is the date that appears in our illustrations; you can enter today's date if you prefer.) When you enter the date, something unexpected happens—instead of a date, you see on your screen a large integer number (30396 in this case). This integer represents your date as the number of days since January 0, 1900. To see the date as a day-month-year combination, you must format the entry.

Fig. 8.3   Unformatted Date

With the pointer still in M1, select RANGE FORMAT DATE and the first of the three date formats—MM-DD-YY. Type [Enter] to define a single-cell range to format, and you'll see another surprising display: a row of asterisks. The asterisks indicate that the cell is not wide enough to display the formatted entry. The date entry requires a ten-character display, but column M is set at a width of only nine characters. To widen the column, select WORKSHEET COLUMN SET, type a Right Arrow, and type [Enter]. The asterisks disappear and the date is displayed as requested.

Fig. 8.4   Formatted Date

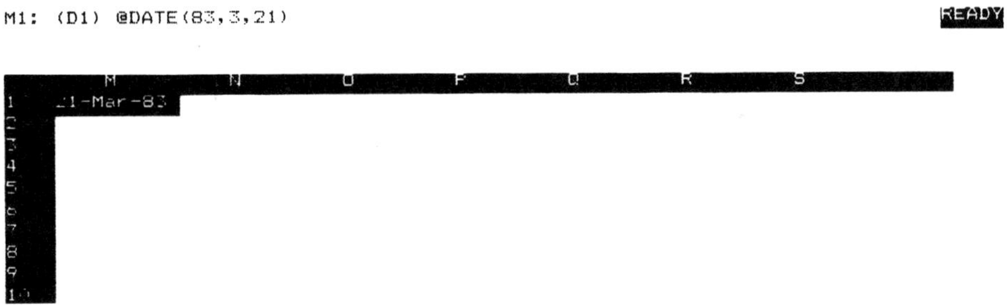

M1:   (D1)   @DATE(83,3,21)   READY

```
        M            N        O        P        Q        R        S
1    21-Mar-83
2
3
4
5
6
7
8
9
10
```

3. Entering and Justifying Text

Now you can move the pointer down to M3 and type the greeting.

Fig. 8.5   The Greeting

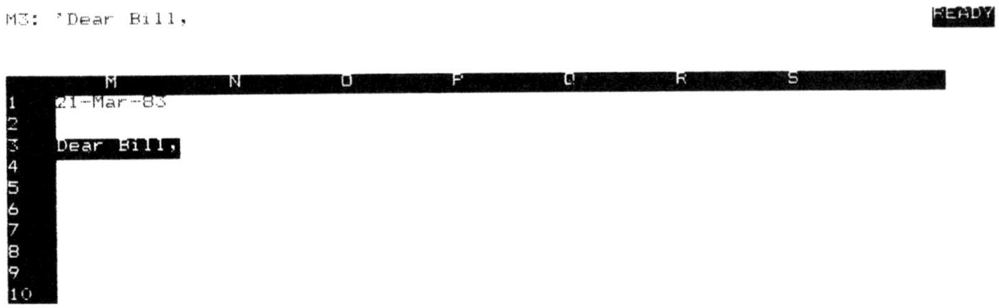

M3:   'Dear Bill,   READY

```
        M            N        O        P        Q        R        S
1    21-Mar-83
2
3    Dear Bill,
4
5
6
7
8
9
10
```

Enter the greeting just as you would a label, but turn [CapsLock] off to get lower and uppercase letters.

189

Move the pointer to M5 and type the first line of the memo *exactly* as it is shown here (including the mistakes):

Fig. 8.6   First Memo Line

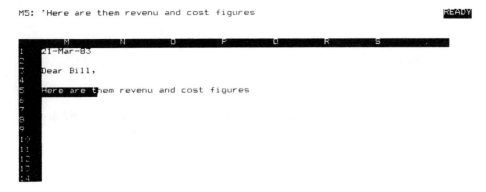

The first sentence contains some mistakes that you'll correct with the EDIT feature later in the chapter. For now, include the mistakes in your memo. As you see, a label longer than the cell simply runs over into the next cell. In fact, the entry is *stored* in only one cell. Enter the line, move the pointer to N5, and you'll see that none of the entry is stored there. If you make an entry in N5, its display "blocks" the overlapping entry.

Fig. 8.7   Overlapping Entry

M5: 'Here are them revenu and cost figures   READY

```
      M        N        O        P        Q        R        S
1  21-Mar-83
2
3  Dear Bill,
4
5  Here are tA new entry blocks the M5 entry
6
7
8
9
10
11
12
13
14
```

But if you move back to M5, you'll see that the full entry is still stored in the cell. Enter the next memo line in M6:

Fig. 8.8   Second Memo Line

```
M6: 'that show the 1st three quarters figures (in $1000's).          READY
```

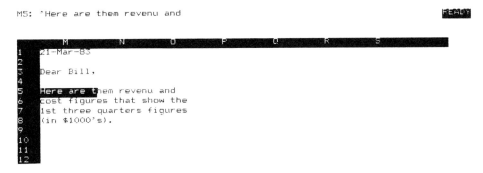

```
       M        N        O        P        Q        R        S
1 21-Mar-83
2
3 Dear Bill,
4
5 Here are them revenu and cost figures
6 that show the 1st three quarters figures (in $1000's).
7
8
9
10
11
12
```

The first thing you notice about the memo is that the lengths of the two lines don't balance. You can realign the entries within a narrower or wider range using the RANGE JUSTIFY command.

Move the pointer to M5 and select RANGE JUSTIFY. Now 1–2–3 asks you for the **Justify range.** This means you must specify the area into which you want the entries adjusted. If you specify a one-line Justify range, that line's entry and all those below it will be adjusted to the width you specify. Type a Period to tack the range down, extend the range to O5 (two Right Arrows), and enter it. The entries in M5 and M6 are adjusted to the three-column width of the Justify range.

Fig. 8.9   Three-Column Justify Range

```
M5: 'Here are them revenu and          READY
```

```
       M        N        O        P        Q        R        S
1 21-Mar-83
2
3 Dear Bill,
4
5 Here are them revenu and
6 cost figures that show the
7 1st three quarters figures
8 (in $1000's).
9
10
11
12
```

To widen the memo, select RANGE JUSTIFY and enter the Justify range M5..Q5. Once again the entries are adjusted to the width of the Justify range.

Fig. 8.10 Five-Column Justify Range

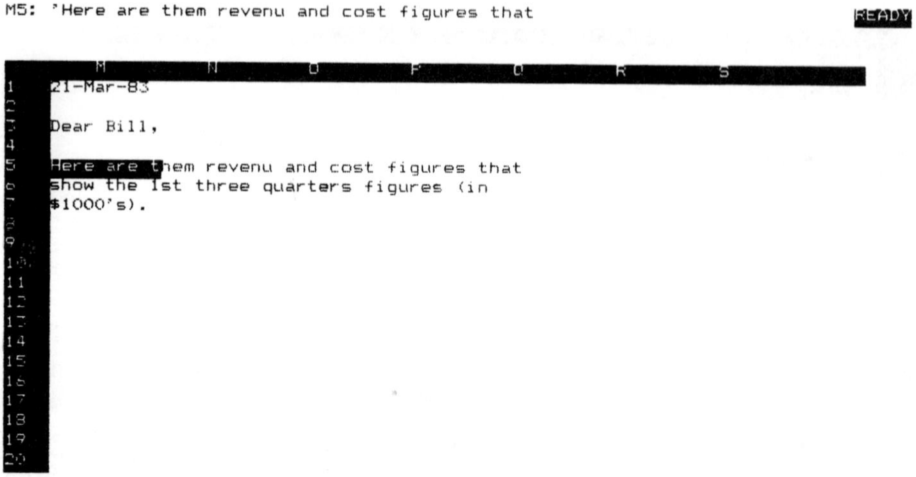

M5: 'Here are them revenu and cost figures that   READY

4. Combining Numbers from a Spreadsheet

Now that the text is properly aligned, you're ready to pull in the divisional summary table. You might be tempted to add the table using the COPY or MOVE commands, but this won't work. You can't simply reproduce the initial table as it exists because it contains two formulas, the @DSUMs, which will be adjusted if the table is relocated. To understand why it won't work, give it a try.

Move the pointer to M9 and select COPY. The range to copy FROM is G9..I14, the first FINANCE data table, and the range to copy TO is M9, the "hook" where you hang the whole range. Enter the two ranges, and 1–2–3 copies the table into your memo—with two major changes. Move the pointer to N10 and N11 and you'll see that the @DSUM formulas no longer point to the DATA and DCRIT areas; they've been adjusted by the COPY command (Fig. 8.11).

Fig. 8.11   @DSUMs Adjusted by COPY

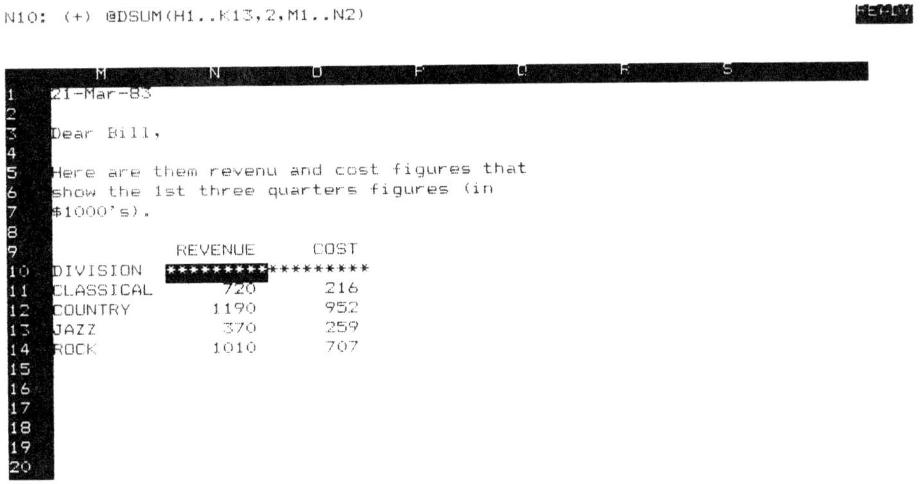

N10: (+) @DSUM(H1..K13,2,M1..N2)   READY

```
        M           N         O         P         Q         R         S
1  21-Mar-83
2
3  Dear Bill,
4
5  Here are them revenu and cost figures that
6  show the 1st three quarters figures (in
7  $1000's).
8
9                REVENUE      COST
10 DIVISION     **************************
11 CLASSICAL        720        216
12 COUNTRY         1190        952
13 JAZZ             370        259
14 ROCK            1010        707
15
16
17
18
19
20
```

What you really want to do is move the table *values* over, ignoring the formulas. In a somewhat indirect way, 1–2–3 lets you do this. Since there's no option for specifying "values only" in the COPY and MOVE commands, you need a different approach. To relocate a block of values (excluding the formulas) within a worksheet, or from one worksheet to another, you must:

1. Push the range you want to relocate out of the worksheet (to a file of its own) with the FILE XTRACT command. XTRACT lets you extract a range with formulas or with values only.

2. Pull the extracted file into its new position in the worksheet (the same or a different worksheet) with the FILE COMBINE command. COMBINE is a very rich command that will COPY, ADD, or SUBTRACT values from a file or a named range into a worksheet. The file is combined at the position of the pointer when FILE COMBINE is invoked.

Before you start the extract, make sure you have a data disk in drive B. 1–2–3 will write the extracted file to your disk. Move the pointer to G9, the upper left-hand corner of the area to be extracted. Select FILE XTRACT VALUES and enter the file name MEMO, to tell 1–2–3 what to

193

call the extracted file. Point out the range to extract, G9..I14, and type [Enter].

Fig. 8.12   Extracting the Table

```
I14: 707                                                                   POINT
Enter xtract file name: memo          Enter xtract range: G9..I14

         G          H          I        J       K       L        M
 1  DIVISION       QTR                RANGES  DISTRIB          21-Mar-83
 2  *                                 100  +
 3                                    200  +++
 4  SUMMARY                           300  +++             Dear Bill,
 5  ENTRIES     REVENUE      COST      400  +++++
 6       12        3290      2134                          Here are them reve
 7                                                         show the 1st three
 8                                                         $1000's).
 9
10              REVENUE      COST
    DIVISION  ****************         
11  CLASSICAL     720        216                           DIVISION
12  COUNTRY      1190        952                           CLASSICAL
13  JAZZ          370        259                           COUNTRY
14  ROCK         1010        707                           JAZZ
15                                                         ROCK
16  ********        1          2        3
17  CLASSICAL     200        240      280
18  COUNTRY       400        400      390
19  JAZZ          100        120      150
20  ROCK          300        350      360
```

Now 1–2–3 will flash the "WAIT" mode indicator and you'll see the disk light flash on as the new file is written to the disk.

Now move the pointer back to M9 in your memo. The FILE COMBINE command will copy the MEMO file into the worksheet starting at the pointer position. COMBINE overwrites any cell in the current worksheet that is overlapped by a non-blank cell in the newly combined file. In other words, only cells with overlapping entries are changed—the rest of the current worksheet remains as is. Because of this partial overlapping effect, you should erase any entries in the area you're "combining into" before invoking the COMBINE command. Use the RANGE ERASE command to clear the table you previously copied into the memo.

Then, with the pointer on M9, select FILE COMBINE COPY ENTIRE and enter the file name, MEMO.

Fig. 8.13   Combining the Table

```
M9:                                              EDIT
Enter name of file to combine: memo
```

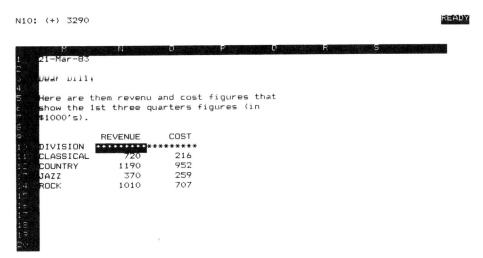

21-Mar-83

Dear Bill,

Here are them revenu and cost figures that
show the 1st three quarters figures (in
$1000's).

1–2–3 locates the file on the disk and copies it into your memo. Because
MEMO was saved with values only, there are no formulas for 1–2–3 to
adjust, and the table is entered correctly.

Fig. 8.14   COMBINE Completed

```
N10: (+) 3290                                    READY
```

21-Mar-83

Dear Bill,

Here are them revenu and cost figures that
show the 1st three quarters figures (in
$1000's).

	REVENUE	COST
DIVISION	*********	*********
CLASSICAL	720	216
COUNTRY	1190	952
JAZZ	370	259
ROCK	1010	707

195

This may seem like a lot of work for such a small table, but keep in mind that the same procedure can be used on tables of any size. You can also use the XTRACT-COMBINE combination to move blocks from one worksheet to another. The THIS YEAR column figures in THISYR, for example, might have been extracted from a summary of a full year's data in FINANCE.

Before you go on, reformat the top table entries in N9 and O9. Move the pointer to N9, select RANGE FORMAT RESET, type a Right Arrow to extend the range, and type [Enter]. Then move the pointer to M10 and enter a new label—CORPORATE.

Fig. 8.15 Table with CORPORATE Figures

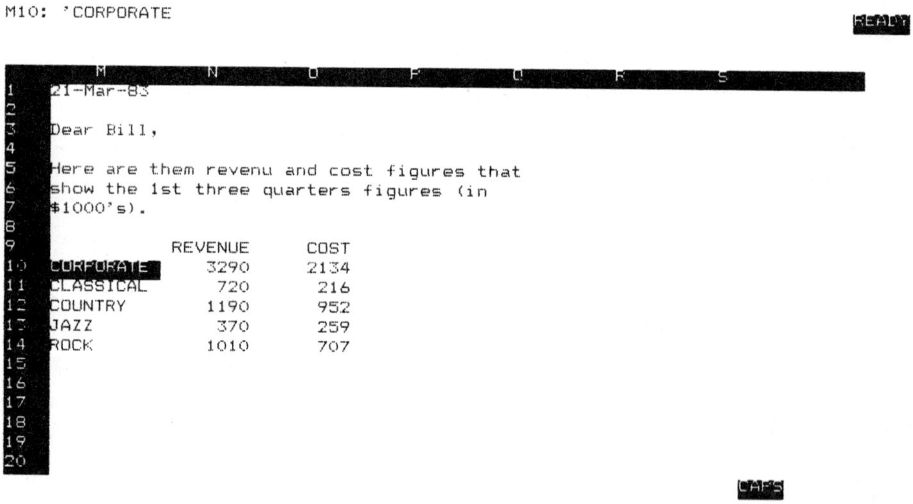

M10: 'CORPORATE

READY

```
        M        N        O        P        Q        R        S
1   21-Mar-83
2
3   Dear Bill,
4
5   Here are them revenu and cost figures that
6   show the 1st three quarters figures (in
7   $1000's).
8
9                  REVENUE     COST
10  CORPORATE        3290      2134
11  CLASSICAL         720       216
12  COUNTRY          1190       952
13  JAZZ              370       259
14  ROCK             1010       707
15
16
17
18
19
20
```

CAPS

5. Extending the Table

Since the memo is stored on the 1–2–3 worksheet, it's easy to expand the memo table to include two formula columns showing dollar profit and profit as a percent of revenue for each division. We'll cover these additions quickly, so if you have trouble remembering how to build and copy formulas, we suggest that you reread Chapter 3. If you feel confident about spreadsheet work in 1–2–3, try to build the columns on your own without reading ahead. The completed table should look like Fig. 8.16.

Fig. 8.16 Completed Memo Table

Q10: (P0) +P10/N10   READY

```
       M          N        O       P      Q      R    S
1  21-Mar-83
2
3  Dear Bill,
4
5  Here are them revenu and cost figures that
6  show the 1st three quarters figures (in
7  $1000's).
8
9            REVENUE    COST   PROFIT PROF %REV
10 CORPORATE  3290     2134    1156        35%
11 CLASSICAL   720      216     504        70%
12 COUNTRY    1190      952     238        20%
13 JAZZ        370      259     111        30%
14 ROCK       1010      707     303        30%
15
16
17
18
19
20
```
CAPS

The formula for calculating dollar profit is Revenue – Cost, or +N10–O10. The formula for profit as a percent of revenue is Profit / Revenue, or +P10/N10. You should format the Q-column entries as percents with no decimal places.

To build the two new table columns:

1. Enter two labels: P9 = PROFIT, Q9 = PROF %REV.

2. Enter two formulas: P10 = +N10–O10, Q10 = +P10/N10.

3. Format Q10, the first percent cell: select RANGE FORMAT PERCENT and type 0 [Enter] Q10 [Enter].

4. COPY the formulas into rows 11–14: select COPY and type P10.Q10 [Enter] (the FROM range) P11.P14 [Enter] (the TO range).

Move the pointer to M16, add the final memo line, and justify it in the range M16..Q16. Add the closure and the sender's name in Q19 and Q20.

197

Fig. 8.17 Memo with Closure

```
Q20:  'Jim                                                       READY
```

```
        M         N        O        P        Q       R       S
1   21-Mar-83
2
3   Dear Bill,
4
5   Here are them revenu and cost figures that
6   show the 1st three quarters figures (in
7   $1000's).
8
9             REVENUE     COST    PROFIT PROF %REV
10  CORPORATE    3290     2134      1156        35%
11  CLASSICAL     720      216       504        70%
12  COUNTRY      1190      952       238        20%
13  JAZZ          370      259       111        30%
14  ROCK         1010      707       303        30%
15
16  Total corporate profits are $1,156,000, well
17  over last year's total profits of $950,000.
18
19                                Sincerely,
20                                Jim
```

6. Editing

As you have observed, there are a few typographical errors at the beginning of the memo. You can correct errors in labels, formulas, or values with the EDIT feature. EDIT is not a command; it's one of the specially defined functions like HELP and GRAPH.

Move the pointer to M5 and type the Edit key (Fig. 8.18).

A copy of the entry appears in the scratch area at the top of the control panel with a small blinking cursor at the end of the line, and the mode indicator is set to EDIT. In EDIT mode you can do the following things:

- Move the cursor around in the entry using the Arrow and Tab keys.

- Delete characters using the [Del] key or the Backspace key.

- Insert new characters by simply typing them in. New characters are inserted to the left of the cursor.

Hold down the Left Arrow and the cursor moves left on the Edit line until it reaches the beginning of the entry. The Right Arrow moves the cursor right until it reaches the end of the entry. [Home] moves the

Fig. 8.18   EDIT Mode

```
M5: 'Here are them revenu and cost figures that                          EDIT
    'Here are them revenu and cost figures that_
```

```
            M       N       O       P       Q       R       S
1  21-Mar-83
2
3  Dear Bill,
4
5  Here are them revenu and cost figures that
6  show the 1st three quarters figures (in
7  $1000's).
8
9           REVENUE     COST    PROFIT PROF %REV
10 CORPORATE    3290     2134    1156         35%
11 CLASSICAL     720      216     504         70%
12 COUNTRY      1190      952     238         20%
13 JAZZ          370      259     111         30%
14 ROCK         1010      707     303         30%
15
16 Total corporate profits are $1,156,000, well
17 over last year's total profits of $950,000.
18
19                               Sincerely,
20                               Jim
```

cursor to the beginning of the entry and [End] moves it to the end of the entry. Shift Tab moves the cursor five characters to the left and Tab moves five characters to the right.

Type [Home], then move the cursor to the "m" in "them," using Tabs and Arrows. With the cursor under "m," type the delete key, [Del], once. The "m" is erased and the line shifts to close the deleted space.

Fig. 8.19   "m" Deleted

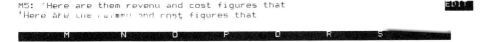

Move the cursor to the space after "revenu" and type an "e." The "e" is inserted to the left of the cursor and the line adjusts to make room for the insert.

Fig. 8.20   "e" Inserted

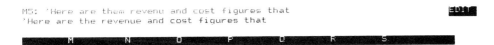

Type [End] and use the Backspace key to erase the word "that." Finally, type "for" and enter the completed line. In fact, the cursor does not have to be at the end of the line to complete the edit. The corrected line looks like Fig. 8.21.

Fig. 8.21 Corrected First Line

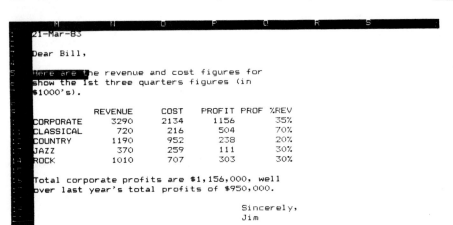

Now move the pointer to M6, type the Edit key, and

a) delete the word "show" and the space following it,

b) change "1st" to "first,"

c) add the words "of 1983" after "quarters," and

d) delete the word "figures."

The corrected line should look like Fig. 8.22.

Fig. 8.22   Second Line Corrected

```
M6: 'the first three quarters of 1983 (in                    READY

     M         N        O        P       Q       R        S
1  21-Mar-83
2
3  Dear Bill,
4
5  Here are the revenue and cost figures for
6  the first three quarters of 1983 (in
7  $1000's).
8
9            REVENUE     COST   PROFIT PROF  %REV
10 CORPORATE    3290     2134    1156         35%
11 CLASSICAL     720      216     504         70%
12 COUNTRY      1190      952     238         20%
13 JAZZ          370      259     111         30%
14 ROCK         1010      707     303         30%
15
16 Total corporate profits are $1,156,000, well
17 over last year's total profits of $950,000.
18
19                              Sincerely,
20                              Jim
```

The corrections have thrown the alignment off, so you'll have to rejustify the first paragraph. You must be careful, though, because you don't want to justify the entire memo—only the first paragraph. Move the pointer to M5 and select RANGE JUSTIFY. So you don't affect the entire memo, specify a block range for 1–2–3 to justify: M5..Q7. If the entries don't fit in the Justify range, 1–2–3 will display an error message and the computer will beep. You won't see the error message this time, because the two entries fit easily in the Justify range. In fact, the three entries have been realigned into two lines.

Fig. 8.23   Realigned Paragraph

```
M5: 'Here are the revenue and cost figures for the           READY

     M         N        O        P       Q       R        S
1  21-Mar-83
2
3  Dear Bill,
4
5  Here are the revenue and cost figures for the
6  first three quarters of 1983 (in $1000's).
7
8
9            REVENUE     COST   PROFIT PROF  %REV
10 CORPORATE    3290     2134    1156         35%
11 CLASSICAL     720      216     504         70%
12 COUNTRY      1190      952     238         20%
13 JAZZ          370      259     111         30%
14 ROCK         1010      707     303         30%
15
16 Total corporate profits are $1,156,000, well
17 over last year's total profits of $950,000.
18
19                              Sincerely,
20                              Jim
```

7. Moving a Block of Entries

The shorter first paragraph has left an extra blank line before the table in your memo. You can't simply delete the blank line, because the DELETE command would eliminate the whole row—including pieces of the database and summary areas to the left of the memo. The alternative is to close up the empty space with the MOVE command. MOVE transfers a range of entries from one location to another. MOVE is unlike COPY in that it erases the range to move FROM after creating the range to move TO. (COPY leaves the original FROM range as is and makes a copy of it in the TO range.) MOVE also "stretches" formulas (addresses don't change when the cells are moved), whereas COPY "adjusts" them (addresses are adjusted to the newly copied position).

Move the pointer to M9 and select MOVE. Build the range to move FROM by pointing right four times and down eleven times to row 20. The complete FROM range is M9..Q20. Type [Enter] and move the pointer up one row to M8, the "hook" on which the TO range hangs. Type [Enter] again, and 1-2-3 moves the entire range up one row.

Fig. 8.24   Completed Memo

M9: 'CORPORATE   READY

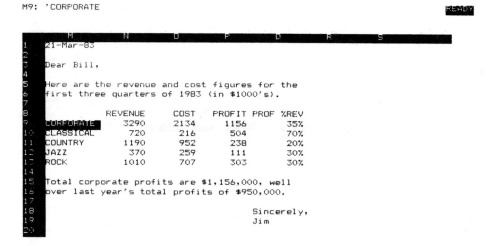

Your memo is now complete and ready to print. You could even build a graph of the PROFIT or PROF %REV figures, print the graph, and send it along with the memo. You know the figures are right (no transcribing errors) because they didn't have to be retyped.

You might choose to save the memo along with the worksheet. When fourth-quarter figures are in, you simply recalculate your summary table, pull the new totals into the memo and adjust the wording to describe the new figures. Your memo will be completed with little effort and very little chance for error. If you have retained the graph by naming it and saving the file, you can generate and print new graphs in a matter of minutes.

Chapter 8 Exercises

FINANCE Exercise

Use the skills you learned in Chapter 8 to do the following:

1. Write a memo about the two-cell table (G16..J20) and include the table in your memo. To accompany your memo, produce a stacked bar chart of the quarterly revenue figures.

2. Use the MOVE command to move the Corporate totals down below the table. Reenter formulas for the total revenue and cost entries so they accurately reflect changes to the table data. When you COMBINE the fourth-quarter figures, you'll have to change only the Division entries; the Corporate sums will adjust automatically.

3. Write a memo of your own on the 1–2–3 worksheet to give you practice with the editing commands. You'll probably find 1–2–3 very convenient for drafting memos, outlines, and other short documents. Outlines are especially easy if you reduce the column widths to 3–5 spaces; the smaller columns provide an easy way to indent.

THISYR Exercise

Here are three ways you can practice with your THISYR worksheet.

1. Write a memo describing the state of Music Corporation's four divisions. Add a section about COUNTRY division's what-if values. Use the XTRACT-COMBINE sequence to pull the table into the memo.

2. Produce a longer reporting letter that pulls pieces of both FINANCE and THISYR into a separate worksheet. Describe the raw FINANCE data in light of LAST YEAR's profits listed in THISYR.

3. Determine the average increase in profits for the divisions and use the average to determine a growth factor for forecasting next year's profits. Add a column to THISYR (call it NEXT YEAR) that multiplies each THIS YEAR profit by the forecasted growth factor.

```
A1:                                                                   READY

      A        B          C          D          E         F        G
1                     LAST YEAR  THIS YEAR   CHANGE   % CHANGE
2
3              JAZZ      123.00    200.00     77.00       63%
4              ROCK      456.00    500.00     44.00       10%
5              CLASSICAL 789.00    800.00     11.00        1%
6              COUNTRY   444.00    400.00    (44.00)     -10%
7
8              CORPORATE 1,812.00  1,900.00   88.00        5%
9
10
11                                         CHANGE
12                             COUNTRY    DIV %     CORP %
13                             WHAT-IF?    -10%        5%
14                              420.00     -5%        6%
15                              430.00     -3%        7%
16                              440.00     -1%        7%
17                              450.00      1%        8%
18                              460.00      4%        8%
19
20
```

PROJACT Exercise

PROJACT uses the PROJDATA table from the Chapter 6 exercise to help you track a project. Build the model a portion at a time, referring back to Chapters 6 through 8 whenever you need help. The PROJACT model helps you control the project as it progresses. In fact, you can use the same model to record your actual HOURS data.

1. Save a copy of your completed model with the name PROJBUD. The data in PROJBUD should be changed only if you actually rebudget the project.

2. Save a second copy of the model with the name PROJACT. You'll use PROJACT to keep track of actual hours, so any changes you make should be saved with the PROJACT file name.

3. Zero all of the HOURS entries in PROJACT by entering a zero in the first row, then COPYing it down the column. 1–2–3 will recalculate the CHARGES and TOTALS as zeros.

4. Now, as weekly timecard data comes in, enter the actual hours worked in the appropriate row. (This presumes that employees keep track of which task they are working on.) Each time you enter new data, 1–2–3 recalculates the CHARGES and TOTALS, and you can reproduce the summary table.

5. If you want to compare budget and actual data, you can enter two new columns, BHOURS and BCHARGES, to your data base. These columns contain the budget data from PROJBUD. Enter the new columns in F and G, right next to the actual data. The new DATA area looks like this:

```
A10:                                                              READY

            A              B          ▪       D      F       F       G
10
11   Rate:                        $35.00 hour
12
13   TASK              TASK #      EMP    HOURS  CHARGES  BHOURS BCHARGES
14   Plan              1           wrb        5      175       8      280
15   Plan              1           jpf       10      350       8      280
16   Plan              1           meb        7      245       8      280
17   Design            2           jpf       26      910      20      700
18   Outline           3           wrb      8.5    297.5       6      210
19   Outline           3           jpf        8      280       6      210
20   Write First Draft 4           jpf       25      875      40     1400
21   Write First Draft 4           meb       26      910      24      840
22   Revise            5           wrb        4      140       8      280
23   Revise            5           jpf        4      140       8      280
24   Revise            5           meb        4      140       8      280
25   Write Final Draft 6           jpf        0        0      36     1260
26   Write Final Draft 6           meb        0        0       8      280
27   -----------------------------------------------------------------
28   TOTALS            6           3      127.5   $4,463     188   $6,580
29
```

6. Enter the Budget data with the XTRACT-COMBINE sequence:

a) Save PROJACT.

b) Retrieve PROJBUD.

c) FILE XTRACT the two budget data columns (D and E).

d) Retrieve PROJACT.

e) FILE COMBINE the budget data starting in F14.

7. Expand your OUTPUT section and you can extract both actual and budget data. You'll have to move the % TOTAL column over to make room for the two new output columns. To calculate actual charges as a percent of budgeted charges, you may want to change the % TOTAL formulas to % BUDGET formulas. The completed extract area looks like this:

```
A30:                                                              READY


        A        B          C        D       E       F       G          H
30
31  CRITERION AREA
32  TASK       TASK #      EMP     HOURS   CHARGES
33                          jpf
34
35  OUTPUT AREA            TOTALS:    73    2555    118    4130        62%
36
37  TASK       TASK #      EMP     HOURS   CHARGES BHOURS BCHARGES % BUDGET
38  Plan        1           jpf      10     350      8      280       125%
39  Design      2           jpf      26     910     20      700       130%
40  Outline     3           jpf       8     280      6      210       133%
41  Write Fir   4           jpf      25     875     40     1400        63%
42  Revise      5           jpf       4     140      8      280        50%
43  Write Fin   6           jpf       0       0     36     1260         0%
44
45
46
47
48
49
```

8. You can also expand the summary table to total both actual and budget data. Again, you may want to replace the % TOTAL column with % BUDGET formulas. Here is an expanded summary area:

```
I1:                                                                    READY

        I       J       K       L       M       N       O       P
1               SUMMARY AREA
2
3               EMP
4               *
5
6                       HOURS   CHARGES BHOURS BCHARGES % BUDGET
7               EMP     127.5   4462.5   188    6580      68%
8               wrb      17.5    612.5    22     770      80%
9               jpf      73      2555    118    4130      62%
10              meb      37      1295     48    1680      77%
11
12
13
14
15
16
17
18
19
20
```

Automating Your Worksheet

1. The Typing Alternative

Alternative Typing is a convenient feature of 1–2–3. It lets you list a series of keystrokes and tell 1–2–3 to carry them out for you. For example, you might list the five keystrokes needed to SAVE an updated version of your file:

/ F S [Enter] R

With Alternative Typing, you can tell 1–2–3 to type the five keystrokes for you.

The list of keystrokes that you want 1–2–3 to perform is called a **macro.** A macro is like a simple computer program—it's a list of instructions that the computer carries out. Think of it as a recipe for a very dumb chef. You write the recipe in the restricted language that the chef understands, and you tell him *every step* that he must take. You write a macro in the language of the 1–2–3 commands and you include every keystroke that you want 1–2–3 to type. You can't tell 1–2–3 "save the file," you must tell it:

/	type a slash to invoke the menu
F	select the FILE command
S	select the SAVE option
[Enter]	accept the default file name
R	select the REPLACE option

If you leave out a step, you'll probably get some confusing results.

It's a good idea to use extra caution when you're working with macros. The precise step-by-step logic of a macro is a little alien to most people, and it's easy to leave steps out or to enter something different from what is intended. Macros do *exactly* what you tell them to do, so use them carefully.

2. How to Build a Macro

Macros are entered on the 1–2–3 worksheet as labels. A long macro may be split into several labels entered in a column. 1–2–3 doesn't care how long each piece of the macro is (though each cell is limited to 239 keystrokes); it simply starts with the first label and performs all the keystrokes there, moves down to the next label, and continues typing keystrokes there. When 1–2–3 reaches an empty cell, it stops typing keystrokes. Figure 9.1 includes a one-cell macro for saving an updated worksheet.

Fig. 9.1   File-Saving Macro

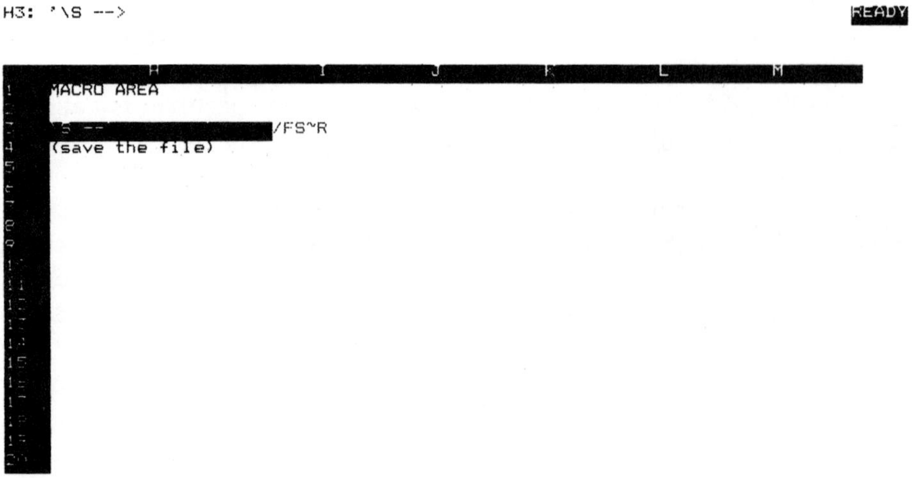

H3: '\S -->   READY

```
       H                 I          J        K        L        M
1  MACRO AREA
2
3  S --                         /FS~R
4  (save the file)
5
```

In a macro, the tilde (~) stands for the [Enter] key; it tells 1–2–3 "type [Enter]."

The first cell in a macro is named with the RANGE NAME command. Macro names are made up of a Backslash and a letter, such as \A, \M, \Z, etc. The special range name associates the letter with the macro. Only the first cell of the macro is named; subsequent cells are included in the macro so long as they follow one after another (with no blank cells in between) down a column. You might name the file-saving macro "\S," for SAVE.

To start a macro, you hold down the [Alt] key and type the letter name of the macro. The [Alt]-letter combination tells 1–2–3 to start typing the keystrokes in the macro. To start the \S macro, you hold down the [Alt] key and type S.

3. A Simple Macro for Saving the Worksheet

SAVE any unsaved work and RETRIEVE your last version of THISYR (including the What-If table that you added in Chapter 5).

Fig. 9.2   THISYR After Chapter 5

A1:   READY

	A	B	C	D	E	F	G
1			LAST YEAR	THIS YEAR	CHANGE	% CHANGE	
3		JAZZ	123.00	200.00	77.00	63%	
4		ROCK	456.00	500.00	44.00	10%	
5		CLASSICAL	789.00	800.00	11.00	1%	
6		COUNTRY	444.00	400.00	(44.00)	−10%	
8		CORPORATE	1,812.00	1,799.00	99.00	5%	
11				CHANGE TABLE			
12			COUNTRY	DIV %	CORP %		
13			WHAT−IF?		−10%	5%	
14			420.00		−5%	6%	
15			430.00		−3%	7%	
16			440.00		−1%	7%	
17			450.00		1%	8%	
18			460.00		4%	8%	

Your worksheet fills the screen almost completely, so we'll build the macro one screen over to the right (starting in column H). Type [Home]

to move the pointer to A1, then type the Tab key once. Tab moves the pointer one page (one screen width) to the right. Now your pointer is in H1 and you are looking at a blank section of the worksheet.

Fig. 9.3   Pointer in H1

Start the new macro area by entering the label MACRO AREA in H1. 1–2–3 doesn't require this label, but it makes your worksheet easier to understand.

Now move the pointer down and over to I3, type '/FS~R and press [Enter]. Your screen should look like this:

Fig. 9.4   Macro Entry

The quote (') tells 1–2–3 that you are entering a label, not invoking the FILE command, but it is not part of the macro itself. Remember—1–2–3 pays attention to every character in the macro (even spaces at the end of the entry), so make sure it's typed *exactly* as shown above (with no spaces).

To tell 1–2–3 this is a macro, not just a simple label, you must name the macro. Select RANGE NAME CREATE, type the name \ S, and type [Enter] to set the range name as I3..I3.

Fig. 9.5   Final Prompt for Range Naming

A final step that isn't required, but will help you keep track of your work, is to make a note of the macro's name and purpose. You can add this "documentation" to the left of the macro. Move the pointer to H3 and type:

      '\ S --->   [quote-backslash-S-space-dash-dash-"greater-than" sign]

Fig. 9.6   Macro with Name Label

Now move the pointer down to H4 and enter a short description of what the macro does. Enter ' (save the file) in H4.

Fig. 9.7   Macro with Documentation

213

The label looks a little messy because it runs into the I column. To make the screen neater, select WORKSHEET COLUMN SET, and type 20 [Enter]. The expanded column gives you plenty of room for comments.

Fig. 9.8   Completed File-Saving Macro

Adding labels that clarify a macro (or a program) is called "documenting the code." You should always include some type of documentation with your macros. It's well worth your time now to add some comments that will help you understand what the macro does when you pick it up again three weeks from now.

Your macro is complete and ready for a first test. You can start a macro from anywhere in the worksheet; your pointer does not have to be in a particular cell to make the macro work. Hold down the [Alt] key and, watching your screen closely, type an S. If you watched closely, you probably saw the menu flash on the screen before the disk started whirring. 1–2–3 shows you what it is doing by displaying the menus and prompts, just as it does when you are typing the commands. However, 1–2–3 types *much* faster than you can, so the display changes very quickly.

You saw the disk light turn on and heard the disks spinning, so you probably think the macro worked correctly. But how can you check it? The easiest way to check this macro is to retrieve the newly saved THISYR. If the file includes your macro, it must have been properly saved and updated. Select FILE RETRIEVE and enter the file name (THISYR, unless you saved new versions under new names). If the file comes back with your \S macro in it, you know the macro worked the way it should have.

To test the macro again, move the pointer [Home] and type [Alt] S—
that is, hold down the [Alt] key and type S. Now if you RETRIEVE the
file, the pointer should be in A1, where it was when the macro did the
SAVE. Select FILE RETRIEVE and enter the file name. Is the pointer in
A1? Type the tab key and see if the macro is still there. If it is, you have a
good, working macro.

Fig. 9.9   Completed Worksheet with Macro

	LAST YEAR	THIS YEAR	CHANGE	% CHANGE	MACRO AREA	
JAZZ	123.00	200.00	77.00	63%	/S -->	/FS^R
ROCK	456.00	500.00	44.00	10%	(SAVE THE FILE)	
CLASSICAL	789.00	800.00	11.00	1%		
COUNTRY	444.00	400.00	(44.00)	-10%		
CORPORATE	1,812.00	1,900.00	88.00	5%		

	CHANGE	
COUNTRY	DIV %	CORP %
WHAT-IF?	-10%	5%
420.00	-5%	6%
430.00	-3%	7%
440.00	-1%	7%
450.00	1%	8%
460.00	4%	8%

Notice how the macro assumes that you are updating a previously
saved file (it just types [Enter] to accept the previously saved file name).
If you were building a macro to handle new files, you would have to use
a different command sequence.

The file-saving macro reduces the number of keystrokes needed to
update your file from five to two. This may not seem like a big savings,
but larger macros (like the one you'll build next) can reduce dramatically
the time you spend typing commands. Also, the [Alt]-S macro lets you
update your file without having to think about 1–2–3 menus and commands; you simply type the [Alt]-S combination.

4. A Graphing Macro

In Chapter 4, you defined a bar graph of the %CHANGE figures in THISYR. So long as you have only one graph associated with your file, you can select it quickly with the Graph key. However, if you have more than one set of graph definitions associated with the worksheet, you must type several keystrokes to view a particular graph. That is, you must do all of the following:

1. Invoke the menu   /
2. Select GRAPH   G
3. Select NAME   N
4. Select USE   U
5. Select the particular graph name

In this section, we're going to build a macro that types these keystrokes for you. Later we'll define a second graph and define a similar macro for it. Finally, we'll combine the two macros in a **user-defined menu**. A user-defined menu is just like a regular menu except that you define its options and what they do. The menus you define are combinations of several macros. The graphing menu you'll build looks like Fig. 9.10.

Fig. 9.10   Complete Graphing Menu

```
H7:  '\G --->
```

```
            H
1   MACRO AREA
2
3   \S --->              /FS~R
4   (save the file)
5
6
7   \G -->               /xmGMENU~
8   (start graph menu)
9
10  GMENU -->            %CHANGE                   PROFPIE
11  Descriptions         Display %CHANGE bar chart Display profit pie chart
12  Select a graph       /GNU                      /GNU
13                       %CHANGE~                  PROFPIE~
14  Quit graph menu      Q                         Q
15  Return to menu       /XMGMENU~                 /XMGMENU~
16
17
18
19
20
```

Like macros, user-defined menus include keystroke-by-keystroke instructions for 1–2–3 to carry out. Only the first cell of the menu is named. Menus are not named with the backslash-letter combination, but with full word names.

Menus are started by a macro, not directly from the keyboard. Therefore a menu must be preceded by a short macro that instructs 1–2–3 to "start the menu." You invoke the starting macro with the appropriate [Alt]-letter sequence, and the macro starts the menu.

Don't worry if this looks confusing now; we'll build the menu a little at a time. Before you start making entries, expand columns I and J to 26 characters wide (using the WORKSHEET COLUMN SET command). You'll need the extra room to see the long label entries in the menu columns.

First, we'll build the macro that selects and displays the %CHANGE graph. The macro that displays the graph is three lines long.

Fig. 9.11   %CHANGE Display Macro

The first line of the macro performs steps 1 through 4 listed at the beginning of this section (/GNU). The second line enters the name of the graph to use, and the third line QUITS the GRAPH menu. The tilde at the end of the second line tells the macro to type [Enter].

Move the pointer to I12 (to leave room for the menu you'll build later), and enter the first line of the macro. Enter a single quote at the beginning to tell 1–2–3 you are entering a label, not invoking the menu. Next, move down to I13 and enter line 2 of the macro. Finally, enter the one-letter line 3 in I14.

Before you test the macro, run through the command sequence by hand. This is the best way to make sure you haven't left anything out of the macro. As you type the sequence, write down each keystroke that you type. Pay particular attention to special keys like [Enter] and the Arrow keys. When you finish the sequence, use your notes to check your macro and correct it if necessary.

To view the %CHANGE graph, type

/GNU%CHANGE[Enter]

Hit any key to clear the graph from the screen (unless you have two monitors). Notice that you are still in the GRAPH menu. Now you see why we need the third line of the macro—the Q tells 1–2–3 to QUIT the GRAPH menu.

You could have put all three macro lines in one label in I11, but it's a good idea to break the macro up into small pieces. Small pieces are easier to follow and easier to correct if you make a mistake.

The macro appears to be complete, so move back to I12 and assign the macro a name. To name the macro \ C (for CHANGE graph):

1. Select RANGE NAME CREATE.
2. Enter the range name: \ C.
3. Type [Enter] to define the range to name as I12..I12.

Before you try the graphing macro, SAVE your current worksheet on the disk. You can use the [Alt]-S macro to save the file in only two keystrokes. Once the file is saved, type [Alt]-C to start the graphing macro. Almost instantly 1–2–3 displays the %CHANGE graph (Fig. 9.12).

If you have only one monitor, type any key to clear the graph. Notice that 1–2–3 QUITS the GRAPH menu for you.

Fig. 9.12   %CHANGE Graph

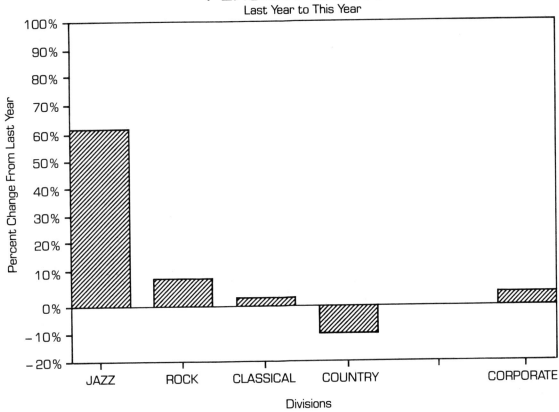

5. A Second Graphing Macro

You may have already defined a pie chart for your THISYR worksheet (we suggested doing so in the Chapter 3 Exercises). If not, define the pie chart now. For the purposes of the macro you need to define only three graph options: the TYPE, the X-AXIS, and the A-RANGE. Later you may want to add titles to the graph.

To define a simple pie chart, follow these steps:

1. Clear the current graph settings

      select GRAPH RESET ALL

2. Define the graph

      select TYPE PIE

      select X-AXIS and enter the column of division names (B3..B6)

      select A-RANGE and enter the column of THIS YEAR profits (D3..D6)

3. Name the graph definition and save the worksheet

      select NAME and enter the name PROFPIE

      select QUIT to leave the GRAPH menu

      type [Alt] S to save the new graph definition with your THISYR worksheet

Without reading further, try to define a second graphing macro on your own. The new macro should display the PROFPIE graph. You can enter the new macro right next to the old one, starting in J12.

If your attempt was successful, you found that the new macro is exactly like the old macro except the graph name (line 2) is PROFPIE ~ instead of %CHANGE ~.

With two graphing macros, your worksheet looks like this:

Fig. 9.13 Two Graphing Macros

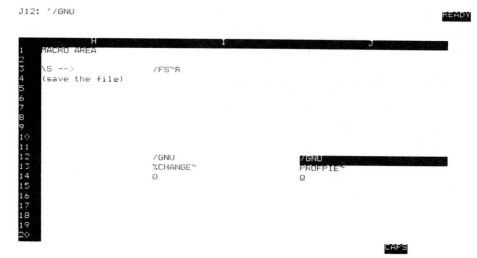

To name the second macro \P, move the pointer to J12, select RANGE
NAME CREATE, type \P [Enter], and type [Enter] again to set the
range to name as J12..J12.

Save the file with the [Alt]-S macro, then test your new macro by
typing [Alt] P. If the new macro doesn't work, compare it to the one in
Fig. 9.11. Make sure there are no extra spaces or other marks in your
macro. Once you have both macros working, you're ready to move on to
menus.

6. From Macros to Menus

You've built two similar macros, both of which display graphs. It would
be simpler if you could combine the two macros so you could start them
with one [Alt] sequence and then select which graph to display. This is
precisely what user-defined menus are for. By defining your own menu,
you simplify the selection of macros and customize the worksheet to
your model and your needs. Figure 9.14 is a menu that combines the two
graphing macros.

Fig. 9.14   Graphing Menu

H7: '\G -->   READY

```
       H                      I                          J
  MACRO AREA

  \S -->                /FS~R
  (save the file)


  \G --                 /xmGMENU~
  (start graph menu)

  GMENU -->             %CHANGE              PROFPIE
  Descriptions          Display %CHANGE bar chart  Display profit pie chart
  Select a graph        /GNU                 /GNU
                        %CHANGE~             PROFPIE~
  Quit graph menu       Q                    Q
  Return to menu        /XMGMENU~            /XMGMENU~
```

221

Column H contains comments that describe what the new macro and menu do. Column I includes your \C macro with some new lines added. The starting macro in I8 includes a command, xm (that means "start the menu"—xm stands for eXecute Menu). The menu is named GMENU, for Graph Menu. Cells I10 and I11 respectively are the first option and first descriptive line in the menu. I12 repeats the command in I8; it tells 1–2–3 to go back to the start of GMENU when you finish looking at the %CHANGE graph.

The additional three lines in column J function just like the lines in column I, except here the menu option and description refer to the second graph—PROFPIE.

Move the pointer to I10 and insert the three new menu lines.

I10 = %CHANGE
I11 = Display the %CHANGE bar chart.
I14 = ' /xmGMENU~

1–2–3 doesn't care whether the entries are in uppercase or lowercase, but you'll probably find the menu easier to read if you make the entries as shown here.

Fig. 9.15 Menu Entries in Column I

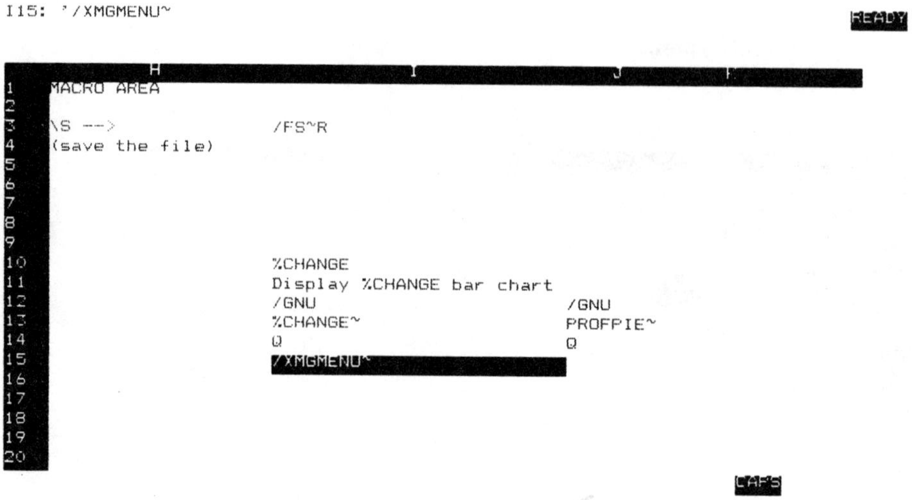

```
I15: '/XMGMENU~                                              READY

        H                    I              J        K
1  MACRO AREA
2
3  \S -->              /FS~R
4  (save the file)
5
6
7
8
9
10                     %CHANGE
11                     Display %CHANGE bar chart
12                     /GNU                   /GNU
13                     %CHANGE~               PROFPIE~
14                     Q                      Q
15                     /XMGMENU~
16
17
18
19
20
                                                      CAPS
```

222

Now move to column J and make the new entries there:

J10 = PROFPIE
J11 = Display profit pie chart
J15 = ' /xmGMENU~

Fig. 9.16   Menu Entries in I and J

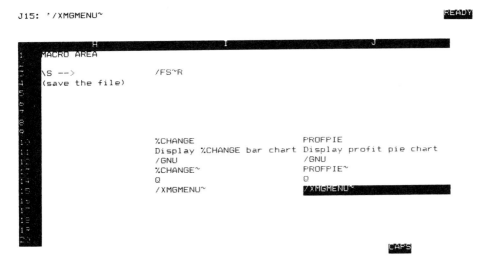

You name a menu just as you name a macro, except the name can be a full word and should *not* be preceded by a backslash. As with a macro, you name only the first cell in the menu. Move the pointer to I10, select RANGE NAME CREATE, and type GMENU [Enter] [Enter]. Now move the pointer up to I7 and enter the command that starts the menu:

I7 = '/xmGMENU~

This one-cell label is really a macro whose function is to start GMENU. Therefore you must name this cell just as you would a macro. Name the cell \ G, for Graph, with the RANGE NAME CREATE sequence.

2 2 3

You've just made several entries on the worksheet, so SAVE a new copy of it on the disk. Your completed menu should look like this:

Fig. 9.17 Completed Menu

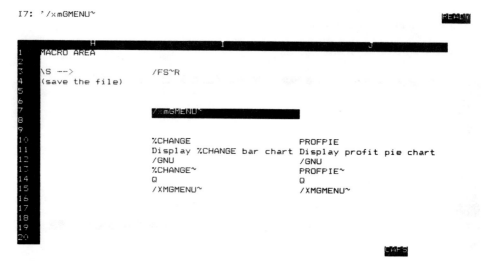

Translated into English, the menu commands mean:

Fig. 9.18 English Menu

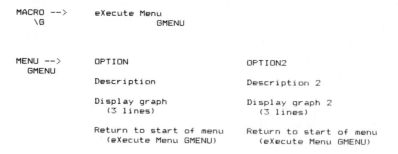

Start the menu now by typing [Alt] G. You should now be looking at a two-option menu of your two graph names. What you're actually seeing are the entries in I10 and J10 plus the first description entry in I11.

Your menu works just like the 1–2–3 menus; if you move the pointer, the description line changes. As before, you can select a menu option by moving the menu pointer to the option and typing [Enter] or by typing the first letter of the option. (You can include more than one option starting with the same letter in your menus, but you'll lose the ability to select by typing the first letter. If duplicates exist, typing the first letter will always give you the leftmost duplicate-letter option.)

Select either graph for viewing. When you finish viewing, type any key to clear the graph. The macro tells 1–2–3 to QUIT the GRAPH menu and re-execute GMENU. To exit the menu, type [Esc].

Your last task is to enter the seven lines of comments in column H. As shown in Fig. 9.19, your completed macro, with documentation, is quite impressive.

Fig. 9.19   Menu with Documentation

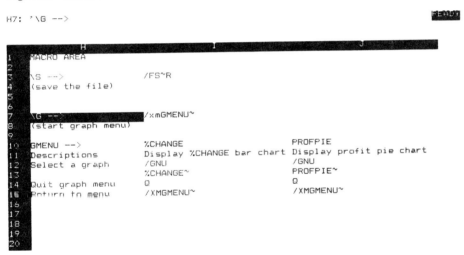

Several other "x" commands (like xm) are used in macros. As you become more expert with 1–2–3, you may want to use these commands to build complicated macros and menus. Many of them are similar to programming commands and may take some time to master. In any case, simpler macros and menus like the ones you just built will handle many of the repetitive command sequences that your worksheets require.

Chapter 9 Exercises

THISYR Exercise

Using what you've learned in Chapter 9, try the following things:

1. Define a third THISYR graph and add it to the GMENU. You might graph LAST YEAR and THIS YEAR profits as paired bars. The TYPE is BAR, the A range is the column of LAST YEAR figures, and the B range is the column of THISYR figures.

2. Add a QUIT option to GMENU. The x-command to quit a menu is /xq~. Remember to add new menu options right next to the current options, with no blank columns in between.

3. Read about other x-commands in your *1–2–3 Users Manual* and experiment with them in your current macro.

STOREMAC Exercise

Enter the following macro in the STORESUM worksheet. This macro produces either of the two summary tables, depending on which menu option you select. Be sure to name the four ranges.

ATABLE	the AREA summary table range
ACRIT	the AREA summary criteria range
CTABLE	the CATEGORY summary table range
CCRIT	the CATEGORY summary criteria range

K1:   READY

```
    K           L                      M                N          O
1       MACRO AREA
2
3
4       \M -->                   /xmMENU~
5       (start menu)
6
7       MENU -->                 AREASUM          CATSUM
8       Descriptions             Summarize by area Summarize by category.
9       Enter 1-cell table range /dt1ATABLE~      /dt1CTABLE~
10      Enter criteria range     ACRIT~           CCRIT~
11      Retun to MENU            /xmMENU~         /xmMENU~
12
13
```

PART IV

Appendixes

Appendix A
Command Summary

WORKSHEET   The worksheet commands let you set up or alter the entire worksheet or one or more of its rows and columns.

GLOBAL   A global setting tells 1–2–3 "do this everywhere" on the worksheet. For example, the GLOBAL COLUMN-WIDTH command sets the width of all columns on the worksheet.

FORMAT   Sets the way numbers are displayed on the worksheet. For example, a one-cell range containing the number 1234.56 can be formatted in any one of nine ways:

Fixed (with one decimal)	1234.6
Scientific	1.23E+03
Currency (with two decimals)	$1,234.56
, (comma) (with two decimals)	1,234.56
General	1234.567
+/−	*********
Percent (with two decimals)	123456.70%
Date	18–May–03 18–May May–03
Text	1234.567

Numbers are displayed in the General format by default.

LABEL-PREFIX   Aligns the labels in all worksheet cells to the left, right, or center. The command assigns a "label-prefix" character

(', ", or ∧) to each label:

LEFT	'YEAR	:YEAR		:
RIGHT	"YEAR	:		YEAR:
CENTER	∧YEAR	:	YEAR	:

Labels are aligned to the left by default.

COLUMN-WIDTH   Sets the number of characters that will fit in all worksheet columns. You can set the width by typing the number, or by expanding or contracting the columns with the Arrow keys.

RECALCULATION   There are six settings that control the order and frequency with which formula entries are recalculated:

NATURAL   Recalculates formulas in order of their dependency. Independent variables are calculated first.

COLUMNWISE   Down each column, a column at a time.

ROWWISE   Across each row, a row at a time.

AUTOMATIC   Recalculates every time the worksheet is altered.

MANUAL   Recalculates only when you type the (Calc) key.

ITERATION   Recalculates all formulas a specified number of times.

PROTECTION   ENABLEs or DISABLEs cell protection. When protection is enabled, you can make entries only in unprotected cells. Cells can be formatted as protected or unprotected with the RANGE FORMAT command.

DEFAULT   Enters the default, or initial, settings.

PRINTER   Sets default printer settings, including margins, page-length, and special printer-setup commands.

DISK   Tells 1–2–3 which disk to access when transferring files between the disk and the worksheet.

STATUS   Displays the default worksheet settings (format, column-width, etc.) and the amount of available memory.

UPDATE   Changes default settings.

QUIT   Leaves GLOBAL menu.

INSERT   Adds one or more COLUMNs or ROWs between existing column or row entries, which are moved to the right when a column is added and down when a row is added.

DELETE   Removes one or more COLUMNs or ROWs. The deleted section is erased and the remaining entries are moved to "fill in" the deleted area. If the deleted section contains entries, they are erased and cannot be recovered (unless they are saved in a file). There is no "undelete" command.

COLUMN-WIDTH   Sets the number of characters that will fit in an individual column. You can specify the width by typing the number or by using the Right and Left Arrow keys to expand or contract the column.

ERASE   Clears the entire worksheet. Unless you save the worksheet before erasing it, you cannot recover your work. You do not have to ERASE the worksheet before retrieving a new file; the new file will replace the current worksheet. (Use the FILE COMBINE command to overlay files.)

TITLES   Sets a portion of the worksheet so that it will not scroll off the screen. There are four TITLES options:

BOTH	sets both row and column titles
HORIZONTAL	sets one or more rows as titles
VERTICAL	sets one or more columns as titles
CLEAR	clears title settings

For example, the top seven rows of this worksheet are set as titles:

Fig. A.1   Worksheet with TITLES

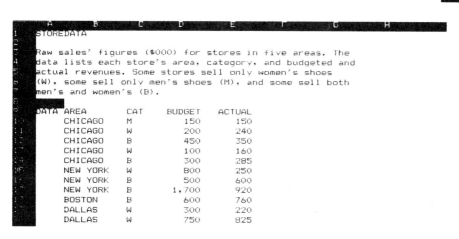

Notice that as the pointer moves down below row 20, rows 1–7 remain on the screen.

Fig. A.2   Worksheet with TITLES Scrolled

A8:   READY

```
        A         B         C         D         E         F         G         H
1  STOREDATA
2
3  Raw sales' figures ($000) for stores in five areas. The
4  data lists each store's area, category, and budgeted and
5  actual revenues. Some stores sell only women's shoes
6  (W), some sell only men's shoes (M), and some sell both
7  men's and women's (B).
25
26 CRIT AREA        CAT       BUDGET    ACTUAL
27                  W
28
29                                               INCREASE/
30 OUT  AREA        CAT       BUDGET    ACTUAL    (DECREASE)
31      CHICAGO     W         200       240       40
32      CHICAGO     W         100       160       60
33      NEW YORK    W         800       250       (550)
34      DALLAS      W         300       220       (80)
35      DALLAS      W         750       825       75
36
37
```

WINDOW   Split the display into two pieces; designation can be either HORIZONTAL or VERTICAL. The two display areas can be set to move together (SYNCHRONIZED) or separately (UNSYN-CHRONIZED). Here is a worksheet with a synchronized vertical window:

Fig. A.3   Synchronized WINDOW

G8: 'AREA   READY

```
      A         B       C        F     G         H         I         J
                                7
   DATA AREA       CAT    8    AREA      SUMMARY BY AREA
        CHICAGO    M      9    *
        CHICAGO    W     10              BUDGET    ACTUAL
        CHICAGO    B     11    AREA      9000      7455
        CHICAGO    W     12    CHICAGO   1200      1185
        CHICAGO    B     13    NEW YORK  3000      1770
        NEW YORK   W     14    BOSTON    600       760
        NEW YORK   B     15    DALLAS    2400      1860
        NEW YORK   B     16    ATLANTA   1800      1880
        BOSTON     B     17
        DALLAS     W     18    CAT       SUMMARY BY CATEGORY
        DALLAS     W     19    *
        DALLAS     M     20              BUDGET    ACTUAL
        DALLAS     B     21    CAT       9000      7455
        ATLANTA    B     22    M         1850      1855
        ATLANTA    M     23    W         2150      1695
                          24    B         5000      3905
                          25
                          26
```

STATUS   Displays the "global" worksheet settings (the default settings for the whole worksheet).

RANGE   Sets or alters an area of the worksheet. The area to set or alter is called a **range** and can be either a cell, a column of cells, a row of cells, or a block of cells.

Fig. A.4   Ranges

These are ranges:

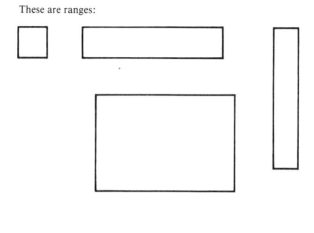

These are not:

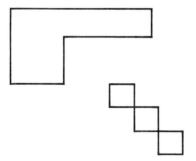

The RANGE settings override any GLOBAL settings in the formatted area.

FORMAT   See GLOBAL FORMAT. There is also a RESET option that returns the cells in the range to the default worksheet format.

LABEL-PREFIX   See GLOBAL LABEL-PREFIX.

233

ERASE   Clears the contents of a range of cells.

NAME   CREATEs a name and assigns it to a range of cells, or DELETEs a previously assigned name. The LABELS option allows you to use a label adjacent to the range (LEFT, RIGHT, UP, or DOWN) as the range name. There is also an option to RESET, or eliminate, all range names.

JUSTIFY   Aligns an area of text within a specified range.

PROTECT   Prevents any entries or alterations to a range of cells.

UNPROTECT   Allows entries or alterations to a range of cells.

INPUT   Limits the movement of the pointer to unprotected cells in a range. INPUT is generally used in combination with a Keyboard Macro for data entry by people who are unfamiliar with 1–2–3. To control input to a simple invoice form:

1. Construct an area of the worksheet to look like the paper invoice form.

Fig. A.5   Invoice INPUT Form

2. Unprotect only those cells where data should be entered (above the dashed lines in this case).

3. Invoke the RANGE INPUT command and define the range as A1 to B11. The pointer will move only to the unprotected cells.

4. Enter the data. Typing the [Esc] or [enter] key *before beginning* an entry ends the INPUT command.

A Keyboard Macro can be used to process a set of entries before new entries are made.

COPY   Copies the contents of one range to another range. When the range to copy FROM contains more than one cell, the range to copy TO is made up of one or more "hooks" on which to hang the FROM range. For example, to copy from A1..A3 into the area B1 to D3.

Fig. A.6   COPY

The TO range is B1..D1, the "hooks" on which the three-cell FROM range is hung. Copied formulas are adjusted to reflect their new position in the worksheet.

2 3 5

MOVE   Moves the contents from one range of cells to another range. The entire FROM range is hung from a one-cell TO range. For example, this sequence moves the entries FROM A1..B2 to the area C2 to D4. Formulas do not adjust when MOVEd.

Fig. A.7   MOVE

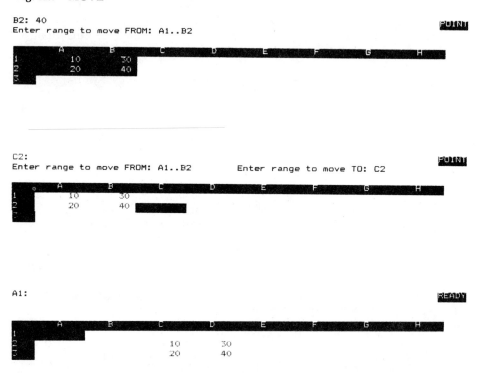

FILE   The FILE commands let you transfer worksheet data or general disk information (such as a directory) between the worksheet and the disk.

RETRIEVE   Loads a file with the extension .WKS from the disk into the 1–2–3 worksheet. You can tell 1–2–3 which file to retrieve by typing its name or selecting it with the menu pointer from a list of available files.

SAVE   Stores a copy of the current worksheet on the disk. The disk copy is called a *file* and is assigned a name, which you enter (in response to the prompt "File to save:"); the file is given the extension .WKS. If a file with the same name already exists, you have the option of either replacing the existing file with the new file or canceling the command.

COMBINE   Incorporates a file into the current worksheet. The new file can overwrite entries in the worksheet (COPY) or its values can be added to (ADD) or subtracted from (SUBTRACT) the current worksheet entries. The combined worksheet is added beginning in the cell where the pointer is located when the command is invoked. Only the entries that are not blank are altered.

Fig. A.8   COMBINE

file to COMBINE

current worksheet

result of COMBINE COPY

result of COMBINE ADD

XTRACT   Saves a portion of the current worksheet in a disk file. You specify the range to extract and the name to give the new file. You can extract all the FORMULAS in the range, or extract only the calculated VALUES.

ERASE   Deletes a WORKSHEET, GRAPH, or PRINT file from the disk. You can specify which file to delete by typing its name or by selecting it with the menu pointer from a list of available files.

LIST   Lists the names of all WORKSHEET (.WKS), all GRAPH (.PIC), or all PRINT (.PRN) files on the disk and displays the amount of free memory available.

IMPORT   Reads the contents of a Print file from the disk into a section of the worksheet. The file can be read as TEXT or as NUMBERS. If you import the file as numbers, any text it contains should be enclosed in quotes. IMPORT is usually used to move data into 1–2–3 from another program.

DISK   Changes the default disk drive. The default drive is the drive 1–2–3 accesses when transferring files between the disk and the worksheet. In a two-drive system the default disk is usually B; the default disk holds your data, while disk A holds the 1–2–3 program disk.

PRINT   Prints a portion of the worksheet on the PRINTER or to a disk FILE. If you print to a disk, the file is assigned the extension .PRN.

RANGE   Set the area of the worksheet to print. You can print the entire file or a portion of the file. If the range to print is wider than your printer paper, 1–2–3 prints as much of the range as will fit on the sheet, then prints additional pieces of the range in strips (Fig. A.9).

LINE   Advances the printer paper by one line.

PAGE   Advances the printer paper by one page. After printing, PAGE will eject to the top of the next page regardless of the number of lines printed.

OPTION   Sets one or more of the options that control how the printed page appears.

> **HEADER**   Sets a line of text to print at the top of each page.

Fig. A.9   Range Wider than the Paper

```
Number Name                      Region     Enviornment        Phylum
     1 Gorilla                   Forest     Tropical forest Vertebrata
     2 Hyaena                    Arid       Savana          Vertebrata
     3 Elephant Seal             Marine     Beaches and shalVertebrata
     4 Bottlenose Dolphin        Marine     Open sea           Vertebrata
     5 Brown rat                 Special    Human dwellings Vertebrata
     6 Cheetah                   Arid       Savana          Vertebrata
     7 Nile crocodile            Freshwater Marshes         Vertebrata
     8 Pink flamingo             Freshwater Marshes         Vertebrata
     9 Galapagos hawk            Forest     Open forest     Vertebrata
    10 Alligator                 Freshwater Marshes         Vertebrata
    11 Red salamander            Forest     Humus           Vertebrata
    12 Boa constrictor           Forest     Tropical forest Vertebrata
    13 Mute swan                 Freshwater Marshes         Vertebrata
    14 Shrike                    Forest     Open forest     Vertebrata
    15 Bearded vulture           Mountain   High mountains  Vertebrata
    16 Herring gull              Marine     Rocky coasts    Vertebrata
    17 Moray eel                 Marine     Coral reefs     Vertebrata
    18 Veiltail                  Special    Aquariums       Vertebrata
    19 Sriped angelfish          Marine     Coral reefs     Vertebrata
    20 Cuttlefish                Marine     Underwater prairMollusca
    21 Mantis                    Forest     Open forest     Arthropoda
    22 Moustached monkey         Forest     Tropical forest Vertebrata
    23 Mouflon                   Mountain   High mountain   Vertebrata
    24 Diamond back rattlesnake  Grass      Scrub           Vertebrata
```

```
Class        Order
Mammalia     Primates
Mammalia     Carnivora
Mammalia     Pinnipedia
Mammalia     Cetacea
Mammalia     Rodentia
Mammalia     Carnivora
Reptilia     Crocodilia
Aves         Phoenicopteriformes
Aves         Falconiformes
Reptilia     Crocodilia
Amphibia     Urodela
Reptilia     Squamata
Aves         Anseriformes
Aves         Passeriformes
Aves         Falconiformes
Aves         Charadriiformes
Osteichthyes Anguillformes
Osteichthyes Cypriniformes
Osteichthyes Chadtodontidae
Cephalopda   Decapoda
Insecta      Dictyoptera
Mammmalia    Primate
Mammmalia    Artiodactyla
Reptilia     Squamata
```

FOOTER   Sets a line of text to print at the bottom of each page.

MARGINS   Sets the amount of blank space at the left, right, top, and bottom of each page. The initial margin settings are:

LEFT	5 spaces from the left
RIGHT	75 spaces from the left
TOP	2 lines from the top
BOTTOM	2 lines from the bottom

1–2–3 reserves a line for the header and footer whether or not they are used, and reserves a blank line between the header and footer and the body of the text. With the top margin set to 0, printing starts on line 3.

BORDERS   Sets one or more COLUMNS or ROWS to be printed as borders. Row borders are printed at the top of each page of printout, column borders are printed at the left of each page of printout. Use borders to print a row of titles or labels along with a range that isn't adjacent to the borders. The BORDER command lets you set titles on the printed page much as the TITLES command sets titles on the screen display.

SETUP   Sets characters that control special features of your printer. For example, many printers can print compressed characters when sent the proper SETUP code (Fig. A.10).

PAGE-LENGTH   Sets the number of lines in your printer paper. The default page-length setting is 66 ines.

OTHER

AS-DISPLAYED   Prints the cell contents as they are displayed on the screen.

CELL FORMULAS   Prints the formulas in each cell as they would appear in the control panel (including format, cell address, and protection status). Formulas are printed one to a line (not as a block) so formula printing can use up a lot of paper.

UNFORMATTED   Ignores automatic page breaks, headers, and footers.

FORMATTED   Prints using automatic page breaks, headers, and footers.

Fig. A.10   Compressed Printing

Dear Bill,

There's good news and bad news when you compare our 1983
performance with last year's figures. CLASSICAL division,
always our biggest seller, shows a healthy 25% growth in
this year's profits. The flashy good news is that we are
bouncing back with the new interest in Jazz and our JAZZ
Division is up an impressive 67%. (Though its margins
aren't what they could be.)

```
              1983 CHANGE SUMMARY
                    ($000)

Division  Last Year This Year    Change  % Change
-------------------------------------------------
CLASSICAL      620       775       155       25%
COUNTRY        330       300      (30)       -9%
JAZZ           120       200        80       67%
ROCK           400       430        30        8%

CORPORATE    1,470     1,705       235       16%
```

The bad news is that ROCK is only up 8% (I would blame that
on the economy) and COUNTRY is down 9% (I would blame that
on us). The attached graph makes it hard to avoid the
conclusion that we should do a serious review of our
COUNTRY Division with an eye to selling it.

                                   Sincerely,

                                   Jim Bickford

241

QUIT   Returns to the main PRINT menu.

CLEAR   Resets printer settings. You can clear ALL settings, only the RANGE settings, only the BORDER settings, or only the FORMAT settings.

ALIGN   Tells 1–2–3 that the printhead is now at the top of the page.

GO   Prints the specified range.

QUIT   Leaves the PRINT menu and returns to READY mode.

GRAPH   Produces a graph of values in the worksheet.

TYPE   There are five graph types: LINE, BAR, PIE, STACKED-BAR, and XY. Samples of the five graph types are shown in Fig. A.11.

X   Defines the set of values or labels used to label the x-axis (the bottom line) of the graph.

A B C D E F   Defines a range of numbers to plot on the graph. You can plot up to six ranges of numbers (A, B, C, etc.) on a single graph. 1–2–3 uses the A–F ranges to scale and label the y-axis (the left-hand line) of the graph.

RESET   Eliminates ALL graph settings or any of the seven range settings (X and A–F). There is also an option to QUIT the RESET menu.

VIEW   Instructs 1–2–3 to draw a graph, based on the current graph settings, on your graphics monitor.

SAVE   Saves a picture of the graph in a disk file. GRAPH files are assigned the extension .PIC and can be printed with the 1–2–3 GRAPH program.

OPTIONS

LEGEND   Labels each data range. The legend appears below the graph.

FORMAT   Sets a format for the entire GRAPH or for one of the A–F ranges. You can format the graph entries as LINES, SYMBOLS,

Fig. A.11   Graph Types

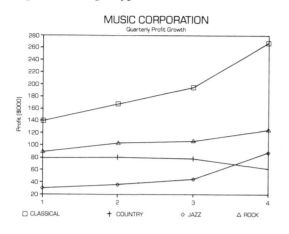

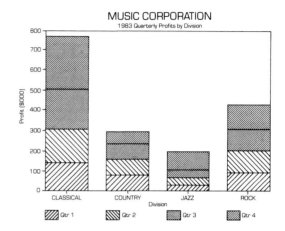

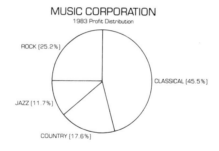

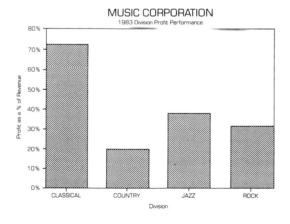

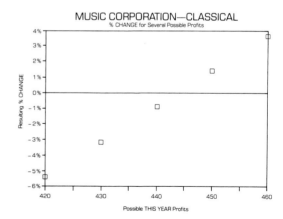

2 4 3

BOTH lines and symbols, or reset them to NEITHER lines nor symbols. There is also an option to QUIT the FORMAT menu.

TITLES   Sets titles for the graph's x-axis (displayed below the axis), for the y-axis (displayed to the left of the axis), or for the whole graph (displayed in one or two lines above the graph).

FIRST   Sets a first title line for the whole graph.

SECOND   Sets a second title line for the whole graph.

X-AXIS   Sets an x-axis title.

Y-AXIS   Sets a y-axis title.

GRID   Displays a grid over the graph. The grid can be set to display HORIZONTAL lines, VERTICAL lines, or BOTH horizontal and vertical lines, or it can be eliminated with the CLEAR option.

SCALE   Sets or formats the axes scale. 1–2–3 will scale the axes automaticaly unless you specify MANUAL scaling. If you use manual scaling, specify upper and lower limits for the scale. You cannot set the scale for a pie chart.

X-AXIS   Sets the x-axis scale in an XY graph.

Y-AXIS   Sets the y-axis scale.

AUTOMATIC   Scales the y-axis automatically.

MANUAL   Scales the graph using the upper and lower bounds you enter.

LOWER   Sets the scale's lower bound.

UPPER   Sets the scale's upper bound.

FORMAT   Formats the y-axis scale using any of the standard formats described under GLOBAL FORMAT.

QUIT   Leaves the SCALE menu.

COLOR   Displays the graph in color.

B&W   Displays the graph in black and white.

DATA-LABELS   Labels the graph's data points with a range of worksheet entries.

QUIT   Leaves the OPTIONS menu.

NAME   Assigns the graph definitions a name. Save the worksheet after naming your graphs and the graph definitions will be saved along with the worksheet. You can USE a currently named graph, CREATE a new graph name, DELETE a named graph, or RESET all graph names.

QUIT   Leaves the GRAPH menu.

DATA   Sets up or analyzes a collection of data.

FILL   Fills in a range of the worksheet with a progression of numbers. You tell 1–2–3 the range to fill, the starting number, the amount by which to increment each number in the progression, and the last number in the sequence.

TABLE   Defines a one-input-cell or a two-input-cell table. Tables are used to summarize the data or to examine how new entries would affect dependent formulas in the worksheet (in other words, to ask WHAT-IF a given series of numbers were substituted for one of the worksheet values).

SORT   Reorders the collection of data. You can define two keys for use with the sort. A key determines the order of the data. For example, if the key were last name, the data would be sorted in order of last name. You tell 1–2–3 what to sort (DATA-RANGE) and what keys will determine the sorted order (PRIMARY-KEY and SECONDARY-KEY). The RESET option clears the sort settings, and the GO option tells 1–2–3 to perform the sort. QUIT leaves the DATA menu.

QUERY   Locates items in a collection of data, or extracts items from the data.

INPUT   Defines the range of the collection of data to query.

CRITERION   Defines a range where the criteria for finding or extracting entries are entered.

OUTPUT   Defines a range where extracted entries are listed. (Actually, copies of the extracted entries are listed in the OUTPUT range.)

FIND   Locates data entries based on some criteria (e.g., name = Smith, profit < 500, etc.).

EXTRACT   Copies all entries matching some criteria to the OUT-PUT area.

UNIQUE   Copies all unique entries matching some criteria to the OUTPUT area. Duplicate entries are ignored.

DELETE   Locates and erases entries based on some criteria.

RESET   Eliminates QUERY range settings.

QUIT   Leaves the QUERY menu.

DISTRIBUTION   Calculates the frequency of distribution of a range of values.

QUIT   Leaves 1–2–3 and returns to the Lotus Access System or the Disk Operating System.

Appendix B
The IBM Keyboard

1–2–3 makes good use of the special keys on the IBM PC. Figure B.1 shows the IBM keyboard highlighting keys with special meaning in 1–2–3. The following list describes how each key is used in 1–2–3. If you have a computer other than the IBM PC, use your *1–2–3 User's Manual* to locate these keys on your computer.

    1. Typewriter keyboard: The majority of the light-colored keys are just like those on a standard typewriter. The letters are arranged in the standard typewriter layout, with a row of numbers and special characters at the top and a space bar at the bottom.

Fig. B.1   The IBM PC Keyboard

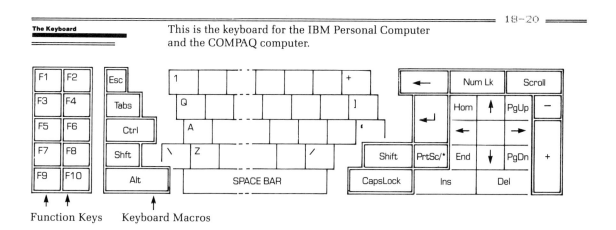

247

2. Hold down a **Shift** key to type capital (uppercase) letters or the top symbol on a key. (Shift 1, for example, is an exclamation point.) The Shift keys are located at either side of the bottom row of letters. They look like short, fat Up Arrows [⬆].

3. The **Escape** key, [Esc], located to the left of the top row of numbers, is used to back out of a command sequence.

4. The **Tab** key, [⇆], located to the left of the Q, moves you one page to the right or one page to the left on the 1–2–3 Worksheet. A page is eighty characters wide. Move one page right by typing a Tab; move one page left by typing Shift Tab.

5. The **Control** key, [Ctrl], located to the left of the A key, is used to select the break function. When you want to interrupt something that 1–2–3 is doing, hold down the Control key and type the [Scroll/Break] key.

6. The **Alternative** key (usually called "alt"), [Alt], lets you give letter keys alternative meanings. [Alt] is located to the left of the space bar. If you find yourself repeatedly typing the same sequence of keystrokes, you can have 1–2–3 do the typing for you by creating an automatic typing sequence called a "Keyboard Macro." Instead of typing the sequence, you simply hold down the Alt key and type its one-letter name, and 1–2–3 performs the keystroke sequence for you.

7. The **Capital Lock** key, [CapsLock], located to the right of the space bar, is like a toggle switch, or ON/OFF key. By typing the key once you switch it to the opposite position—to OFF if it was ON, and vice versa. With the [CapsLock] on, any letter you type will appear as a capital. Number and symbol keys are not affected by CapsLock. 1–2–3 displays the message "CAPS" in the lower right-hand corner of the screen when the [CapsLock] is switched on.

8. During editing, the **Backspace Delete** arrow, [←], deletes the character one space to the left of the pointer; [←] is the first gray key to the right of the row of numbers at the top of the keyboard.

9. The **Enter** key, [↵], the large gray key to the right of the letter keys, tells 1–2–3 that you have completed whatever you were typing and want to "send" the information to 1–2–3. The last step in most typing sequences is to [Enter] what you have typed.

10. The **Print Screen/*** key, [PrtSc], located to the right of the right-hand Shift key, lets you print a picture of whatever is on the screen. You must hold down the shift key to select the print screen function. The asterisk part of the key, [*], is used as the "times" sign in multiplication.

11. The **Numbers Lock** key, [NumLock], located to the right of the back-space delete key, is a toggle for turning the nine keys below it into a numeric keypad. 1–2–3 displays a "NUM" message in the lower right corner of the screen when NumLock is toggled on. When NumLock is toggled off these keys have other meanings.

12. The **Scroll Lock** key, [Scroll Lock], located to the right of the NumLock key, is a toggle that changes how your view of the worksheet is adjusted when you move the pointer. 1–2–3 displays a "SCROLL" message in the lower right corner of the screen when scroll lock is toggled on.

13. The cluster of nine square keys directly below NumLock control pointer movement.

Fig. B.2   Pointer Movement keys

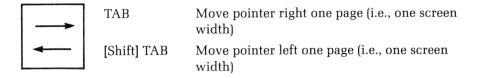

TAB	Move pointer right one page (i.e., one screen width)
[Shift] TAB	Move pointer left one page (i.e., one screen width)

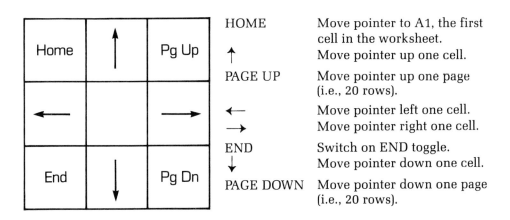

HOME	Move pointer to A1, the first cell in the worksheet.
↑	Move pointer up one cell.
PAGE UP	Move pointer up one page (i.e., 20 rows).
←	Move pointer left one cell.
→	Move pointer right one cell.
END	Switch on END toggle.
↓	Move pointer down one cell.
PAGE DOWN	Move pointer down one page (i.e., 20 rows).

Chapter 2 (section 3) discusses all the pointer-movement keys in detail. These keys can also be used as a numeric keypad when the NumLock is toggled on. Your common use of these keys will be for pointer movement, though.

14. The **Insert** key, [Ins], located to the right of the CapsLock key, has no special function in 1–2–3.

15. The **Delete** key, [Del], located to the right of the Insert key, is used to delete characters during editing.

16. The **Plus** and **Minus** keys, [+], [–], are used for addition and subtraction.

17. At the left of the keyboard are ten dark keys labeled F1 through F10. These are the **Function** keys. They are used to perform specially defined 1–2–3 functions with only one keystroke. The ten function keys perform these functions.

[F1]	HELP	Displays a Help screen.
[F2]	EDIT	Edits the contents of a cell
[F3]	NAME	Displays defined range Names.
[F4]	ABS	Defines a cell as an Absolute value.
[F5]	GOTO	Moves the pointer to [GoTo] a cell.
[F6]	WIND	Jumps from one Window to another.
[F7]	QUERY	Performs the last Query sequence.
[F8]	TABLE	Performs the last Table sequence.
[F9]	CALC	ReCalculates all the formulas in the worksheet.
[F10]	GRAPH	Generates the Graph last defined.

Appendix C
Formula Listings
for Exercises

Chapter 3.   THISYR Exercise

```
C1: "LAST YEAR              C5: 789
D1: "THIS YEAR              D5: 800
E1: "CHANGE                 E5: +D5-C5
F1: "% CHANGE               F5: (P0) +E5/C5
B3: 'JAZZ                   B6: 'COUNTRY
C3: 123                     C6: 444
D3: 200                     D6: 400
E3: +D3-C3                  E6: +D6-C6
F3: (P0) +E3/C3             F6: (P0) +E6/C6
B4: 'ROCK                   B8: 'CORPORATE
C4: 456                     C8: @SUM(C3..C6)
D4: 500                     D8: @SUM(D3..D6)
E4: +D4-C4                  E8: +D8-C8
F4: (P0) +E4/C4            F8: (P0) +E8/C8
B5: 'CLASSICAL
```

Chapter 3.   EVALUATE Exercise

```
A1: 'EVALUATE
C1: 'Date
D1: (D1) 'April 20, 1983
A3: 'Evaluate several characteristics of a list of numbers.
A6: "THE LIST:
B6: U 4
C6: U 22
D6: U 16                    A12: "MINIMUM:
E6: U 34                    B12: @MIN(B6..F6)
F6: U 9                     A13: "COUNT:
A9: "SUM:                   B13: @COUNT(B6..F6)
B9: @SUM(B6..F6)            A14: "STANDARD
A10: "AVERAGE:              A15: "DEVIATION:
B10: @AVG(B6..F6)           B15: @STD(B6..F6)
A11: "MAXIMUM:              A16: "VARIANCE:
B11: @MAX(B6..F6)           B16: @VAR(B6..F6)
```

Chapter 3.   TABLE Exercise

```
A1:  'TABLE
C1:  'Date
D1:  (D2) 'April 20, 1983
A2:  '@Copyright 1982 John M. Nevison Associates
A4:  'Sum the rows and columns of a table of numbers.
A5:  'The rows are projects and the columns are quarters.
C8:  "         QUARTER
F8:  "PROJECT
A9:  "PROJECT
B9:  1
C9:  2
D9:  3
E9:  4
F9:  "TOTALS
A11: 1
B11: (F0) 200
C11: (F0) +B11*1.2
D11: (F0) +C11*1.2
E11: (F0) +D11*1.2
F11: @SUM(B11..E11)
A12: 2
B12: (F0) 400
C12: (F0) +B12*1.5
D12: (F0) +C12*1.5
E12: (F0) +D12*1.5
F12: @SUM(B12..E12)
A13: 3
B13: (F0) 700
C13: (F0) +B13*1.1
D13: (F0) +C13*1.1
E13: (F0) +D13*1.1
F13: @SUM(B13..E13)
A14: 4
B14: (F0) 300
C14: (F0) +B14*1.65
D14: (F0) +C14*1.8
E14: (F0) +D14*1.8
F14: @SUM(B14..E14)
A15: 5
B15: (F0) 500
C15: (F0) +B15*1.25
D15: (F0) +C15*1.25
E15: (F0) +D15*1.25
F15: @SUM(B15..E15)
A16: "QUARTER
A17: "TOTALS
B17: @SUM(B10..B16)
C17: @SUM(C10..C16)
D17: @SUM(D10..D16)
E17: @SUM(E10..E16)
F17: @SUM(F10..F16)
```

Chapter 3.   SALES Exercise

```
A1:  'SALES
C1:  "Date
D1:  (D1) @DATE(83,4,29)
A3:  'Compare budgeted vs. actual profits for a company's five
A4:  'sales areas. The table shows the difference in profit and
A5:  'calculates actual profits as a percent of budgeted profits.
D7:  ^Better/
E7:  ^Actual
D8:  ^(Worse)
E8:  ^as a % of
A9:  'Area
B9:  ^Budget
C9:  ^Actual
D9:  ^Than Budget
E9:  ^Budget
A11: 'Chicago
B11: 1200
C11: (F0) 1185
D11: +C11-B11
E11: (P1) +C11/B11
A12: 'New York
B12: 3000
C12: (F0) 1770
D12: +C12-B12
E12: (P1) +C12/B12
A13: 'Boston
B13: 600
C13: (F0) 760
D13: +C13-B13
E13: (P1) +C13/B13
A14: 'Dallas
B14: 2400
C14: (F0) 1860
D14: +C14-B14
E14: (P1) +C14/B14
A15: 'Atlanta
B15: 1800
C15: (F0) 1880
D15: +C15-B15
E15: (P1) +C15/B15
A16: \=
B16: \=
C16: (F0) \=
D16: \=
E16: (P1) \=
A17: 'Corporate
B17: (C0) @SUM(B11..B15)
C17: (C0) @SUM(C11..C15)
D17: (C0) +C17-B17
E17: (P1) +C17/B17
```

Chapter 5. THISYR Exercise

```
C1:  "LAST YEAR
D1:  "THIS YEAR
E1:  "CHANGE
F1:  "% CHANGE
B3:  'JAZZ
C3:  123
D3:  200
E3:  +D3-C3
F3:  (P0) +E3/C3
B4:  'ROCK
C4:  456
D4:  500
E4:  +D4-C4
F4:  (P0) +E4/C4
B5:  'CLASSICAL
C5:  789
D5:  800
E5:  +D5-C5
F5:  (P0) +E5/C5
B6:  'COUNTRY
C6:  444
D6:  400
E6:  +D6-C6
F6:  (P0) +E6/C6
B8:  'CORPORATE
C8:  @SUM(C3..C6)
D8:  @SUM(D3..D6)
E8:  +D8-C8
F8:  (P0) +E8/C8
E11: 'CHANGE
D12: 'COUNTRY
E12: 'DIV %
F12: 'CORP %
D13: 'WHAT-IF?
E13: (P0) +F6
F13: (P0) +F8
D14: 420
E14: (P0) -0.0540540541
F14: (P0) 0.059602649
D15: 430
E15: (P0) -0.0315315315
F15: (P0) 0.0651214128
D16: 440
E16: (P0) -0.009009009
F16: (P0) 0.0706401766
D17: 450
E17: (P0) 0.0135135135
F17: (P0) 0.0761589404
D18: 460
E18: (P0) 0.036036036
F18: (P0) 0.0816777042
```

Chapter 5. INTEREST Exercise

```
A1:  'INTEREST
C1:  'Date
D1:  'April 20, 1983
A3:  'Computes a sum growing at three
A4:  'different interest rates.
A6:  "RATE >
B6:  (P0) U 0.1
C6:  (P0) U 0.12
D6:  (P0) U 0.15
A7:  "YEAR
B7:  ^SUM
C7:  ^SUM
D7:  ^SUM
A8:  0
B8:  (F2) U 100
C8:  (F2) +B8
D8:  (F2) +C8
A9:  +A8+1
B9:  (F2) (1+B$6)*B8
C9:  (F2) (1+C$6)*C8
D9:  (F2) (1+D$6)*D8
A10: +A9+1
B10: (F2) (1+B$6)*B9
C10: (F2) (1+C$6)*C9
D10: (F2) (1+D$6)*D9
A11: +A10+1
B11: (F2) (1+B$6)*B10
C11: (F2) (1+C$6)*C10
D11: (F2) (1+D$6)*D10
A12: +A11+1
B12: (F2) (1+B$6)*B11
C12: (F2) (1+C$6)*C11
D12: (F2) (1+D$6)*D11
A13: +A12+1
B13: (F2) (1+B$6)*B12
C13: (F2) (1+C$6)*C12
D13: (F2) (1+D$6)*D12
A14: +A13+1
B14: (F2) (1+B$6)*B13
C14: (F2) (1+C$6)*C13
D14: (F2) (1+D$6)*D13
A15: +A14+1
B15: (F2) (1+B$6)*B14
C15: (F2) (1+C$6)*C14
D15: (F2) (1+D$6)*D14
A16: +A15+1
B16: (F2) (1+B$6)*B15
C16: (F2) (1+C$6)*C15
D16: (F2) (1+D$6)*D15
A17: +A16+1
B17: (F2) (1+B$6)*B16
C17: (F2) (1+C$6)*C16
D17: (F2) (1+D$6)*D16
A18: +A17+1
B18: (F2) (1+B$6)*B17
C18: (F2) (1+C$6)*C17
D18: (F2) (1+D$6)*D17
```

Chapter 5.   TIMELY Exercise

```
A1:  'TIMELY
C1:  'April 21, 1983
A2:  '@Copyright 1982 John M. Nevison Associates
A4:  'Compute the expected completion times for a table of tasks.
A5:  'Each task is given a low, likely and high time estimate.
A8:  'TASK
B8:  "LOW
C8:  "LIKELY
D8:  "HIGH
E8:  "EXPECTED
A9:  'Plan
B9:  1.5
C9:  3
D9:  4
E9:  (F2) ((2*C9)+((B9+D9)/2))/3
A10: 'Design
B10: 2
C10: 2
D10: 5
E10: (F2) ((2*C10)+((B10+D10)/2))/3
A11: 'Outline
B11: 1
C11: 1.5
D11: 2
E11: (F2) ((2*C11)+((B11+D11)/2))/3
A12: 'Write First Draft
B12: 5
C12: 7
D12: 13
E12: (F2) ((2*C12)+((B12+D12)/2))/3
A13: 'Revise
B13: 2
C13: 3
D13: 5
E13: (F2) ((2*C13)+((B13+D13)/2))/3
A14: 'Write Final Draft
B14: 3
C14: 5
D14: 10
E14: (F2) ((2*C14)+((B14+D14)/2))/3
B16: '       Total project time:
E16: (F2) @SUM(E9..E14)
F16: 'days
```

Chapter 5.   PROJECT Exercise

```
A1:  'PROJEST
C1:  'Date
D1:  'April 30, 1983
A3:  'Compute total project time and cost estimates at a standard hourly
A4:  'rate. The project is divided into tasks, some of which include more
A5:  'than one employee. This project is estimated in hours and summarized
A6:  'in days.
A8:  'Project Completion Time:
C8:  +D28/8
D8:  'days
A9:  'Project Cost:
C9:  (C0) +E28
A11: 'Rate:
C11: (C2) 35
D11: 'hour
A13: 'TASK
B13: "TASK #
C13: "EMP
D13: "HOURS
E13: "CHARGES
A14: 'Plan
B14: 1
C14: "wrb
D14: 8
E14: +D14*$C$11
B15: 1
C15: "jpf
D15: 8
E15: +D15*$C$11
B16: 1
C16: "meb
D16: 8
E16: +D16*$C$11
A17: 'Design
B17: 2
C17: "jpf
D17: 20
E17: +D17*$C$11
A18: 'Outline
B18: 3
C18: "wrb
D18: 6
E18: +D18*$C$11
B19: 3
C19: "jpf
D19: 6
E19: +D19*$C$11
A20: 'Write First Draft
B20: 4
C20: "jpf
D20: 40
E20: +D20*$C$11
B21: 4
C21: "meb
D21: 24
E21: +D21*$C$11
A22: 'Revise
```

```
B22: 5
C22: "wrb
D22: 8
E22: +D22*$C$11
B23: 5
C23: "jpf
D23: 8
E23: +D23*$C$11
B24: 5
C24: "meb
D24: 8
E24: +D24*$C$11
A25: 'Write Final Draft
B25: 6
C25: "jpf
D25: 36
E25: +D25*$C$11
B26: 6
C26: "meb
D26: 8
E26: +D26*$C$11
A27: \-
B27: \-
C27: \-
D27: \-
E27: \-
A28: 'Totals
B28: 6
C28: 3
D28: @SUM(D14..D26)
E28: (C0) @SUM(E14..E26)
```

Chapter 6.   FINANCE Exercise

A1: "DATA
B1: "DIVISION
C1: "QTR
D1: "REVENUE
E1: "COST
A2: 4
B2: 'CLASSICAL
C2: 1
D2: 200
E2: +D2*0.3
A3: 10
B3: 'COUNTRY
C3: 1
D3: 400
E3: +D3*0.8
A4: 7
B4: 'JAZZ
C4: 1
D4: 100
E4: +D4*0.7
A5: 1
B5: 'ROCK
C5: 1
D5: 300
E5: +D5*0.7
A6: 5
B6: 'CLASSICAL
C6: 2
D6: 240
E6: +D6*0.3
A7: 11
B7: 'COUNTRY
C7: 2
D7: 400
E7: +D7*0.8
A8: 8
B8: 'JAZZ
C8: 2
D8: 120
E8: +D8*0.7
A9: 2
R9: 'ROCK
C9: 2
D9: 350
E9: +D9*0.7
A10: 6
B10: 'CLASSICAL
C10: 3
D10: 280
E10: +D10*0.3
A11: 12
B11: 'COUNTRY
C11: 3
D11: 390
E11: +D11*0.8
A12: 9
B12: 'JAZZ
C12: 3

D12: 150
E12: +D12*0.7
A13: 3
B13: 'ROCK
C13: 3
D13: 360
E13: +D13*0.7
A15: 'CRIT
B15: "DIVISION
C15: "QTR
D15: "REVENUE
E15: "COST
B16: 'ROCK
A18: 'OUT
B18: "DIVISION
C18: "QTR
D18: "REVENUE
E18: "COST
B19: 'ROCK
C19: 1
D19: 300
E19: 210
B20: 'ROCK
C20: 2
D20: 350
E20: 245
B21: 'ROCK
C21: 3
D21: 360
E21: 252

Chapter 6. PROJDATA Exercise

```
A1:   'PROJDATA
C1:   'Date
D1:   'April 30, 1983
A3:   'Compute total project time and cost estimates at a standard hourly
J3:   'EMP
A4:   'rate. The project is divided into tasks, some of which include more
J4:   '*
A5:   'than one employee. This project is estimated in hours and summarized
J5:   'SUMMARY TABLE
A6:   'in days.
K6:   "HOURS
L6:   "CHARGES
M6:   "% TOTAL
J7:   "EMP
K7:   @DSUM(DATA,3,SCRIT)
L7:   @DSUM(DATA,4,SCRIT)
M7:   (P0) +L7/$L$7
A8:   'Project Completion Time:
C8:   +D28/8
D8:   'days
J8:   "wrb
K8:   22
L8:   770
M8:   (P0) +L8/$L$7
A9:   'Project Cost:
C9:   (C0) +E28
J9:   "jpf
K9:   118
L9:   4130
M9:   (P0) +L9/$L$7
J10:  "meb
K10:  48
L10:  1680
M10:  (P0) +L10/$L$7
A11:  'Rate:
C11:  (C2) 35
D11:  'hour
A13:  'TASK
B13:  "TASK #
C13:  "EMP
D13:  "HOURS
E13:  "CHARGES
A14:  'Plan
B14:  1
C14:  "wrb
D14:  8
E14:  +D14*$C$11
A15:  'Plan
B15:  1
C15:  "jpf
D15:  8
E15:  +D15*$C$11
A16:  'Plan
B16:  1
C16:  "meb
D16:  8
E16:  +D16*$C$11
```

Chapter 6.   PROJDATA Exercise (Cont.)

A17: 'Design
B17: 2
C17: "jpf
D17: 20
E17: +D17**$C$11
A18: 'Outline
B18: 3
C18: "wrb
D18: 6
E18: +D18**$C$11
A19: 'Outline
B19: 3
C19: "jpf
D19: 6
E19: +D19**$C$11
A20: 'Write First Draft
B20: 4
C20: "jpf
D20: 40
E20: +D20**$C$11
A21: 'Write First Draft
B21: 4
C21: "meb
D21: 24
E21: +D21**$C$11
A22: 'Revise
B22: 5
C22: "wrb
D22: 8
E22: +D22**$C$11
A23: 'Revise
B23: 5
C23: "jpf
D23: 8
E23: +D23**$C$11
A24: 'Revise
B24: 5
C24: "meb
D24: 8
E24: +D24**$C$11
A25: 'Write Final Draft
B25: 6
C25: "jpf
D25: 36
E25: +D25**$C$11
A26: 'Write Final Draft
B26: 6
C26: "meb
D26: 8
E26: +D26**$C$11
A27: \-
B27: \-
C27: \-
D27: \-
E27: \-
A28: 'Totals
B28: 6
C28: 3

D28: @SUM(D14..D26)
E28: (CO) @SUM(E14..E26)
A31: 'CRITERION AREA
A32: 'TASK
B32: "TASK #
C32: "EMP
D32: "HOURS
E32: "CHARGES
C33: "jpf
A35: 'OUTPUT AREA
C35: "TOTALS:
D35: @SUM(D38..D71)
E35: @SUM(E38..E71)
F35: (PO) +E35/E28
A37: 'TASK
B37: "TASK #
C37: "EMP
D37: "HOURS
E37: "CHARGES
F37: '% OF TOTAL
A38: 'Plan
B38: 1
C38: "jpf
D38: 8
E38: 280
F38: (PO) +E38/$E$35
A39: 'Design
B39: 2
C39: "jpf
D39: 20
E39: 700
F39: (PO) +E39/$E$35
A40: 'Outline
B40: 3
C40: "jpf
D40: 6
E40: 210
F40: (PO) +E40/$E$35
A41: 'Write First Draft
B41: 4
C41: "jpf
D41: 40
E41: 1400
F41: (PO) +E41/$E$35
A42: 'Revise
B42: 5
C42: "jpf
D42: 8
E42: 280
F42: (PO) +E42/$E$35
A43: 'Write Final Draft
B43: 6
C43: "jpf
D43: 36
E43: 1260
F43: (PO) +E43/$E$35
F44: (PO) +E44/$E$35

Chapter 6.   STOREDATA Exercise

```
A1:  'STOREDATA
A3:  'Raw sales' figures ($000) for stores in five areas. The
A4:  'data lists each store's area, category, and budgeted and
A5:  'actual revenues. Some stores sell only women's shoes
A6:  '(W), some sell only men's shoes (M), and some sell both
A7:  'men's and women's (B).
A9:  'DATA
B9:  'AREA
C9:  'CAT
D9:  "BUDGET
E9:  "ACTUAL
B10: 'CHICAGO
C10: 'M
D10: 150
E10: 150
B11: 'CHICAGO
C11: 'W
D11: 200
E11: 240
B12: 'CHICAGO
C12: 'B
D12: 450
E12: 350
B13: 'CHICAGO
C13: 'W
D13: 100
E13: 160
B14: 'CHICAGO
C14: 'B
D14: 300
E14: 285
B15: 'NEW YORK
C15: 'W
D15: 800
E15: 250
B16: 'NEW YORK
C16: 'B
D16: 500
E16: 600
B17: 'NEW YORK
C17: 'B
D17: 1700
E17: 920
B18: 'BOSTON
C18: 'B
D18: 600
E18: 760
B19: 'DALLAS
C19: 'W
D19: 300
E19: 220
B20: 'DALLAS
C20: 'W
D20: 750
E20: 825
B21: 'DALLAS
C21: 'M
D21: 400
```

```
E21: 295
B22: 'DALLAS
C22: 'B
D22: 950
E22: 520
B23: 'ATLANTA
C23: 'B
D23: 500
E23: 470
B24: 'ATLANTA
C24: 'M
D24: 1300
E24: 1410
A26: 'CRIT
B26: 'AREA
C26: 'CAT
D26: "BUDGET
E26: "ACTUAL
C27: 'W
F29: 'INCREASE/
A30: 'OUT
B30: 'AREA
C30: 'CAT
D30: "BUDGET
E30: "ACTUAL
F30: '(DECREASE)
B31: 'CHICAGO
C31: 'W
D31: 200
E31: 240
F31: +E31-D31
B32: 'CHICAGO
C32: 'W
D32: 100
E32: 160
F32: +E32-D32
B33: 'NEW YORK
C33: 'W
D33: 800
E33: 250
F33: +E33-D33
B34: 'DALLAS
C34: 'W
D34: 300
E34: 220
F34: +E34-D34
B35: 'DALLAS
C35: 'W
D35: 750
E35: 825
F35: +E35-D35
```

Chapter 7.   FINANCE Exercise

```
G1: "DIVISION
H1: "QTR
J1: "RANGES
K1: "DISTRIB
G2: '*
J2: 100
K2: (+) 1
J3: 200
K3: (+) 3
G4: 'SUMMARY
J4: 300
K4: (+) 3
G5: 'ENTRIES
H5: "REVENUE
I5: "COST
J5: 400
K5: (+) 5
G6: @DCOUNT(DATA,0,DCRIT)
H6: @DSUM(DATA,2,DCRIT)
I6: @DSUM(DATA,3,DCRIT)
K6: (+) 0
H9: "REVENUE
I9: "COST
G10: 'DIVISION
H10: (+) @DSUM(DATA,2,DCRIT)
I10: (+) @DSUM(DATA,3,DCRIT)
G11: 'CLASSICAL
H11: 720
I11: 216
```

```
G12: 'COUNTRY
H12: 1190
I12: 952
G13: 'JAZZ
H13: 370
I13: 259
G14: 'ROCK
H14: 1010
I14: 707
G16: (+) @DSUM(DATA,2,DCRIT)
H16: 1
I16: 2
J16: 3
G17: 'CLASSICAL
H17: 200
I17: 240
J17: 280
G18: 'COUNTRY
H18: 400
I18: 400
J18: 390
G19: 'JAZZ
H19: 100
I19: 120
J19: 150
G20: 'ROCK
H20: 300
I20: 350
J20: 360
```

Chapter 7.   STORESUM Exercise

```
G8: 'AREA
H8: 'SUMMARY BY AREA
G9: '*
H10: "BUDGET
I10: "ACTUAL
G11: 'AREA
H11: @DSUM(DATA,2,ACRIT)
I11: @DSUM(DATA,3,ACRIT)
G12: 'CHICAGO
H12: 1200
I12: 1185
G13: 'NEW YORK
H13: 3000
I13: 1770
G14: 'BOSTON
H14: 600
I14: 760
G15: 'DALLAS
H15: 2400
I15: 1860
```

```
G16: 'ATLANTA
H16: 1800
I16: 1880
G18: 'CAT
H18: 'SUMMARY BY CATEGORY
G19: '*
H20: "BUDGET
I20: "ACTUAL
G21: 'CAT
H21: @DSUM(DATA,2,CCRIT)
I21: @DSUM(DATA,3,CCRIT)
G22: 'M
H22: 1850
I22: 1855
G23: 'W
H23: 2150
I23: 1695
G24: 'B
H24: 5000
I24: 3905
```

Chapter 7.   PROJSUM Exercise

J1: 'SUMMARY AREA
J3: 'EMP
J4: '*
K6: "HOURS
L6: "CHARGES
M6: "% TOTAL
J7: "EMP
K7: 188
L7: 6580
M7: (P0) 1
J8: "wrb

K8: 22
L8: 770
M8: (P0) 0.1170212766
J9: "jpf
K9: 118
L9: 4130
M9: (P0) 0.6276595745
J10: "meb
K10: 48
L10: 1680
M10: (P0) 0.2553191489

Chapter 8.   FINANCE Exercise

M1: (D1) 30396
M3: 'Dear Bill,
M5: 'Here are the revenue and cost figures for the
M6: 'first three quarters of 1983 (in $1000's).
N8: "REVENUE
O8: "COST
P8: "PROFIT
Q8: 'PROF %REV
M9: 'CORPORATE
N9: 3290
O9: 2134
P9: 1156
Q9: (P0) 0.3513677812
M10: 'CLASSICAL
N10: 720
O10: 216
P10: 504
Q10: (P0) 0.7
M11: 'COUNTRY
N11: 1190
O11: 952
P11: 238
Q11: (P0) 0.2
M12: 'JAZZ
N12: 370
O12: 259
P12: 111
Q12: (P0) 0.3
M13: 'ROCK
N13: 1010
O13: 707
P13: 303
Q13: (P0) 0.3
M15: 'Total corporate profits are $1,156,000, well
M16: 'over last year's total profits of $950,000.
P18: 'Sincerely,
P19: 'Jim

Chapter 8.   PROJACT Exercise

A11: 'Rate:
C11: (C2) 35
D11: 'hour
A13: 'TASK
B13: "TASK #
C13: "EMP
D13: "HOURS
E13: "CHARGES
F13: "BHOURS
G13: "BCHARGES
A14: 'Plan
B14: 1
C14: "wrb
D14: 5
E14: 175
F14: 8
G14: 280
A15: 'Plan
B15: 1
C15: "jpf
D15: 10
E15: 350
F15: 8
G15: 280
A16: 'Plan
B16: 1
C16: "meb
D16: 7
E16: 245
F16: 8
G16: 280
A17: 'Design
B17: 2
C17: "jpf
D17: 26
E17: 910
F17: 20
G17: 700
A18: 'Outline
B18: 3
C18: "wrb
D18: 8.5
E18: 297.5
F18: 6
G18: 210
A19: 'Outline
B19: 3
C19: "jpf
D19: 8
E19: 280
F19: 6
G19: 210
A20: 'Write First Draft
B20: 4
C20: "jpf
D20: 25
E20: 875
F20: 40

G20: 1400
A21: 'Write First Draft
B21: 4
C21: "meb
D21: 26
E21: 910
F21: 24
G21: 840
A22: 'Revise
B22: 5
C22: "wrb
D22: 4
E22: 140
F22: 8
G22: 280
A23: 'Revise
B23: 5
C23: "jpf
D23: 4
E23: 140
F23: 8
G23: 280
A24: 'Revise
B24: 5
C24: "meb
D24: 4
E24: 140
F24: 8
G24: 280
A25: 'Write Final Draft
B25: 6
C25: "jpf
D25: 0
E25: 0
F25: 36
G25: 1260
A26: 'Write Final Draft
B26: 6
C26: "meb
D26: 0
E26: 0
F26: 8
G26: 280
A27: \-
B27: \-
C27: \-
D27: \-
E27: \-
F27: \-
G27: \-
A28: 'TOTALS
B28: 6
C28: 3
D28: @SUM(D14..D26)
E28: (C0) @SUM(E14..E26)
F28: @SUM(F14..F26)
G28: (C0) @SUM(G14..G26)

Chapter 8.   PROJACT Exercise (Cont.)

A31: 'CRITERION AREA
A32: 'TASK
B32: "TASK #
C32: "EMP
D32: "HOURS
E32: "CHARGES
C33: "jpf
A35: 'OUTPUT AREA
C35: "TOTALS:
D35: 73
E35: 2555
F35: 118
G35: 4130
H35: (PO) 0.6186440678
A37: 'TASK
B37: "TASK #
C37: "EMP
D37: "HOURS
E37: "CHARGES
F37: "BHOURS
G37: "BCHARGES
H37: '% BUDGET
A38: 'Plan
B38: 1
C38: "jpf
D38: 10
E38: 350
F38: 8
G38: 280
H38: (PO) 1.25
A39: 'Design
B39: 2
C39: "jpf
D39: 26
E39: 910
F39: 20
G39: 700
H39: (PO) 1.3
A40: 'Outline
B40: 3
C40: "jpf
D40: 8
E40: 280
F40: 6
G40: 210
H40: (PO) 1.3333333333
A41: 'Write First Draft
B41: 4
C41: "jpf
D41: 25
E41: 875
F41: 40
G41: 1400

H41: (PO) 0.625
A42: 'Revise
B42: 5
C42: "jpf
D42: 4
E42: 140
F42: 8
G42: 280
H42: (PO) 0.5
A43: 'Write Final Draft
B43: 6
C43: "jpf
D43: 0
E43: 0
F43: 36
G43: 1260
H43: (PO) 0

Chapter 8.   PROJACT Exercise (Cont.)

```
J1:  'SUMMARY AREA
J3:  'EMP
J4:  '*
K6:  "HOURS
L6:  "CHARGES
M6:  "BHOURS
N6:  "BCHARGES
O6:  '% BUDGET
J7:  "EMP
K7:  127.5
L7:  4462.5
M7:  188
N7:  6580
O7:  (PO) 0.6781914894
J8:  "wrb
K8:  17.5
```

```
L8:  612.5
M8:  22
N8:  770
O8:  (PO) 0.7954545455
J9:  "jpf
K9:  73
L9:  2555
M9:  118
N9:  4130
O9:  (PO) 0.6186440678
J10: "meb
K10: 37
L10: 1295
M10: 48
N10: 1680
O10: (PO) 0.7708333333
```

Chapter 9.   THISYR Exercise

```
H1:  'MACRO AREA
H3:  '\S -->
I3:  '/FS~R
H4:  '(save the file)
H7:  '\G -->
I7:  '/xmGMENU~
H8:  '(start graph menu)
H10: 'GMENU -->
I10: '%CHANGE
J10: 'PROFPIE
H11: 'Descriptions
I11: 'Display %CHANGE bar chart
```

```
J11: 'Display profit pie chart
H12: 'Select a graph
I12: '/GNU
J12: '/GNU
I13: '%CHANGE~
J13: 'PROFPIE~
H14: 'Quit graph menu
I14: 'Q
J14: 'Q
H15: 'Return to menu
I15: '/XMGMENU~
J15: '/XMGMENU~
```

Chapter 9. STOREMAC Exercise

```
L1:  '\M -->
M1:  '/xmMENU~
L2:  '(start menu)
L4:  'MENU -->
M4:  'AREASUM
N4:  'CATSUM
L5:  'Descriptions
M5:  'Summarize by area
N5:  'Summarize by category.
```

```
L6:  'Enter 1-cell table range
M6:  '/dt1ATABLE~
N6:  '/dt1CTABLE~
L7:  'Enter criteria range
M7:  'ACRIT~
N7:  'CCRIT~
L8:  'Retun to MENU
M8:  '/xmMENU~
N8:  '/xmMENU~
```

Index

267